M. R. Hamilton was born in Lancashire, England. She studied Literature at the University of London and later Creative Writing. Time spent as a teacher, as well as extensive travels in Europe, Asia, Africa, North and South America offered a rich vein in which to tap. *The Narrow Gate* is her first novel. She lives in South West France.

For Mum and Dad.

For Jim…

"Somewhere on the other side of this dark night…"
Carol Ann Duffy

M. R. Hamilton

THE NARROW GATE

AUSTIN MACAULEY PUBLISHERS
LONDON * CAMBRIDGE * NEW YORK * SHARJAH

Copyright © M. R. Hamilton 2022

The right of M. R. Hamilton to be identified as author of this work has been asserted by the author in accordance with section 77 and 78 of the Copyright, Designs and Patents Act 1988.

All rights reserved. No part of this publication may be reproduced, stored in a retrieval system, or transmitted in any form or by any means, electronic, mechanical, photocopying, recording, or otherwise, without the prior permission of the publishers.

Any person who commits any unauthorised act in relation to this publication may be liable to criminal prosecution and civil claims for damages.

This is a work of fiction. Names, characters, businesses, places, events, locales, and incidents are either the products of the author's imagination or used in a fictitious manner. Any resemblance to actual persons, living or dead, or actual events is purely coincidental.

A CIP catalogue record for this title is available from the British Library.

ISBN 9781398446106 (Paperback)
ISBN 9781398446113 (ePub e-book)

www.austinmacauley.com

First Published 2022
Austin Macauley Publishers Ltd®
1 Canada Square
Canary Wharf
London
E14 5AA

With thanks to my late parents for all the detail of their war experiences. My late husband, Jim, children, Kate and Scott, for their forbearance while I wrote this book. Readers – Robert Hampson, Alison McLeod, Steve Jeffries, Sharon Maslin, Tif and Jenny Harris, Anne Rawnsley. Veronique Baxter – for originally showing faith in me. Mike Slattery for his legal help and advice. Jenny Blaker for her help in Native American research. RAF Burtonwood Heritage Centre. Thanks also to the editing and production team at Austin Macauley. Plus all of those – too numerous to mention – who have encouraged me along the way. A heartfelt thanks to you all.

Prologue

North East Montana
America
1951

I know he is awake. The slope of his back sharpens as he pulls himself from sleep, inhaling deeply, stopping; he exhales with a sigh. There is irritation. I lie still, my breathing shallow, my eyelids, like the restless wings of a butterfly flutter as I struggle to keep them closed. He fidgets with himself under the covers, thinking I am sleeping, but I am not. I am waiting.

Before blue-black pales into dawn, he raises himself in one movement, stretches oblivious of my stare, enjoys that rush of energy through his body. His muscled calves push against the hem of his night-shirt, hands clenched in fists either side of his head, elbows outstretched. He relaxes. At the bed he casts a closed glance, at once resentful and needy, shakes his head slowly as though in disappointment or some imagined rebuke.

He is beautiful. His triangle of muscle from shoulder to tapering waist still soldier-firm; a perfect machine, and if I didn't know better, I would want him, want to feel him here beside me, inside me, but I do know better, and my ache has been replaced with something else.

He pulls his night-shirt over his head and throws it on the bed. Uninhibited, because he thinks I don't see him, he scratches his sun-patched body, kneads the dented shoulder—detritus of war, his hooked penis bobbing somewhere between sleep and arousal, then whispering something under his breath, drags his dungarees and tee-shirt from the chair and goes from the room. Even at this stage of wakefulness there is anger at some unbidden ghost, some dream-time conflict. It crackles in the air. I feel it on my skin, in my teeth. Then the sweet click of the latch as he closes the door behind him.

Downstairs, he scuffles in the kitchen making waking up noises. I hear Berry meow. Silky. Delicious. Imagine her rubbing against his legs, murmuring sweet hellos, jumping up onto the dresser her back arched, before being brushed to the floor in a careless sweep.

I feel bad about Berry.

I hear water pumped; the kettle placed heavily on the range. The screen-door snaps then footsteps over the yard until the barn door creaks open its morning yawn. I imagine the sweet dung smell like a blanket wafting into the outside air. Buckets clang. There is a restlessness in the barn, a calf lets out a plaintive bellow, a few chickens squawk, then stillness for a while. The caw-caw of a crow suddenly pierces the quiet, reaching out like a vengeful siren call over the land, only to be swallowed up in the layers of air. I sense the wheat, as far as the mind can see, yellowing. Spilling like a quiet sea, maturing, ready for harvest.

This is the day.

I turn my back on his side of the bed, curl foetal-shaped, into the cupped mattress, and wait. The impatient tick tick tick tick, of the clock arms me; I am ready to detonate.

Snaking around me like a winding sheet is his scent, still in the air, in the bed, a faint smell of hops and something metallic. I breathe in, close my eyes against the grey dawn and drown my lips and face into the softness of my upper arm. I smell my mother's milk, her skin; sun-warmed sweet cheese, her breast pushing at me like a great soft pillow, suffocating. I smell it in my dreams, and other smells: apple-wood embers, lemon curd, the inside of my father's windjammer.

But *this* smell, here and now, I *shall* forget.

At the sound of the barn door, I go to ground, curl my legs tight, my body closed. I shut my eyes and continue to listen, my heart an insistent percussion. Everything before has been leading to this.

He crosses back over the corral, the yard. I hear the slight drag of his heels on the baked ground. The screen door snaps again as he slips bootless up the stairs. In the shower I know he is scrubbing himself red with the loofah, washing something away. His ritual over, he returns to the kitchen, makes strong coffee, the sharp bitterness of which I can smell through the floorboards. He will drink half and leave the rest, breakfast at Meg's fifty miles away on highway eighty-six, where he will flirt with the waitress, who will think I am lucky.

In town he will find a bar, sit in shadows—predatory, sad—surrounded by misfits. If capable, he will wind back somehow in the early hours. Otherwise, he will find someone willing, return sullen in the morning when he will shower and scrub until his skin smarts. Again.

I wait until the sound of his pickup on the clay road is a pricking whisper in the distance then slide from the bed and tread softly to the window, avoiding loose floorboards. I must not wake Sheila, though it is doubtful she will leave her room today. When her son 'goes off', she prefers not to acknowledge it. I pull back the drapes, notice a prairie sparrow brushed up and balancing on a fence post, observe the smallest sway of the wheat, nudged by an insistent breeze. I look through the silken ochre and purple strata of dawn to the Dutch white house on the horizon, sitting like a painted galleon, sailing on the morning sky.

I have watched this house for five years, the only other one on the prairie for miles. My Noah's Ark. I imagine all the rodents of the earth scrambling for it, knowing that harvest is near; the birds of the air, searching for a landing in this sea of wheat. Birds I do not see now: woodpeckers and wagtails, finches, blackbirds, thrushes. Woodland creatures I remember from home: dormice and hedgehogs, foxes, red squirrels and shrews. And people. Memories. A ship's cargo increasing as each day passes, as each recollection twists its blade.

I move from the window, shudder, scrunch my eyes tight shut.

Now he is gone I can begin. I wash quickly then slip into clothes I made ready yesterday; green shirt-waister and brogues. I tread noiselessly down the stairs carefully stepping over the last one lest it yawns and creaks. I brush my hair quickly, grown wild and weedy in this wilderness, scoop it up into a bun. In my head I hear music: *The Ride of the Valkyries*, Dad's gramophone belting it out, remember that different sense of entrapment: youth, concealing, as I have increasingly begun to think, what we all essentially are: alone. I pour myself a glass of water.

When I go into the barn, the weaner calves swirl their pupils nervously showing the whites of their eyes, stop chewing, see it is me, then resume. I breathe in their smell, experience the reflex association: my pony Tara—from a time buried deep, far from the agonies of adulthood. I pull out the rusted bicycle that I have secretly treated with gun oil to loosen the cogs. Last week I mended a puncture, the way my father showed me, licking the inner-tube till it hissed with my spittle. I wheel it out of sight of the windows, behind the barn.

In the kitchen I remove the money, scratched together over three years, from under the loose floorboard at the back of the pantry. Mice have nibbled at the edges. No matter. I strap it to my belly with tape, where it pinches and pleats my skin. I pack a small bag with food and water. Nothing else. I leave, then return, scribble an afterthought: *Please look after Berry.*

Outside, I stand for a moment, take it in, the house that I am leaving. The life. See the crawl space that separates it from the earth, think of times I have hidden there grateful for its refuge, the rustle of snakes and scratch of insects in the night, until alcohol or anger or both have worn through his system.

The windows are eyes. I imagine a woman, obscured by window-glint, grey-washed, standing back behind a curtain in a room with mad wallpaper, watching. Outside, the dark red paint on the timbered laps bleeds into grey close to the ground where parts of the earth clamber onto it. Summer-dried mildew and tall weeds with fluffy heads like *Old Men's Beard*, turn the red grey brown and mottled, give the house an impression of having grown out of the earth, or of nature taking back its own.

The wood is curled and split on the corners where the paint has worn off and winter has got in, as though the house is peeling off its face. The roof has the merest tilt. There is a tiny round window in the gable, an eye that looks out over the land, concealing secrets. Extensions, like arms on each side, give the house a clumsy look. On the left, *his* room; a forbidden landscape, where he keeps his private things and his pleasures.

Even when he was away during the war, his mother never entered, ignored the key that hangs on a nail outside, not touched by anyone but him. *Fear is the key*, I said in jest when first this was pointed out to me. Her lips tightened in a snarl, but in her eyes, I sensed not just a warning but real fear. There is a porch out front with wide shabby steps, down which I have just walked for the last time.

I do not look back as I wobble over tyre-trenches down the only road out of here, my hands shaking as I rattle along, the sun coming up hot on my back. To reach where the Amish people live, at the white house, I must cycle a long route around; no road connects the two houses. Strangers, especially settlers, overcomers, are not welcome in these parts.

I find some pleasure riding into the sunrise. I remember things: …*faster Ali faster*, down, down through the dappled forest, the coconut musk of gorse drifting down from the hillside above…

I push the pedals hard until I am fair racing along. I feel myself waking, my body alive as though from hibernation. Wings sprout from my back and I am flying. From up here I see the miles of wheat, nothing but wheat. I see the farm getting smaller and smaller…

When I come close, I see the white house is bigger than I thought, how it seems to lean towards me. I am tempted to laugh out loud, caught in a fairy-tale; I am a ubiquitous Gretel looking for refuge and smile at the thought of the candy house, shudder at the idea of being consumed. A large windmill structure dominates the yard and sails creak and whine in the lazy breeze. There is no doorknocker, I thump three times with my fist and wait, listen to my heart knocking in my chest. After some time, the door cracks open.

'Yes…hello…'

'I am from the McCullough farm, I…' Not my farm, never my farm.

'Who is it, Heidi?' I hear a voice deep within the house echoing clarity of enunciation that is both disapproving and curious, inlaid with Pennsylvania Dutch.

'Papa, it is a woman from the McCullough farm.' Heidi is about sixteen, her bottom lip hangs open, suggesting sensuality and a little stupidity. She wears the clothes of the Amish. Her eyes are the palest I have ever seen. She stares without inhibition.

'Ask her what she wants.'

'What do you want?'

'Can you help me? I have no transport. I need to get to the cross on Highway Eighty-Six. I need to know if your father or a brother, perhaps, could take me in your buggy…please.'

'That's a long way.' She looks out to the distance as she visualises the journey.

'I can pay. I can get a Greyhound from there…' I hear the shrill note of pleading in my voice and am embarrassed.

'Come in, please. Sit down here. I will speak to father.'

As I move inside, she steps back. Did she bow slightly? One arm is sweeping me in, palm upwards, eyes downcast. A saintly beauty nestling in marble skin. She is vacant but welcoming and it is good to feel the close physical presence of another human being. I resist the urge to make inane pleasantries before she clops away down the hallway, a loud phantom, looking back suspiciously as though I might disappear, her gait displaying remnants of babyhood.

A smell of polish and something else swims in the air: sickly like lilies, but there are no flowers. The room is plain and dark. I sit on the edge of a hard and upright chair, my feet tucked neatly together, my small bag on the floor beside me where it looks untidy. I feel my back rigid and arched. I play with my fingers, examine my nails and try not to sniff in the pulsing silence. I see my reflection in the glass of a painting of Christ's resurrection that leans out from the wall: I am washed-out, white, super-imposed, just a girl, though a woman of twenty-eight.

The table has been set for breakfast: a white loaf sliced on a wooden board, six glasses of water; the same amount in each glass. A bowl of oranges in the middle is the only colour. An open bible rests on the mantelpiece.

I hear voices whispering in the next room. I wait, practising penance, silently mouthing a Latin mass in time: ...*et expecto resurrectionem mortuorum et vitam venturi saeculi...*

'Good morning, Mrs McCullough.'

'Good morning...sir.' He is very tall and straight-backed, good-looking even, in an austere way: grey sprinkled and weathered brown with a stiff beard stretching from ear to ear that gives his chin a slightly protruding look. He walks right up to my chair, so close I must side-step to stand up comfortably. He does not offer his hand but is smiling. A quick efficient smile. His eyes blink as he does so.

'What is it that I can do for you exactly, Mrs McCullough?' He reminds me of someone.

'I'm sorry, I know this is an unusual request, but I need to get to Wolf Point as soon as possible...today. I wonder can you take me as far as the cross. I know it's a long way...I can pay.' My accent cuts the air, my vowels clipped, flat. My palms are sweating.

'I don't want to seem unhelpful but...what about your husband? Why does he not take you?'

'He isn't here.'

'Can't you wait for him to come back?'

'No...no, I can't. It's complicated.'

'I see.'

Silence. I wait for him to speak. He waits also. I see him thinking, weighing me up, making judgements about me. I feel my head swelling, adrenaline. Eventually, he speaks:

'We don't get many opportunities to meet our neighbours.' He looks through the window as though I am still somehow out there, scratches his beard, looks at the floor. Another quick smile.

'No, no…that's true…'

'You must forgive us, Mrs McCullough, if we have not extended the hand of friendship to you.' He nods his head as though in affirmation of this fact.

'Please…don't mention it…I know it's difficult.' I am lying.

'Yes, it is. It is difficult.' He is resting his right elbow in his left palm. His right hand is stroking his beard. He has the same ice eyes as his daughter's, which do not look at me.

'The Amish they, we…tend, in these parts at least, to live separately, you see…'

'Yes, I understand. I'm sorry if I have invaded your—'

'No, don't concern yourself with that. I'm wondering how we could have helped you.'

'You can help me now?' I try to control my voice, keep it low.

'I hope so, Mrs McCullough…Please, sit down.'

He draws a chair up to mine. I feel a sudden shiver.

'You are cold?'

'No, no…' I offer a weak smile like winter sunshine. It does not penetrate.

'You have been here some years, I think?'

'About five…yes. I came here from England.'

'Yes, I know something of that.' I can imagine how I have been discussed, knowing what I know now.

'Yes…well.'

'So. You were in England during the war?'

'That's right.'

'That must have been hard for you?'

I smile again, incline my head, my face tight. How could I tell this man that however bad it was, for me it was living? Fun. That I left the largest part of me in the wreckage of my wake. That everything since has been a pale shadow.

'It is hard to leave one's mother country, is it not?'

'Yes… I have family there, brothers…'

'And family here too, of course.'

I feel the beads of perspiration begin to run down my temples, down my back into my waist. Pools collect at my feet. Water is rising. Cold water. Get out of the boat…My instinct tells me to swim. I resist it. My best chance is here.

'Would you like some water? You have been energetic, I see.'

'Thank you.'

'In fact, join us for breakfast? I think…yes. We have finished our prayers.'

'No…really…'

'I insist. Please, unless you have eaten already? Heidi… Heidi, set another place for breakfast. Tell your mother that Mrs McCullough will be joining us.'

Mrs Schouten, wide-mouthed, strong-boned, emits an air of honed duty as she places food on the table. Smiles under lowered eyelids. She and her three daughters flutter noiselessly like dark moths around a light. The son, an adolescent, whose arms and legs seem too long for his body, slinks in shyly from the sun-filled outside, walking hay onto the floor.

'Samuel, Samuel…please… Clean your shoes. This is Mrs McCullough.'

I notice Mr Schouten has a habit of holding his left arm close to his side and shrugging his shoulders as though pulling something up. I wonder if I am making him uncomfortable.

I feel like a circus exhibit. A midget in a room of giants. I sit where I am bidden, notice the two girls Ruth and Anna exchange furtive glances with Heidi who, wide-eyed, bites her loose lip. I abruptly stand again as no one else is seated.

'The Lord in his wisdom has provided us with food this day. He has brought a stranger to us, we bid her welcome at our table. May the Lord be thanked for his bounteous mercy. Amen.'

'Amen.'

A few large pieces of darkly rich carved furniture sit ornate, out of context, like trees in a desert. I cannot resist running my fingers along the waxen grain, feel the gloss of old oak, as I make my way to the library, where I have been asked to wait. Each room leads onto the next in this large square house. Doorways look through doorways. The sun filters in under half closed blinds, dust motes perambulate down yellow shafts of light losing themselves in shadowy corners. The wooden floors, whose high wax speaks as I walk, are gold with wheat-glow.

I wait. So many books. I close my eyes and breath in the mustiness, run my fingers along their spines. I have not had books since I came here except for the ones I brought with me from England, now dog-eared and disintegrating.

Most are religious texts, but not all. Picking one at random, I sit and shrink into shade, open the book whose brown curved pages crack in the silence. But I cannot read, my body is demanding action; the momentum contained over weeks like trapped energy. My knees jitter, hands shake. I stare into space, sense old spirits.

'Ah, you like to read, Mrs McCullough?' I did not hear him come in. I jerk back into my situation. 'I'm sorry if I made you jump.'

'No…it's all right. I really must…'

'Don't worry, all in good time. It is not too unpleasant sitting here, I think?'

'No. It's very nice.'

I think of Mrs Schouten and wonder about her relationship with her husband, wonder if she feels safe with him. Wonder what *she* knows. I cannot imagine them making love, though there is something animal in the way he moves, taut, nervous, a restrained energy. There was something wistful in her demeanour at breakfast. I watched the arch tenderness with her children, the furtive glances at me under thick lashes. No-one asked why I was there, flotsam washed up at their door.

Suddenly, I want *my* mother. Need to hear her peal of laughter, sharp enough to strip paint. I smile.

'That's better. Now …what are you reading?'

I lift the cover. He tilts his head to read the spine.

'You like philosophy?' He raises his eyebrows, looks surprised.

'I don't know really…I just picked it up.'

'Hmm…Schopenhauer. *The World as Will and Idea*. Strange you should pick that one… not the most accessible, but you might enjoy it. Philosophy is…is like watering the flowers in your soul. Though, of course, it is God who planted them.'

I am silent.

'Would you like to borrow some books maybe?'

'I like books…reading.'

'What else do you do to occupy your time?'

'I don't know really.'

'You have been to our workroom, no? We believe that creation is ongoing. That we should use the gifts we have been given, you understand? By these means we can survive in this world economically, but also provide an outlet for...shall we say—our darker energies? Do you create Alice? I may call you that?'

'Yes, yes of course. I used to paint a little, write poems and stories, you know, when I was younger.'

'Excellent. And now?'

'No. Not now.'

'Ah, now I see. Yes. You know...when we have—*the blues*—as they say here,' he leans forward as though sharing a private joke, smiling as he enunciates the phrase clearly, his eyebrows raised in mock complicity, '...creating can be very...what is the word now? Cathartic. Yes. We can be just who we want to be in our heads, even if we feel, perhaps, that life has given us little...control? In our minds we can be free. Tell you what...'

He walks over to a desk, turns a key and pulls open the lid. He pulls out a pristine hardback notebook. He draws a new pencil from a pot of them and presents them to me. 'Here, this can be your beginning. Write down who you are, your life. Keep a diary, a journal if you like.

'No one can take away your imagination, my dear. I think you may find it will help.' I take the proffered gift limply, half-smile my thanks.

'I suppose I...I need to explain why I am here Mr Schouten...I...'

'No. That is between you and God. Only what is necessary. You mentioned to my daughter a Greyhound bus? You know, of course, there is only one weekly bus to the city, on a Friday, yesterday, which is what I assume you want to do?'

'Oh no...no, I didn't know.' He cannot imagine the effect this knowledge has upon me. I hold in my lips to avoid panic or sudden tears. All the planning, months, years of it; how could I have missed that?

'Perhaps you could begin by telling me your destination, Mrs McCullough?'

'England...eventually.' I regret it as soon as I have spoken.

'England?'

I might as well have said the moon.

'England. So. You want to go to England? Now?' He smiles and folds his arms, leans back slightly.

I feel stupid. I want to stand up, assert myself, but I cannot.

'Yes...it's difficult to explain.'

'I'm sure, I'm sure. Would I be right in assuming that Mr McCullough does not know of this? He maintains his raised eyebrows, his head tilted in a questioning pose that already knows the answer.

'I am in a difficult situation…I am… I have no-one else to ask.' My fingers grip the Schopenhauer too tightly, I notice him cast a quick glance at them. He is nervous for his book. He twitches his shoulders.

'You have God, my child. God will always help us, no matter what the difficulty may be. *Ask and it shall be given.*' Suddenly he is on safe ground, he rocks back on his heels; confident in the truth of the advice he offers. 'Marriage…life with another person is not always straightforward, is it? But life is not always about feelings. You are young…' Piety gives his face a waxen look, not quite human. His eyes crinkle, but he doesn't smile.

Now I know where I have seen this look. Mr Brown, English teacher, ageing bachelor. The only male in my all-girls' convent school before the war. His nervous twitch. I hear his voice suddenly: *There are two kinds of intelligence, Alice Conroy: Emotional intelligence of which you suffer an excess, and intellectual intelligence, which you would be well advised to cultivate. Your essays, how shall I say…suffer from an indulgence of personality, altogether too visceral. I suggest, if you must immerse yourself in female writers, then give the Brontë's a rest for a while and concentrate on Austen. An ironic view of the world might temper your tendency towards…excess.* I look up at Mr Schouten.

'God has not listened. Believe me, I have tried.' He winces. Something sinks inside me.

'God always listens.' He pulls up a chair, looks at the floor. Rubs his palm with the thumb of his other hand. There is a smell of grass around him and something freshly ironed. His trousers are loose across his groin, but I know from the movement of his hands, by the downturn of his mouth, it is always there; an awareness of the burden he carries between his legs; pink, damp, nestling, being ignored. He is a man after all.

'If He has not responded to your prayers, my dear, it is because you are not meant to do …whatever… No-one said that life should be easy.'

'Please. I have waited a long time…I must do this.'

The ground is falling away. He is not listening. Please God, if you are, help me now.

'Yes, I think I am understanding you. You wish to leave your husband…and children?'

'No children…sadly, well, perhaps not sadly in the circumstances.'

'So, there was a reason then.'

'Pardon?'

'Hmmm. This is difficult for me…you understand? Forgive me…When you married you made a solemn vow, did you not, Mrs McCullough, to remain with your husband for good or bad?'

'Yes, yes of course…but things change…I am not a child, Mr Schouten.' I am needled, he is patronising me.

'We are all God's children, if I may correct you…and there are no buts in God's holy law, my dear. Everything is very clear.' He stands, moves behind me and looks out of the window to restrain an emerging irritation. I can see by his movements that this is a man used to being obeyed. Outside, the family is doing farm chores and he is momentarily distracted. I hear Samuel chasing a chicken. I am suspended, on a plateau of uncertainty, feel my independent act, years of dreaming, planning, ebbing away. 'What sort of example would I, a minister, set my family, if I were to aid you in this…action? You can, perhaps, see that I am trapped between the horns of a dilemma?' He moves around, looms in front, a steamroller, he is going to flatten me. I am silent.

Then, like a southerly breeze in winter, he warms.

'But it is not simple. Jesus says *if anyone asks you to go one mile, go with him two miles. Give to him who begs from you, and do not refuse him.* So. I think…yes, this house can be a retreat for you, for a day or two. Give us both time to think. There is no hurry, is there? The bus has gone. If I decide I can help you in some way, I shall do so. I shall pray for guidance.'

As I stand, my eyes pricking, fogged, he moves in front of me, grips my forearms with his hands. He looks me in the eyes, full of earnestness. He will not help me. I can feel it. I pull against him but feel the tide pulling me in and know I am going nowhere.

'Come, come now, all will be well. Trust in God. There is purpose in your coming here. And now I have much work to do, and you have many books here?' He smiles, lets go of my arms and rests a hand on my shoulder.

…Therefore, do not be anxious about tomorrow, for tomorrow will be anxious for itself. Let the day's own trouble be sufficient for the day.

As the day leans forward, I follow the stream of sunlight into a south-facing parlour, its shutters creating blades of diagonal light across the room. I am like a greyhound in the starting box, every muscle, every cell hot with contained energy, waiting to burst out.

Suddenly, a clatter of laughter from the barn. Then silence. I look around me. See that I am in a workroom. Spools and bobbins of silk trail ends onto the floor where there are woven baskets piled high, a stash of wicker and raffia in the corner leaves a carpet of sandy coloured bits around it. There are unfinished tapestries of bible scenes, cushions of needlepoint, adorned with windmills and flowers, stacked high. There is even some fine art hanging and propped against the wall. I resist the urge to charge at it, pull it to the floor, destroy it all. Scream. Instead, I take slow measured steps and try to see a way forward.

At a long worktable in the centre of the room are signs of their continuing industry. There are four places and at each is a work in progress. It seems they are all good at something different. I sit at one, run my hands along the table edge, and am transported suddenly, not without a fleeting fondness, to a worktable like this one, where bawdy women and quiet men with raised eyebrows, saucy smiles playing around their mouths, made hats for fashion-starved women recovering from the poverty of rations, in a warehouse in Broughton, England. It smelt of this room.

I pick up a needle and some tartan braid, I begin to loop and roll it until I have a perfect bow. I sew it quickly into place, decorate it with a piece of scarlet velvet that seems discarded, and with a small sense of achievement, leave it to be found.

Over lunch, Heidi wants to know all about England, especially the weather: 'And tell me, does it rain all day, every day? If so, it must be tiresome? English people must be very damp?' She makes everyone laugh. They laugh easily. Samuel reminds me of my older brother. He lifts his left eyebrow in just the same way when he smiles lopsidedly. I wish we could have been friends; too late now that I am leaving. I smile as though her question were rhetorical. I cannot speak of home here.

When they talk amongst themselves, I daydream, thinking of what it is I would say were I able, but there are only sense impressions, colours, sounds. Like trying to recall the essence of a loved one that has died. My energy is fading to a tiring nostalgia.

An urgent whinny from their horse outside reminds me of Tara, her neigh caught on the breeze blowing in from The Pike.

'More potatoes, Alice…come eat.'

'Ah yes...' My response is perfunctory. I am somewhere else. The whole situation is surreal.

At sundown, when the family has finished their chores and the minister has come in from the fields, we talk. Of marriage and sacrifice. Of God and love. Later, beside the narrow bed they have fixed up for me, a candle burning on the bedside table, I feel like a confessor that must do penance. On my knees, hands clasped like a small child I try to pray: *In my bed I lie, heavenly Father, hear my cry...*

Maybe I am wrong, *mea culpa*. Maybe there is another way, *mea maxima culpa*. Maybe. My Catholic guilt engulfs me. Doubt like illness weakens me.

This was not the way to do it.

Trained in obeisance from the moment of my birth, I need sanction. Permission. The black crows gather on my shoulder: every nun that ever taught and caned me, priest that nurtured and threatened hell-fire, father who worshipped, yet discarded me, and husband that forces his fingers up between my legs then beats me for not being grateful. All in the name of love. Love of God. Love of man. Love of power. I am love's slave: prisoner of my conditioning.

I climb into the high bed, stiff cotton sheets crackling as I push into them. Before I lie, sleepless, entombed, I sit for a moment and run my hand over the journal that Mr Schouten has given me, remembering one like it that smelt of the sea, whose every scribbled page contained luxurious, horrific, extraordinary details of a life. I pick up the pencil by my bed, open the first page and write at the top: *Journal of an Overcomer*. Underneath:

North East Montana
America
1951

One day, someone will know...

Finally sleep comes. Luxurious oblivion. Faithless though, it departs before the end of night and leaves me staring at a tall ceiling in a strange house four thousand miles from where I want to be, with the conviction that I have been seduced. Again.

And now, a prodigal wife, I return. I am being driven back. Mr Schouten has *seen* to everything, he says. My husband is waiting for me.

This faith is quicksand, sucking everything in; there is no air and I cannot pull myself from it. Weariness tugs at my limbs, dread makes me very still. Life is pulsing from me. Mr Schouten drops me at the bottom of the track, thinks it is better for me if I appear unforced.

'*Enter by the narrow gate*; my dear, as Jesus tells us in Matthew, *the way is hard that leads to life…*'

He says some kind things, his face earnest, oblivious. He places a bible in my hands 'for guidance' and then he is gone. His horse and buggy blur in the distance. Only the faint clop of hooves and the thump in my chest fill up the silence. On a perfect blue sky, the white house in the distance shimmers in the heat, a mirage of an upside down galleon sailing away and with it the hopes and dreams of every waking moment since first I realised exactly what I had done.

I walk up and sense a presence. I retch. I am twenty-seven years old, a bird caught in the thresher.

I get closer to the house, notice a rag hanging from the fence-wire. No…too heavy for a rag. Something in the act of falling, as though from the sky. The wind whips up my skirt, pushes me forward, fills my mouth with hair. Then drops. There is a scent in the air. The pulse in my neck quickens, there is a tingling in my scalp. Up close, I see the price I have paid. It is newly done. Red oil, thick and viscous, runs in tiny rivulets along the track. The rag is Berry. She is tied by her tail to the wire. Her throat has been cut.

'There is a way out of every dark mist, over a rainbow trail.'
Navajo song

Book One

Chapter One

Hebden Bridge
England
1933

> Cinderella,
> Dressed in yella,
> Went upstairs,
> To kiss a fella.
> By mistake,
> Kissed a snake,
> How many doctors,
> Did it take...1...2...3...4...

'Ali...ALI...Walter's at the door, stop skipping and see what he wants will you?'
'Hiya Walter.'
'You coming down to the stream?'
'The boys are out at footie practice...'
'Yeh I know, what about you?
'Give me two secs.'

Fine mizzle made tiny droplets on his eyelashes, on the blond hairs of his forearms. The faint, snail-trail scar on his right cheekbone showed pearly and crinkled in his morning smile. His hands: winter white, vaguely freckled, fingers too long for his age gesticulated in the pale air as he explained what he had in mind for our outing. His bicycle leans haphazardly against his hip as his body jerked in enthusiastic anticipation.

Mam stood on the threshold as we left, arms folded over her bosom, humming *I've got you under my skin* along with the radio in the parlour. She raised her eyes to the sky, tutting and shaking her head in that exaggerated way she has at the inclement weather and then at the clothes I had chosen: an old woollen dress that was too short, worn thin at the elbows, thick long socks and wellington boots. She sighed loudly. Her smile of submission wondered when her little girl would begin to show signs of being female. With two older brothers and Walter always hanging around, she shrugged at the inevitable, planted a peck on a rosy cheek, pushing back my black uncombed curls that immediately fell back over my face, as I rushed through the open door with my net and bucket onto a bike to disappear down Horsehold, a shouted goodbye lost on the slipstream of our departure.

We cycled down over Blackpit Lock, along the towpath beside the black and shiny canal; a shifting tableau patterned by a restless sky and the reflection of wavering top and bottom houses stacked on hills that seemed to lean over as though they would topple at any moment. Our usual place, just behind the pump house, was at the very base of the valley. One of our secret places.

'Do you think if we put the frogspawn in a bucket and tip it in your pond, it'll grow?'

We squatted on the bank of the shallow, clear stream that meandered through the meadow getting lost in reeds and weeds and small culverts, only to reappear, a gentle gurgle farther on. This was our favourite spot. The stream widened slightly, and the eddying water created pools in which all sorts of interesting *stuff* was to be found. It was a place for trysts. A place of revelation.

I poked at the water with a twig, trying to separate the individual eggs from the huge dollops of dotted jelly that stuck resolutely together, still basking in the glow of being asked to come. Usually, I was tagging along with my two older brothers, but Walter didn't seem embarrassed to be seen exploring with just a girl, as Vincent would have been. Mam was cooking Sunday lunch listening to the BBC, probably glad to have the place to herself. Sunday was boring unless there was an adventure in it.

There was still a faint smur, but it was warm, and a watery sun struggled through the wet mist, the kind of weather you get in Yorkshire in May. Walter was gazing intently at the skaters that flitted and jumped across the glassy surface of the water. I looked at our reflection, our cheeks chubbier as we leaned over. I copied Walter biting his lip, his serious air. He was two years older than I and knew what was what.

'Nah, it needs to be left alone,' he said finally, with a flourish of responsibility.

'Why, they're just eggs.'

'See, what you're doing with that stick'll cause mayhem.' He frowned at the seriousness of this pronouncement, nodding slightly. It was his mother speaking.

'Mayhem?'

'Yeh.'

'Frogs don't think like that, they live, or they don't. Mayhem is for humans.'

'Ali, you're ten years old, stop talking like your dad.'

'It's like saying: "the dirt on your shorts is profound".'

'*Profound*? You're such a blinking smarty-pants.'

'It means *a lot*. I heard Mrs Walker say it to Maggie Riley, *you are profoundly disorganised*. It's too big a word for such a little thing, if you see what I mean. Oh, but look, some have hatched, there see…look…there.'

Walter shifted so that his body leaned into mine. He was unconscious of this shared intimacy, of the warmth I felt through my dress, of the smell of him: fresh, clean, an odour of swimming pool and starch.

'What, where?'

'Baby tadpoles.'

'Tadpoles *are* babies; if they weren't, they'd be frogs. Or eggs. But yeh…we could take those in a bucket and see whether they grow into respectable citizens of the frog community.'

'Now who's a smarty-pants? Be a shame to take them away from their brothers and sisters though…'

'What happened to "mayhem"? *Frogs don't think like that…*'

'What?'

'You are daft, you. Come here, I'll do it.' He wrestled the bucket from my hands gently, in a *let me open that door for you* kind of way. I smiled, handed it over, unaware of the deference I showed him. I watched as he tried and failed to scoop the tadpoles with the bucket.

'Walter?'

'Yeh?'

'Why haven't *you* got brothers or sisters?'

'Pass that…that thing.'

'Tell me.'

''Cause I haven't.'

'No, that thing there, the net thing.'

'Didn't your mam want more kids?' I sat back on the bank while I pondered this new thought, watching the spawn glide over the edge of the net, thinking how lonely it must be for him.

'Well, she couldn't, could she? Not on her own. You do know about er...all that?'

'What? Oh yeh, 'course. Well, I think so. At least, bits of it. Pat told me.'

'How does she know?'

'Her Mam told her I think.'

'Blimey. Does your Mam talk to *you* like that?'

''Course not. Pat's your age. I'm just a kid. But you know, in the playground…'

'Yeh, I know.' Walter looked up from the task in hand as though something had caught his attention.

'Can't imagine Mam and Dad doing it…but then they must have done it at least three times,' I offered.

'At least my Mam only had to do it once.' He laughed out loud, dropping the net into the water. 'Whoops…Still it can't be that bad or there wouldn't be any more people.'

I looked at Walter and imagined doing it with him, whatever 'it' was—kissing when you were naked and holding and stuff and shuddered thinking about it. I think it was the first time the concept of practical romance entered into the scheme of things.

'Ali! Here give us that stick, you're making it all muddy.'

Two damselflies flitted over the surface of the water, dipping, hovering, darting. Then they stuck together for a little while. I pointed.

'Do you think they're doing it?' I said.

'Probably. It's spring. Everything mates in spring, except people, they only do it when they want children.'

'Oh. It's probably some primeval urge in animals to procreate that we've dispensed with.'

Walter sat up and laughed at me.

'Ali, the way you talk, you sound like a professor or something.'

'Don't be daft.'

'No, really. Everyone thinks you're clever—you seem older than ten.'

I felt my cheeks burn. Walter made me feel noticed in a way that no one else did.

'Just as well eh, or you'd feel you were baby-sitting?' I poked him with the stick I had resisted relinquishing, to cover my embarrassment. Walter just looked at me whilst grabbing the end of it, attempting to control my wand-like waving as though he didn't know what to say.

'Anyway, your Mam. Didn't she though?'

'What?'

'Want more kids.'

'Suppose so, but Dad went away and then he died.'

'Oh yeh. Don't you miss him. I can't imagine not having my dad.'

'Dunno, I never met him. Here, grab that.'

'That's funny. Never meeting your dad. Didn't he like you?'

'Told you, he never saw me. Hold it still—you're spilling it…'

'What happened to him?'

'Oh Ali, you know all this.' Walter tipped the tadpoles he'd caught in the net into the bucket of stream water that I held, along with some of the spawn that had slithered in.

'Tell me again.' I pulled my legs from under me and sat, making myself comfortable as though I was about to be read a story.

'He was in that big war; you know years ago in France. He was in the trenches.'

'Trenches?'

'Big holes in the ground, I think, that the soldiers dug and then hid in.'

'France must have been full of holes at the end. Was he a soldier?'

'Yeh. Mam and him were sweethearts, engaged.'

'Did they write to one another?'

'Suppose so.'

'Love letters?'

I thought about how romantic that was, waiting for your man to come home from the war while you missed him and wept all over the place.

'Then he got home, with medals and stuff.'

'Have you seen the medals?'

'Yeh. Mam keeps them in a box now. She caught me betting with them at marbles: Dad's medals for Jack's gob-stoppers—a whole packet. She went mad with me.'

'Did you lose?'

'What?'

'The game of marbles. Your dad's medals.'

'Yes…No. Mam had to go around to Jack's ma and get them. I had to give the gob-stoppers back. Ali, do you want to know or not?'

'Yes. Sorry.'

'Anyway, they got married and he took over Grandma's shop in the town. But he didn't like it.'

'What? Marriage? Or the shop?'

'Dunno really. I suppose he'd changed, being away so long.'

I thought about that. How could someone change just because they'd been away for a while? It didn't make sense.'

'Perhaps he met someone else while he was away.'

'Don't think so. He missed the war, I think, but that was over…and he left. So, it was just Mam and me. It's the reason she's like she is. I think he hurt her a lot, leaving her like that when she'd waited so long and being pregnant an' all.'

'But what happened to your dad?'

'He died soon after, that's all. Dunno really, Mam doesn't talk about it. Maybe he killed himself.'

'But why would he do that if he'd just been married?'

'Why do you want to know?'

'I'm interested, hey…you're spilling it, urghh, I've got frogspawn down my wellie. Pick up the tadpoles, they'll die…'

'C'mon Ali, hold this and I'll take the other, I'm gonna pour them into the pond in the garden and see what happens.' I followed him as he got on his bike and started to cycle away. Walter assumed my complicity in all things and because he did, I felt it was right. I was the youngest, and a girl, used to being the lowest in the order of things.

We ran along the back end of the alley that squeezed itself between each pair of houses, to the patchy lawn that stretched narrow to the pond at the end. The borders were overgrown with cow parsley, elder, oxeye daisies, dandelions, and a rusty old bicycle leaned up against the fence alongside dustbins and bits of old discarded furniture. We had spilt some of the water, our bikes rocking from side to side as we stood on our pedals pressing down hard against the incline to his house, the dappled light scribbling and flashing through arcs of foliage on the buckets of glistening sludge.

As we flopped and squatted on our haunches by the weedy water, I looked up at the back of Walter's house and noticed the upstairs curtain twitching. His mother, I knew, would be standing behind the glass, watching; the way that lonely women do, while life was going on somewhere else.

'Your mam must be sad, Walter? What does she do all day with no one to look after?'

'If she's not in the shop, she cleans the house. Sometimes she goes out.'

'I couldn't bear to be alone like that with no one to love me.'

'I love her,' he said quickly.

It was an unwitting moment, a spontaneous defence of the lovability of the gaunt, difficult woman with whom he shared his life, a side he would never reveal in front of the boys.

I watched him as he watched the window where he knew she was. I noticed his smile and upward nod and saw for the first time that Walter and his mother were close in a way I hadn't realised before. *He* would never treat a woman the way his father had treated her.

'What shall we do when we're old, do you think?' I said, out of the quiet that had settled upon us.

'How old, like Mam do you mean?'

'No silly, not old, old. You know seventeen or eighteen.'

'I'm not sure. I'd like to travel a bit—maybe visit London. Then live in Manchester and work in an important office doing stuff. Get married, I suppose.'

'I want to go to college, be a teacher like Mrs Taylor. She's my favourite. When she talks about books, it's as if she…sparkles.'

'*Sparkles?* You're mad, you are.'

'And have lots of children so I don't end up like your Mam.'

'You'd have to find a husband first, one that understands the way our Ali ticks.'

'The way *I tick*?' I hadn't thought until that moment *I ticked* any differently to anyone else.

'Yeh. You're special, our Ali…' He stared straight at me, utterly unselfconscious, 'you know, like a boy, but hey, kind, clever. I don't know…different.'

We walked our bikes back up Horsehold, having cycled miles around the lanes until hunger forced us home. The sun pushed through the opaque sky making steam on the lane, the newly green hedgerow fragrant with hawthorn in the afternoon still. The effort of the steep incline to my house created tiny pearls of sweat on Walter's upper lip and temples. Then he did something. After leaning his bike up against the wall, he looked out over the moor behind the house, and then back at me in a way he hadn't before. He took a long slender hand out of his pocket, and gently, deliberately, lifted a curl from my forehead.

'You have the bluest eyes I've ever seen, Ali Conroy,' he whispered, as though unable to summon more volume. He coughed his embarrassment.

I could smell the rubber from his handlebars, see the fresh dirt in his fingernails. I didn't speak. I knew something significant had passed between us. We were just kids but…something shifted; his demeanour like that of an infant practising the facial expressions it would one day need, suggesting an inner world that seemed to have attained a greater degree of complexity and wit than his years would suggest. A faint smile lingered around his mouth. He lowered his eyes, turned around, grabbed his bike and disappeared down the hill.

That night I dreamed of him. In my dream he was telling me he wanted to be my hero. I was skipping, counting, ignoring him…

Down by the river,
Down by the sea,
Johnny broke a bottle
And blamed it on me.
I told Ma,
Ma told Pa,
Johnny got a spanking,
So ha ha ha…1…2…3…

When I woke the next morning, my face was wet. I felt a brooding disquiet. Some childish premonition: one day I would lose him and with that, part of me too. But then, I remembered it was just a dream. I was hungry, could smell bacon, toast, hear the clatter and chatter of family downstairs, my brothers arguing, the scraping of breakfast chairs, the radio news blaring. If I didn't get down soon it would all be gone.

I pulled back the curtains flooding my little room with the soft May light of a perfect morning. I pulled on my school uniform without washing and ran barefoot down the stairs.

Chapter Two

America
1933

'I don't care what the hell they tell us, I ain't selling my wheat for that price. *It's the Depression* they say, *people are starving an' your fields full of grain.* They told us to increase production—*feed the nation,* so I buy all this land and machinery with money I ain't got... goddamn it. We clung on by our fingernails during the so-called *dustbowl crisis* and now this. Well, I sure as hell didn't cause it. How do I cover my bills if I sell for that? I'd rather burn it. Boy, get in, we're done here.'

Jed McCullough climbed into his truck and started driving away before his son had seated himself. Carl grabbed the dashboard and leaned out to get the door, swung wide, as his father threw the vehicle into reverse and then around fast, out of the market and away from Scobey.

'Yessir, I'd rather burn it', he repeated under his breath as he pulled out onto the highway.

'God*damn* it,' he shouted with a rising cadence, banging a fist down hard onto the steering wheel, his unshaven face hollow as he pulled against it, eyes darting from side to side. 'First the drought and nothing, now I've got some yield, they won't pay. You'll have to leave school now, no more molly-coddling for you, boy. I need the help, can't afford to keep employing Billy now.'

'But Ma thinks—'

'Ma should keep her thoughts to herself an' do what she's good at.'

Jed gripped the steering wheel so tight, Carl knew better than to argue. ''Sides, you're fifteen now, time you quit all that mumbo jumbo. You got no need for it. What use are books? You can't eat them. I'll get your Ma to tell the school next time she's in town. You won't be going back.'

'But Billy's wife just had another kid. What'll *he* do?' Carl grasped at reasons to deflect his father's decision.

'Billy'll just have to find something else. He ain't my problem.'

Carl stared at the straight road ahead, impotent. School was the only way out of here, the only break from *them*. Living so far from everyone, friends were scarce. Tom and Willie lived as far on one side of County High as he did the other. Couldn't even say goodbye. And girls. Just when things had started to happen—Daisy Markham…

'Can I just go in to get my things, y'know, say thanks an' that to folks?'

'No need. I'll swing by the school and do the necessary next time I'm passing. Don't want you getting excited though, you'll be up at six and work a full day. Understood? If things get better, you might even earn something. Now quit jabbering, I need to think.'

They were the only farming family left thereabouts; the others given up on Roosevelt's promises and gone. Jed McCullough got farm equipment cheap—no one had need of it now. Nobody knew how the McCullough's had survived when everyone else had packed up and gone. There was talk. Even so, they *got by* living on bread and potatoes. The cattle had long gone. In the winter, no fuel and no money, it was subsistence—no more.

When the truck came in through a wide gap in the wire fence—the missing gate chopped up for firewood—Carl jumped out while the tyres spat dust into the air. He ran in, up the steps, letting the screen door slam behind him. In his room he kicked his door shut and fell onto the bed, his face creased and red. After a moment he picked up a pillow and threw it hard across the room. It hit a framed photo of the family, which fell off the wall and smashed, mixing tiny shards of glass with curled grey feathers from the burst pillow.

'Darn it. *Darn it*. I hate my life,' he screamed, muffled, into the bedclothes. '…trapped in this God-awful hell-hole…' He wailed like a small child beating his pillows with clenched fists. All his dreams of college, girls, friendships of any kind, of life outside here all turned to dust. How he hated his father.

There were footsteps outside his door, the tap tap of his mother's shoes—tentative, cautious.

'Carl?' There was a hesitant, soft knock on the door. 'Carl? You okay, honey?'

She opened the door a crack, saw the glass, the feathers and slowly closed it again.

Carl heard the tap tap again on the stairs, the creek near the bottom, then voices. They were, in turn, upended and questioning, 'why can't you leave Carl out of it, he's just a boy…' and thumping, like a hammer knocking on a block of wood: "Shut your mouth, woman, can't you see this is about survival?' More shouting, more hammering. Then quiet. Carl knew what was coming. He heard the furniture go over—what was left of it. The loud silence of his mother. The slam of a door and a bucket being kicked down the steps into the yard. The truck started up again outside, reversed, then screeched off exhaling a cloud of dust in its wake, that even horizontal on his bed, Carl could see rising into the still air like smoke from a fire.

Later, as he sat at the table waiting for whatever food was available: watery soup with a few onions, bread with the last of the lard smeared over it, his mother was silent, nursing her anger as she always did in self-hate. He wondered, looking at her, whether she'd always been this way, this passive victim. He'd seen photos of her laughing and pretty. Where had she gone? Her lip was cut and swollen, the side of her face bruised and grazed. And there was a weariness in her that made her look much older than her years. As Carl stared at the ghostly figure limping silently around him, all he could think was that at least it wasn't him. This time.

Chapter Three

England
1939

'My history teacher thinks I'm *lovely*.' Walter's voice was buttery, vowels sliding thick through laughter.

I watched his mouth, the words perfunctory. 'Lovely, that's what she said. Don't join up. You're too lovely.' He closed his eyes, pushed up his lower lip in that way he had, nodded his head in confirmation, his body loose and open. He pushed his hands into wide, frayed pockets. Rocked back on his heels.

'Myopic, is she?' I rasped, neatly sidestepping when he attempted to nudge me into the hedge. 'Too slow.'

He narrowed his eyes, reaching forward as though to show me how slow he was. I didn't move. His smile said he conceded defeat, instead he brushed the dishevelled hair from my forehead with his fingers, his eyes circling my face. 'Only sixteen and too clever by half.' I stared, provocative; pushed the boundary. He half whistled, took a deep breath and gave me that sideways look that told me to behave.

Mam said we were just kids. She didn't understand.

Walter looked at his watch. 'Heck…I'll miss my bus.' He started to walk backwards down the hill, over the canal, his legs crossing one behind the other in a plaiting movement.

'Are we going up top tonight?' I threw after him, feeling the sudden vacuum. 'We could take Tara, she needs the exercise, I can't ride her just yet…'

'I'll call after school.' He turned, leaned into a run, his teenage wave barely rising from his hip.

I watched him, gangly, colt-like, trotting down the cobbled street, his sandy hair flopping in rhythm, just the right side of ginger. Books slithered under his arm, his shirt hanging out as he turned the corner and disappeared into Holme Street. Since that day up on Blackstone Edge, I started to take care how I looked around him and began to worry just a little. I walked on, turned left into Market

Street and waited at the stop for the bus to St Jo's, casting a lingering glance behind to check he wasn't rushing back to say something sweet; the kind of thing he did in my idea of him. He wasn't.

It was steep. Tara pulled against the slope, her dappled forelegs taking the strain. A sheen of sweat coated her neck and flanks, seal-like, muscles moving to and fro beneath her skin. She chewed at the snaffle, snorted and snatched at tall grasses, smelt of hay and too long in the stable.

A low sun shone gold on the beck where bits of it stretched flashing smooth on the water like coloured glass, curving over stones, around grassy banks. Squinting, Walter's expression was lean and easy, the play of a smile always lingering or anticipated, his temples beaded with perspiration in the heavy warmth that hung about the evening.

He glanced behind him, at the sky.

'Cu Nims,' he said almost inaudibly, a slight frown settling, like flaws in marble.

'Cu Nims?'

'Cumulus Nimbus. Storm clouds.'

'A storm?'

'Not yet.' He inhaled sharply, then looked at me pointedly, as though absorbing the duplicity of his perception.

But the sun was warm that day in 1939, the breeze balmy. The sort of day you live your life for, not for the things that happen, but for the promise of what may.

I heard a skylark and stood for a moment shielding my eyes from the sun. High, it dipped and danced, dropped and fluttered. I looked to the ground, stepping carefully, then realised it was too late in the year for nesting. Walter walked on, as always, separate, his gaze flooding the landscape, every distant crevice filled with it. He loved the vastness of things. He appeared always to be searching, seeing things for the first time, yet not quite seeing.

He noticed changes: the springiness of the moorland after rain but would not see a small pony slowly getting bogged down in it. He would wonder at the size of the rocky outcrops, their stratum, see in them the manifestation of a jaw or claw, but not observe the colours of the lichen creeping over their surface like yellow snowflakes. He enjoyed his walks with a pretty blue-eyed girl, oblivious to the fact that she was always a few steps behind, easy in his wake; utterly in love with him.

When he turned, his gaze lapped at me, eddied around me creating the sensation of sinking, like feet in an incoming tide.

I became thirsty around him, wanting to be quenched, my body moving like a hunted mate that knows all the steps, that wants to be *taken*, but coy, converting my instincts to romance, to a conditioned idea of the way it *should* be and willing him to conform to it.

He raised his eyebrows, a look that warned me; he knew me too well and walked on.

Walter had man's legs: sandy haired, sinewy; solid muscled thighs, the legs of a swimmer.

'I'm going over to Burnley tomorrow after the gala to see how old you have to be to enlist. Murray says eighteen,' he threw over his shoulder, pushing a sideways glance at me.

'Why?' Catching up, I pulled him back and made him look at me. I stared big-eyed, waiting, and felt the grown-up world like a tidal wave suddenly encroaching. He looked at my hand on his arm, felt the tremor in it. 'I…I…just want everything to stay the same. Please don't do it, Walter?'

Unusually, he felt rigid. He looked away at the sky, then back at me, not quite smiling. Then with a sharp intake of breath, he cast a glance back to where we had been, his head tilted to one side, his bottom lip pushed up, measuring, fulminating a response.

'How bird-like you are, Ali. Airy, like a wisp of wind would blow you away. Everything's changing. Why will you not see what's coming? For someone so clever…'

'What?'

'There *will* be a war, no matter what Chamberlain does or says. It's going to happen, and I won't have a choice. We're so young, y'know? Everything is in a state of flux. We can't make promises—you know that. You'll be the best reason to come back…' He pulled me over to him, held me so close my breath escaped as a sigh, his arms crossed over my back. 'To miss you, I have to go first and going *is* inevitable. Life isn't about standing still, Ali, we must move with it or stagnate, and you need to prepare yourself. I know from Mam…' He took a deep breath. 'Look…it's just not our time.'

I didn't speak, just stared into his chest. He leaned back, pulled up my face to his, ran his finger down my cheek.

'Your eyes…the colour of cornflowers. Have I ever told you that?' I nodded. 'Yeh, well…You look like a kid with your hair clipped back, your girl-clothes. But you're not a kid, are you, our Ali?' I wanted him to carry on. 'This how you'll always be, set up here, high, like one of those birds that has wings but can't fly…' Walter was the first to see it. 'You have to make life happen; it won't come to you. This is your territory, mine too, but to appreciate it, maybe we have to have something to compare it to, you know?'

'But…'

'We're so…we need more. Of life, I mean.'

My jaw trembled. I didn't want him to see and put my hands to my mouth in a misread gesture.

'You're so melodramatic.' He laughed off the moment and it was gone, kissed my forehead, relaxed. 'Let's stop for a while, Tara can graze, can't she? Hey look.' He pointed into the distance. 'Stoodley Pike… clear as a bell, looks like a lighthouse on a cliff edge don't you think? You could imagine the sea over yonder, but it must be fifty mile at least.'

He shielded his eyes. I climbed up behind him, tried to see the world as he did. I saw the sky like a lid, framing the earth, the detail of distant cloud slowly changing; animals and monsters appearing and disappearing, painted for our pleasure.

'What about you swimming the channel?' I turned my back to him, looking down into the cotton grass that tickled my legs.

'Look around you. What is there here for me? I want to travel, Ali. I want to know what's over the next hill. I may get lucky with my swimming; get my name in the papers for five minutes. Then what? Get sucked in. Take a job in the shop and spend the next fifty years giving *tick* to hard-up pensioners. You wouldn't love me then.' He turned around; a question hung around his eyes. 'Life has to be about more than that, doesn't it? I don't know, maybe war will give us that.'

'Who said I loved you?' I poked him in the ribs, teasing, ignoring the irony of his words. I turned and ran.

'Come here. You need punishment, you do.'

He gave chase, laughing at my squealing, grabbing me around the waist, bringing me down in one easy movement.

'Try!'

I lay back on the grass giggling.

'Worm! I am not a rugby ball.'

He flopped beside me, his face just above mine. He had the face of an artist, or at least my idea of one; gentle, strong, haunted in some way. I noticed again the slight cross in his front teeth that pushed forward his top lip. His full pale mouth, his freckles. His green eyes, with the merest fleck of hazel, the lashes that brushed my cheek as his lips grazed my neck and throat. The honed bone structure, the slight furrow between his brows, the rasp of his chin. My *Angular Saxon*.

I looked up into space, enjoying the rise and fall of his breathing, his lemony swimming pool smell, while Tara trotted on and stopped at a greener patch on the hillside. He laid one arm around my head, the other lay across me, picking grass. I reached over and stroked the baby-smooth skin of his upper arm. Like a breeze caressing the surface of a pond, his skin goose-bumped; rippled into tiny points.

'Ned went down to Bovingdon last week for training.' I plucked a sheaf of grass to chew.

'I know, I talked to him. He must be one of the first, lucky blighter…' He stopped himself, shook his head wincing slightly, wishing the thought unsaid. 'Are you all right about it?'

'Oh…you know. On the radio, it's all happening to someone else. Then it's your brother. It'll be Vincent next…then you.' A wisp of cirrus crossing the sun threw a shadow. 'I think if you all just sat tight, it may blow over.'

'Oh Ali. Ned will be alright in the AFV's. He'll be a mechanic; he won't be going anywhere dangerous. He'll have the time of his life. I know how close you two are, but don't worry. He's young, wants to be where the action is. You can understand that can't you?' He traced the tip of his index finger down the inside of my collar, closed his eyes.

I didn't answer. A faint buzzing of insects filled the silence. I pondered whether *I* should want to be where the action is.

'And what about us women, when you've gone. What're we supposed to do?' I pouted, attempting to hide the sense of panic that had nestled in my breathing.

'Oh well, if it's going to ruin your social life, I'll tell the war office to make it up with Hitler pronto, can't have our Ali and her pals bored now, can we!'

He leant over, kissed my throat; cotton-wool kisses. He mumbled almost inaudibly, stroking me like a cat.

'Mmm…'

'The house seems bigger.' Schooled in maintaining composure, I stared at the sky.'

'I want to…'

'I'm trying to persuade Mam to let me have his room…' a crack in my voice. I inhaled, took hold of his face, held it back. He pulled against me, kept on kissing, barely touching me, the flutter of a leaf, soft breeze on moist skin.

'I want…to write…' he made circles with his index finger on my belly through the gap between the buttons on my dress '…all over you.'

'You have,' I whispered.

Opening his eyes, he made me look at him. I stroked his lips with a grass stalk. He blinked, a playful expression sliding onto his face.

'Come here.'

I began humming as he kissed me again, then singing *I don't want to play in your yard. I don't like you anymore, you'll be sorry when you see me, sliding down our cellar door. You can't holler down our rain-barrel, you can't climb our apple tree. I don't want to play in your yard, if you won't be good to me.*

'Holler?'

'Holler.'

'You're always singing that…'

'My Mam used to sing it when we were small, her Mam sang it to her. I can't remember all the words.'

'I wish we could…' Brows raised; his eyes asked the usual question. He touched my lips with his finger. 'You have a baby's mouth.' I pulled a face. 'No really. Sometimes, when you're dozing, your bottom lip moves back and forth in a suckling motion. I've seen you. And you stroke a bit of cloth or something, with your thumb and forefinger.' He demonstrated.

I hadn't realised he knew, felt embarrassed suddenly. It had to be silky, a clothes label or a feather, my…thing. Whenever I found one, I would keep it somewhere, touch it when I felt the need.

Even had I let him, he wouldn't try and seduce me. We were too close; for us it would be more than experimentation and we both knew it.

'We can't,' I said, without conviction. 'You do want me though, don't you?' I stroked his belly where his shirt had ridden up.

'You're such a tease! Stop it.' He laughed. 'Your Dad'd kill me!'

'Anyway, it's a mortal sin.'

'No one would know.' His eyes glazed.

'I'd know. And if we did it and used a Johnny, that's another sin.'

'God! I can't believe you left-footers.'

'Don't start that. Anyway, I don't want to. I mean, I want to…I *want* to', I kissed him, licked his lips lightly, knowing what I was doing and enjoying the effect, then pushed him away, '…but not yet. I'd feel guilty. You lot can do whatever you want. No repercussions. No morals.' I put on my superior look.

'Don't let my Mam hear you say that. She already thinks you're above yourself.'

'Oh, your Mam. She's just jealous. Wants you all to herself, mummy's boy!' I plucked a handful of grass and threw it at him.

'Hey! Come here you. I'll teach you who's a mummy's boy.'

He rolled onto me letting me feel his weight. Kissed me on the mouth. He was such a good kisser. I was always trying to explain this feeling to the girls at school. Jane McLaughlin had done it, gone the whole way. She said using a Johnny was like eating a toffee with the paper still on. Expelled from school, pregnant. One day she was there, handing in homework: *Ambition in Macbeth*; the next she was gone. One of the girls said she was working at Woolworth's. Her name wasn't to be mentioned.

Walter's hand crept down towards my breasts—forbidden territory, but I let him. Felt my nipples pucker to his touch through my thin cotton dress, aware of tumbling into a promised sublimity.

'Do you want babies, Walter?' I whispered through my arousal trying to regain some sort of equanimity.

'Not at this precise moment,' he groaned.

'I do. Loads.'

He threw himself back laughing, counting 'one, two, three…' collecting himself.

'There's a name for girls like you!'

'Don't you dare, Walter Bradshaw.'

It was a game.

We lay still, felt the setting sun on our faces, ants on our ankles. The grass tickled my neck, frog spittle made damp patches on my frock. The sky slowly changed its pattern. I emptied my mind, thought of nothing except clinging to the surface of my revolving earth, infinitely moving, in infinite space.

Suddenly, waving my arms like wings, I sprang from the ground and sprinted up the hill. Tara, startled, broke into a canter.

'Last one in is mardy…'

Up ahead, the tarn waited, still. A pale mirror of a darkening sky; fire-gold. Solid. Around it a dense fringe of tall grasses and reeds leaned into it.

Despite my start, Walter beat me easily to the edge, tearing at his shirt, tripping on his undone shorts.

'You see water and you can't wait to get your keks off,' I shouted.

He stopped at the steep edge where the tarn was deepest.

Time stopped.

I paused, breathless, watched him concentrate. I did not exist. He stood, eyes closed, very still. He counted softly to himself. After five heartbeats he leapt. High. Looped somehow, and entered the water straight, toes pointed, insteps curved like a ballerina. Circles spilled out. The wake lapped at the edge. Down, down he went. He told me: light and sound ceased, just a murky glow and muted murmur. Cold streaked across his body and woke in him primeval beginnings. He had scoured the oceans, combed the depths. Swimming was in him before he was born.

He was in a place I couldn't go. He told me that sometimes, when everything was right, when he was focused so that nothing else existed, he could swim around in the depths with no need to breathe.

Sometimes a hint of iridescence, blue-black and green, flashed as he rolled between strokes. The strike of his feet on the wake, a mighty tailfin. Time, space and matter shifted.

When he returned, triumphant, a hero, I could hardly believe how puny he looked. My *Angular Saxon* was still just a boy. His white chest and awkward arms maintaining balance while he trod water.

'Where were you?'

'I was watching.'

I stood in a short petticoat, my frock beside me, folded. He told me later, much later, how small I looked standing there. Perfect. My hair curling, dark, shot through with sun. My knock-knees. Told me how that moment was the one.

I hovered on the edge, my arms outstretched like a cormorant eyeing my prey, biding my time, knowing that when I was ready, he was a fish I would scoop from the water and take to my nest to consume. Then I jumped, dropped flat beside him, plunging deep into the green, pulling him under. As we surfaced, he held me. Said he would always be there to catch me.

Chapter Four

England
1940

'Why can't you stay in Hebden? Why Manchester?' Mam didn't look up when I read out the letter from the War Office, her face fixed. She banged down the iron, hunched her shoulders, wisps of hair fell over eyes that stared like a hare in headlights. 'Why?'

'Because that's where the factories are. It might be fun.' I tried to suppress a smile that slid over my face at the prospect as I waited for the predictable response.

'Fun! You've no idea, young lady…'

I looked to Dad who lowered his newspaper and winked at me.

'Look Mam, it's all right.' I squeezed the top of her arm in the reassuring gesture Dad had used for years; affection weakened her. 'They've found digs for me in…where is it…Middleton Junction? I'm not going into the jungle.'

'Oh yes you are.' She banged down the iron again. 'Middleton Junction! It's a dump. Harry Ford, you know him, rough as muck. He's from there. His garden's an eyesore, no wonder his wife left him. Rob you as soon as look at you, common as pork pie. There'll be two an ha'penny like him in Middleton Junction.'

Dad snorted, I groaned, only the merest look from Mam revealed her awareness of being outside the circle.

'And there'll be soldiers everywhere looking for a good time. You're a country girl. They'll eat you alive. Not to mention the air raids. Remember the blitz last Christmas? The city was a smoking ruin, dead babies in the streets…and where will you go to mass?'

'Oh Mam… Mam, stop.' She ceased her ironing for a moment, fixed her gaze out of the kitchen window, across the garden to the moors. 'Stop being so dramatic.'

'It's just, you know, with Ned and Walter gone, now Vincent…' Her voice wavered and trailed off.

'Yes, and I'm stuck here…' I barked. She closed her eyes, the iron poised in an upturned hand. 'Sorry Mam, I didn't mean that, but…well, I'm young, everyone else has gone. I want to go too.'

'Nowt'll happen to her, love. She's only down't road,' Dad said, tutting and snapping his newspaper. One son in action. The other bound for somewhere soon. 'Stop your fretting, Kathy. In case you hadn't noticed, she's a girl…she'll only build the bloody things, not fly 'em. She's going nowhere.'

'Oh Dad, you're so practical. Such ambition you have for me.' I sidled onto the arm of his chair, slipped my arm around his neck, kissed his balding head.

'Don't say *nowt*, Bernard, please,' Mam spat. 'Alice, get off the arm of that chair, you'll break it…'

Ned's visit home after eight months away and a frantic evacuation from Dunkirk had fuelled the fire of anxiety. Mam had folded and unfolded the letter he couldn't send, telling of things unimaginable: *…all you could see were abandoned trucks, burned out tanks, flattened villages. Bodies…* She'd found it in his pocket, dog-eared and smelling of army surplus, when doing the laundry.

Eight days after the date on the letter, Ned had walked up the path to our front door. Five o'clock in the morning. The milkman had given him a lift in the wagon up Hebble End. He stood on the back listening to the dawn chorus and the clopping of hooves, falling asleep bolt upright, until it got too steep for the horse. After walking the last three hundred yards up Horsehold, he had to hammer on the door for a full five minutes before Mam, cursing, then crying and laughing, let him in. He pulled the mattress off the bed and slept on the springs in his uniform. Dog-tired. Crawling with lice.

Later, Mam sat beside him, a stiff joy set on her lips, watching his face, touching him, his shoulder, his hand, seeing past the man to the boy; his preoccupation with the way things worked, his bicycle in bits over an oily kitchen floor, his apologetic and satisfied smile. Then she noticed me staring at her and a feminine complicity manifested in a sad smile, spread between us in recognition of our powerlessness.

We drank his health with home-made apple wine.

'To Ned,' Dad toasted, standing up, eyes shining, his lips fat with love and alcohol.

'To Ned,' everyone chorused.

Ned told us he was lucky. The *Lady of Mann* passenger ferry he had boarded at Brest was attacked by Stuka bombers on the way over. Six thousand on board.

'We made it though, sailed into Mill Bay without a scratch. Not everyone did. I can't tell you how good it felt.'

Two weeks later, he left for the Middle East. Went out on the *Empire Pride* to join the Army of the Nile. When a letter arrived some weeks later, mostly blanked out by the censor, it said the food on board had been dreadful; he missed Mam's cooking. He didn't say they'd had to zig-zag all the way. U-boats.

*

Nearvarna, hand painted in nine different colours, was tacked crookedly onto the architrave above the front door. Inside, the smell of vegetables boiled too long and the tinkle of a pan lid simmering, together with a décor of dingy yellow anaglypta, filled me with drear cheerlessness. The unlit fire and brown tiled surround, the colour of a grubby dog, added to my sinking feeling

Upstairs, our bedroom window looked down onto the outside privy, which when flushed, growled like the slow dull thud of thunder. Beyond it was a view over the narrow yard, past the coal-shed, onto the shiny slate roofs of the neighbouring houses, and an urban landscape that stretched dark and smoky into infinity.

There were two small beds crammed into the room, separated by an old cupboard, inside which was a chamber-pot for night-time emergencies, and above, a bedside lamp whose electric wiring looked precarious. A small teak coloured wardrobe, whose door was crooked and wouldn't close, and a painted chest of drawers with two handles missing, stood side by side opposite the beds, leaving two feet of space for manoeuvre.

In the tiny bathroom across the landing, the howl from the hot water tap as air moved around the system, and which no one ever got around to fixing, could be heard all over the house so that sneaking in late meant no night-time wash, or one in icy water.

Our house, one of row after row of parallel red brick terraces, was not what I had in mind when I thought of moving to the city. Outside, weeds pushed through the grey gravelled front square and a rusty bike leant up against the crumbling white-washed sill of the window. Ragged children ran in and out of each other's houses and there was an endless yapping, accompanied by the occasional blast: 'Will some bugger shut that bloody dog up?'

Leading to the corner shop, an alleyway ran along the side of the house where litter blew into crevices and skinny dogs and cats strayed, leaving calling cards that would make me curse as I dashed each morning for my bus. My new home had the feeling of something utterly unlovable.

'Hiya, I'm Lily Parkinson. What do you think about all this then? Flippin' excitin' I'd say, though this room is a bit poky for two.'

'Ali Conroy. Pleased to meet you.' I offered my hand, which then dropped by my side, untaken.

'Which bed do you want?' An alley cat choosing her territory.

'I don't mind, you choose.' I felt instinctively I should defer to this bottle blond that strutted and tutted. I was only just eighteen, Lily was twenty-one, a world away.

'All right. This one'll do.' Lily flopped down on the bed that I knew she would take, having already put her bag on it, and the other being up against the wall under the window that rattled a nervous tic when the wind blew.

I put down my bag, uncertain what to do next.

'What d' ye think of the landlord and his wife then?'

I shrugged. What did she want me to say? 'Not sure.'

'Definitely dodgy, if y'ask me.' Lily lay back, kicking off her shoes. 'He's got an alki's nose. And *her,* she won't die wondering; surprised she's still standing.' She pulled a sour face and laughed.

I caught sight of my face in the dressing table mirror: pink, wide-eyed, halfway between amusement and horror.

After getting off the bus each morning, walking under the railway arch, then ascending the steep rise on the other side, I never failed to notice the mill's edifice soaring over me, its name highlighted on the tower in white brick that glinted in the sharp morning light. The office, where I was employed, was deep in its belly.

Behind high frosted windows, reflecting flickering fluorescent lights that gave me a headache, I stared, day after day, from the one clear pane that looked out over the clutter of the factory floor, where part-built aeroplanes sat waiting for their creators to finish so they could roar into life, and wondered when I would. I seemed destined to stare from windows waiting for life to begin.

I remember feeling I had been swallowed alive.

Each time I tried to lose myself in a book to deflect the stultifying boredom, the manager's secretary, Mrs Mandy Buck, known as Randy Mandy, would rip me from the pleasant distraction by yelling like a market vendor: 'Alice Conroy, a' thee readin'? Get thee face out't book. You know't bloody rules.'

That voluminous backside had eyes in it.

I tried to get involved in the ledgers, the orders, the accounts, but two or three hours a day saw the work finished and filed. The rest of the time I gazed absently at the noiseless goings on of the factory floor, dreaming of what I *could* be doing and with whom. I fiddled with my nails, crimped my hair, stared into a powder compact mirror that Lily had given me and decided my nose was too small, lips too thick and how much prettier I would be if I were blonde.

The world, I felt, was going on somewhere else. After a fortnight, when I had to stop myself lying supine on the floor, such was the soporific effect of the flickering yellow light and the absence of occupation, I asked to be moved, said my sanity depended on it. Within a week, I was sent up the road to Chadderton, to the aircraft factory A. V. Roes: Avie Rose as we called it, like some red-cheeked winsome lass, to join Lily, building gun turrets on Lancaster Bombers, and belling the ends of the hydraulic pipes on the Cerabin Tanks. They were short-staffed now that production had increased.

As I left, Randy Mandy gave me a useful tip for the future: 'Ye gorra lot to learn, young lady. Remember to do as your told, take yer nose outta yer arse and keep yer fingers out of other people's pies…'

When I entered the huge, dirty carcass of a building, and saw mostly women wearing overalls and snoods, doing what looked to me like men's heavy work, I began to think I should have stayed put, but the factory noise and activity, punctuated by bursts of laughter reminded me why I was there. The few men, discharged for some reason or too old or unfit to fight, hovered around me like wasps to jam, as they did, apparently, with all pretty, newly conscripted girls. My new roommate was delighted at my transfer and introduced me, with a comic air of self-imposed authority, to everyone she thought was worth the trouble.

I decided to like Lily, enjoy her bossy energy, her rebelliousness, her scarlet toenails, high insteps and four-inch heels that made marks on the lino causing Percy, our landlord, to whinge in the mewling way he had. Her tight skirts, plunging necklines and a stare that was calculated to stop a man in his tracks always won him around. *Get off with you*, he would whimper with a wave of his hand, never removing his eyes from her cleavage.

Lily said that I should get my nose out of my books and get some real education; said I needed to mix with the hoi polloi, get my hands dirty, have myself *a bit of city*. I had to admit, beside her, I looked pretty dull.

'And you're bonny enough, but there's so much more you could do.'

She painted my nails, let me borrow her red shoes, drew stocking seams with eye pencil. When we were going out, she showed me how to use gravy browning to tan our legs. I said they smelled of Sunday lunch. Lily said only posh people said 'lunch'. She told me not to wash my face with soap, said cold cream would keep me *kiss-fresh*. She talked a lot about sex.

The deal was, I would teach Lily to dance, Lily would 'educate' me. While I experimented with make-up, Lily waltzed around the gaps between the beds, a pillow for a partner, trying out steps I had taught her, crooning *I'll be with you in apple blossom time…* or jigging to Tommy Dorsey or Eddie Fisher on the radio. Percy would bang on the ceiling with the old trumpet he couldn't play, to shut us up. At which point the focus of conversation between us always turned to the landlord and his wife.

'She's got delusions of grandeur, that one, her ruddy nose in the air and nowt in her pocket. Champagne taste and beer income.' I would pretend to be distracted as though only half listening. 'She's got an arse on her like the back end't tram and I reckon there's blokes hailing from every blinkin' tram-stop in South Manchester, getting on and off like there was no tomorrer.

'Just listen,' Lily prattled, 'you can hear them at it.' I *had* heard men coming in and out all times of the day and night, the slam of the front door a familiar sound in the early hours. We couldn't imagine what Percy was doing while all this was going on. Counting the money?

'…An' the pair of 'em smoke like ruddy Rainser Brew power station. My red shift stinks of stale tobacco. Reckon it's the *having it off* that pays for it. How else could they afford all the fags?'

Lily could sleep through anything: the blackout with its sounds of ack-ack in the distance, the yapping dog and mewling infant next door, the whine of the air raid sirens or the howl of the hot water tap. Even the squeaking springs of the bed in the room along the hall. I envied her; wished I could switch off as I lay exhausted, a jumble of thoughts and random images in my head: the steep hill up Horsehold, a flash of Stoodley through the mist, Mam's chipped teacup with the pink flowers, the worn arms of Dad's chair, Ned's bicycle leaning askew in the hall, April violets, Vincent's hands... Night after night I lay wide-eyed in the dark, staring at the gradually lightening square of grey window in a stupor of sleeplessness, sad and happy at the same time, the soft cushion of Lily's breathing beside me.

It was at night that Walter would drift in and out of my thoughts, the warm feeling at the base of things; the constant, in a world that seem to change by the minute. But both of us were exposed to experiences and influences the other couldn't share or censure and it preyed on my mind.

During his training in Seaton Carew, I hadn't seen him once. Since he moved to Driffield, closer to home, we had some contact. On my visit there though, we spent the entire two days skirting around each other, he not knowing quite what to do with me, being out of context as I was, in his new soldier's life. I felt overly gay in bright colours, pristine in white gloves, as if I were somehow outside of the war. At first, holding hands, kissing, hugging, had seemed perfunctory. It was as though our previous relationship risked being consigned to childhood, something to be embarrassed about.

Then just as I was leaving, as I stood on the steps of his barracks, eye-to-eye with him, I saw the hesitation, the awkwardness in his demeanour. He took hold of both of my arms, his face creased and taut. He bit the inside of his mouth, frowned, looked away, then back at me seemingly unable to articulate what was troubling him. It wasn't like him. Then he moved a curl from my brow, held it away from my face and pressed his mouth where it had been. He sighed and held me there.

'This is my favourite place, just here,' he whispered into my hair. His voice was choked. He ran his lips back and forth along my forehead. 'Here, underneath these curls, this white skin, whiter than the rest, perfectly smooth and hiding all those secrets. There's no one like you, Ali Conroy, not to me. We're two halves of a whole, always have been. I didn't expect to miss you so much...As long as I can remember, you've always been there.'

But since Driffield, something had changed. I suppose life was just too busy. Lily, probably jealous, said I mustn't let grass grow. I thought about our letters. Mail seemed to take an age. Longer than those I received from Vincent at his training base. Even letters from Ned eventually got through, though being Ned, chunks of them were censored; he always said too much or nothing at all.

One night, by the light of a torch, yellow in the darkness, I read and re-read the letter I had recently received from Walter. It was full of his life as a soldier in training. He told me about Jack, a friend from home, killed in the Atlantic. Poor, poor Jack…his Mam…He asked about Ned and Vincent, and all the usual stuff, but I kept skipping to the bit at the end: *I've got leave in a fortnight. Do you think you'll be able to get some time off? I want to come over. I miss you, Ali. I need to see you. Perhaps you could fix something up for me? This may be the last opportunity to be together before I go.*

In a spidery hand that wobbled against the bedclothes, the other hand angling the torch, I started to write a reply. I tried to make it breezy, push away the fear at the root of everything. I told him about my dubious landlord and lady, the lack of food with the rationing; though Percy seemed to have no shortage, waistline like a hula hoop. I wrote that Ned was in Tobruk with the Australians…Told him I missed him. Almost told him I loved him.

I yawned and clicked off the torch to sleep when the sirens started. I heard the whining of the Junkers and there were searchlights moving all over the sky, visible even through the blacked-out windows. There was the dull whistle of dropped bombs and then silence. I held my breath, counted.

Suddenly, two of the window-panes blew in with the blast, tiny shards of flame all over the bedroom floor. I grabbed Lily, yelling at her to get out, grab her gas mask and follow me onto the landing where Percy screamed at us to get under the stairs, the rumble of delayed thunder making the house shudder. We squealed, falling over each other, as we tumbled down the stairs. I wanted my family, Mam's arms around me. Nobody moved until it was over. I remember the thick rubber smell of the gas mask, no saliva in my mouth. I remember I was very still, finding a place within myself away from the horror outside.

The next day we saw that Murray Road, three streets away, had taken a direct hit. Just disappeared. We could smell the devastation, the cordite; everything was burning. Lily and I held each other and wept to see the great empty space in the knowledge of how many had died. It could have been us. Clouds of smoke, like spectres, hung in the still air, haunting the scene. The ground was a river with all the hoses trying to put out the fires. I saw a sailor in uniform arrived from somewhere, a kit bag over his shoulder, just standing there in front of nothing, shivering.

Chapter Five

England
1941

I leant back on straight arms, half smiling. *Snow White*, he said. Silent for a while, we pointed our faces toward a milky sun.

He smelt different: Brylcreem, boot-polish; like a stranger that I knew. When I spoke, my voice was husky, lowered, the way it is in church. I was embarrassed, wanted to be close, but couldn't breach the barrier between us. I cleared my throat, leaned forward, fiddled with my sleeve, all the while feeling a nervous ache in my groin, while Walter, looking distracted, lay back, his head resting on his hands staring into space. His brow was knotted, as though through the tree's awning, up in the sky, something was of immense interest. Some minutes passed, the air heavy. When we spoke, it was at the same time, then laughter and silence again. We talked around things, reminiscing. Not touching.

Feeling the comfort of the stronger sun breaking through, I lay back too, closed my eyes and gently rested my head on Walter's outstretched elbow. I thought back to the morning when he'd said I'd changed, and I wondered about that. He loved the red dress that Lily had given to me, but said I looked *too good*. He didn't explain, though I knew what he meant. He watched as soldiers broke their step, turned their stare upon me and saw that I liked it.

Light-hearted banter blew about between us as we shuffled around Manchester like two people lost in their shared world. Everywhere there were men and women digging, clearing away rubble, sweeping the edges of tattered lives into sacks. The whiff of old cement, like the crypt of a church, made of the Spring air something ancient. Despite the renewed shock of the proximity of war, I was conscious of a certain gaiety in my manner, a sense of my place in things. My perceptions were heightened—everything in contrast, as though seeing for the first time the opposite of my mortality. War, I thought, was fun.

I enjoyed Walter in his uniform. I wanted to touch him, play, claim ownership—my own toy soldier—all grown up and smelling like a man. People nodded to us. An old man lifted his hat, his sad, wintry eyes diluting his cheery greeting, making me turn to watch him walk away, wondering what it was he saw.

Beneath the gaiety, was an unspoken need and small actions became charged: a sideways glance from Walter, lips slightly apart, as though controlling something that required a great deal of concentration, made me aware that what had been fermenting for years had come to fruition. We were ready, had become adults with adult needs. Gone was the freedom of our childhood where physical proximity was uninhibited, unguarded, where words were just that and not laced with innuendo or purpose.

There was the added sense that if we didn't seize the moment, there may not be another or at least not for a long time. There was only one way that could be done and we both knew it. A slow brush of my thumb across the back of his hand caused an involuntary shudder, an intake of breath. He bit his lip, kept his eyes on the pavement. I knew what I was doing, or at least, I thought I did. What passed between us was the recognition that our parallel lives were gradually converging.

There were too many people around. On a whim we decided to get out of the city and randomly took a bus from the cathedral going North.

Heaton Park was closed. Military police guarded the gates, MOD notices said *Keep Out*, which we ignored and slipped in where a broken fence had been used as an unofficial entry point, the grass worn down by heavy boots. We could see, through the perimeter woodland of beech and oak, thousands of forces tents, a canvass city squatting in a pale and limpid sun.

In the distance, we saw Heaton Hall, a honey-coloured mansion requisitioned for forces use. Keeping out of sight we wandered behind it, through a copse where Walter helped pull me up a steep incline, my face brushing his shoulder, his hands strong around my waist.

'Breathless already?' He smiled, releasing me.

I shot him a look.

At the top of the hill, the white stuccoed bell tower stood round and proud, with a view that reached out beyond Manchester, some five miles distant, to the Pennines. Walter stared toward the city, hands in his pockets as though in a dream. I watched his back as I ran a hand over the curve of the walls reading the detritus of lovers: *GC & BJ. Be mine. Until we meet again. We were here.* Wished Walter would leave his, or at least turn around and use the moment.

Instead, he stood silhouetted against the sky, the ground in front of him falling steeply away toward a lake some hundred feet below. I noticed his muscled calves push out the trousers below the knee, his hips slender and boy-like, his elbows stuck out by his sides like fins. He swayed slightly, a slight shimmer about his body. I had a sudden urge to do or say something rash. Instead, I stared at his back, mute. He turned and gave me a long lopsided smile as though reading my thoughts, biding his time.

As we sidled off in uncertain silence, he stretched out a hand to me and helped me down the slope. We wandered for a little while to a wilder part of the park, each apparently deep in thought, and after some minutes came upon a pretty sun-lit clearing on a downward slope. I let go of his hand and ducked inside the canopy of a huge weeping beech that touched the ground in a full circle around me, the sunshine filtering through its bare branches in waving spangled light.

'Come over here, Walter, I've found a cave.'

And now we lay on his overcoat, unspeaking, tense, our time together ticking away, while the grand powers that controlled our lives made plans for our futures, oblivious to the small passions of Ali Conroy and Walter Bradshaw. A few minutes passed, then Walter leaned over, took hold of my collar whispering 'sod the bloody Pope', and kissed me. Light airy kisses, his mouth pulling softly at mine, his tongue brushing, feather-soft against my lips. We smiled at the same time, then laughed softly, relieved that the wall had been breached.

The kisses became firmer, surer, until I felt he was almost sucking me into him, his tongue probing, predatory. Caresses became less tentative, more exploratory, until he stopped suddenly. His breathing uneven, he looked at me, at my lips, open slightly. I saw the veins on his translucent eyelids, the eyebrows with their curve leading to the indents of his temples that pulsated. His mouth a blurred pinkness, and the dark, uncertain invitation in his normally pale eyes.

'No…you're not Snow White…are you?' he whispered. It wasn't a fairy story anymore.

He lay against me, one arm under my neck, the other cupping my face as though the long anticipation of this moment had somehow paralysed him. It was the first time for both of us, and we lay, uncertain precisely how these things went.

I waited, closed my eyes, a montage of our lives thus far accelerating through my mind, wondering how we had managed, finally, to get to this; as though everything before had been leading here: the end of something, the beginning of something else.

My hands shaking, I took the initiative, loosened the buttons of his shirt and slid my hand inside, feeling his bare flesh, the shape of his torso, its hollows, feeling the faint new brush of hair high on his chest. This one aspect of his manhood made me shiver in anticipation and not a little fear; despite growing up with three men, I had never seen or touched a naked man.

Walter's eyes opened wide, staring at this new boldness, and I saw that he was trembling. I lay very still, felt the dampness of the grass on my legs, smelt the winter foliage, saw the confusion of black branches above us beating against a sky that seemed cracked and which might suddenly fall, showering fragments of delicate blue glass.

Walter's hot breath on my face, the brush of his uniform against my skin, the perception of my youth, the war…the way he stroked me gently, then not so gently, from my face down the length of my body and back again; over and over like the sea creeping and drawing on the sand, my heartbeat pulsing in rhythm as though existence itself had an echo that we had somehow locked into…and I knew, whatever life offered up to me in the future, this day, I would remember always.

'I want you, Walter…'

The smell in the chill air was of earth and something salty like sea. Walter's eyes were pressed shut. His hands pulled up my dress then he lowered his face to my breasts. His kisses light as gossamer ran down my body, while sliding his hand inside my panties, just touching, stroking the down, then he kissed me there lightly.

His face was flushed as he moved on top of me, his lips swollen with desire, the weight of his body surprisingly heavy. I felt submissive, given over to him, felt an overwhelming love that informed all my instincts; I relinquished control, pushed into the hard uneven ground, yet floating, high, drifting in a warm current of air. I felt my body absorb him, when suddenly he pulled back…

'We can't. Oh God, we can't, Ali. What are we thinking?'

I felt a dropping pain, an ache. I saw him above me, moving away, my red dress hitched up, body exposed, panties around my thighs, ugly white in the winter light. Foolish.

'What…what?' I whispered.

'I love you, Ali. I've always loved you. You are everything…you have no idea. I'm leaving tomorrow, I can't remember you like this; what might happen to you… just like my father left my mother. I, we can't. I didn't think we…didn't think you…I haven't got…I can't go away and leave you. Ali…I could be away for years. Oh God. Christ. Fuck…oh fuck.' He cursed, shouted, punched down on the earth with both fists with an anger I had never seen.

He lay back on the grass, breathing hard. There were tears rolling down his face.

'We can, Walter, come here, come to me. It's what I want. It's probably what your mother wanted. I love you, that's all that matters. Whatever happens afterwards is fine, I'm not a child anymore. Come here…come.'

After a long hesitation, where despair mixed with desperate longing, he moved back and as he entered me, his salty tears fell onto my face and down my neck mingling with my own.

It was over quickly but was loving and tender. The last piece of the jigsaw. When we lay back, we looked to each other for a long time, complicit, a softness in our gaze, a half-smile playing around our lips.

'When I come back…in a month, a year maybe…will you…be mine, Ali Conroy? Will you make this inadequate man whole? Will you do that? Will you?' Tears still streamed down his face.

'Walter Bradshaw, you soppy git, you know I will,' I whispered.

The next day, he returned to barracks. Four weeks later he left on a troop ship bound for somewhere. Not even *he* knew.

In eight months, I had only one letter.

Chapter Six

America
June 1942

Carl kicked a stone along the sidewalk, the rasp of denim the only sound in the unseasonably hot midday still. Dust covered his boots and floated in a fine mist into the turn ups of his faded Levi's. Stale, yeasty air, like the smell of fermenting beer, reached under his arms, around his waist, became a film that smeared itself on his upper lip and temples in a glistening grease of milky sweat. His hands, thrust deep into gaping pockets, jingled *two-bit* coins.

Seeing the reflection in Walgreen's window, he almost didn't recognise himself. He stopped, pushed spread fingers through a dark quiff, observed his frayed face set against the backdrop of the colour-washed town square. Or what passed for a square. No more than a crossroads in truth. This sure was a one-horse town; this sure was one boring pile of shit. He kicked the stone hard into the gutter and spat.

Life. You buckled down to work on the farm and spent what leisure time you had, shopping for tractor parts in Sears, loafing for company in Hovey's Milk Bar and moaning about the price wheat was fetching, maybe afterwards stopping by the Green Derby for a beer and a half-interested gawp at the girls who passed the window, most of whom you went to school with, most of whom were, let's face it, ugly. Ugly and tight-arsed.

Or you got out.

He stopped at the bus terminus, the only place in town with a bench. A place where teenagers, kids, hung around of an evening, nothing better to do, a place where the local hookers did what little midnight business there was.

He sat, lit up, cupping his hands in habit against a non-existent breeze. Two guys, he knew by sight, were staring at an empty road, waiting for the Greyhound bus.

'Time is it?' the shorter of the two asked limply, wiping his neck with a handkerchief.

'Quarter after twelve,' replied a lanky, languorous type without looking at his watch. He leaned against the bus post and dragged deeply on his cigarette.

'S'late then.'

'It'll be here, relax. Frightened Aunt Maisie's going to ride on out here and stop you?'

'Naw. Just keen to get there 'fore I change my mind.'

'Now's the time to do it if you're going to. Once you sign on the dotted line, you belong to Uncle Sam.' He smiled, dipped his chin, raised his eyebrows. Carl, elbows on knees, face down, cigarette smoke curling around his head, listened in, sensed there was something here for him.

'Whatever. I gotta get out of this place 'fore I go crazy. Anything's better than being buried alive here.'

Carl dropped his guard and spoke.

'You the boys from over at Miller's place?' knowing they were.

'Sure.' The two eyed each other.

'You found something worth leaving for?' Carl couldn't help noticing their overnight bags and smart shoes.

'Maybe.' The lanky one offered.

'Going to enlist, that's what.' The shorter one said, standing up straight and raising his chin. 'We're going to join the army. Go to Europe. Get outta here once and for all.' A broad smile covered his face.

'Truly?'

'Rumour is, Pearl Harbour an' all, we'll be called anyways. Figured we'd get there first.'

'What do you have to do?' Carl stamped out his cigarette, anxious that the bus didn't arrive too soon.

'Why? You interested?'

'Maybe.' Carl caught the lanky one's eye.

'Just get on the bus, I guess.'

Carl started calculating. Thought about how much money he had on him, whether the pickup was parked safe, the effect on his father. Moreover, what his father would do to him if he did this. Kick hell out of him, that's what he'd do. Not for fear of losing him. Not for love. But for inconvenience, for taking control and for the farm. But his mother, what about her, if he wasn't there? She surely would get it if he didn't. But hell, you can't plan your life around other people's shit.

He stared up the road, panned around at the only town for seventy miles, the tangle of overhead cables a bleak mesh fanning out from the centre spoiling what prettiness there might be, as though the town itself were caught in a giant web, its inhabitants going about their daily lives unaware that they were being ever so slowly but inevitably consumed. He curled his lip at the seedy wooden buildings leading off the junction, the clapboard church with its billboard up against the picket fence: *Come to me all ye that are heavily burdened and I will refresh ye*, alongside: *Mary Brown's pregnancy classes. Saturday 2 till 5. Coffee and muffins. All welcome.*

He stared down the road. A fine line of tarmac through a prairie of wheat. Not a bird in the sky. Nothing. He looked back. As he did so, the Greyhound bus, edged onto the horizon in a shimmer of heat-haze like a great lumbering beast, pushing, driving its way through the hot dense air, because it could. Because it had somewhere to go. He stood up. Reached in his back pocket for a wallet.

'Count me in.'

'Boy, you sure fill the doorway. Come in, come, I won't bite.' A khaki man with a shaved rugby ball head and a collar so tight his neck spilled over it like tied pork fat, stood in the room trying to be taller and slimmer than he was, a smell of carbolic soap and shoe polish wrapped around him, pervasive as smoke. He almost smiled when Carl entered, economically lifting one side of his mouth only.

'Thank you, sir.'

'I'm Sergeant Bush and you are? Relax, you're not in the army yet.' He tapped a pencil against his other hand like a schoolmaster about to begin chastising an unruly child.

'Carl McCullough, sir.'

'How old are you, son?'

'Twenty-three.'

'Step on the scales please. Whoa…big boy. You work out?'

'Farm work sir.'

'Where are you from?'

'Northeast.'

'So. You're a farmer?'

'That's right.'

'And you want to join the army?'

'Yes, sir.'

'And who's going to look after the farm?'

Carl shifted from one foot to the other, kept his hands clasped behind his back, pushed forward his face in a gesture meant to look confident, but which made him look as though he may lose his balance. 'My father…sir.'

'Is he happy about this?'

'Doesn't know yet.'

The sergeant paused, raised an eyebrow, went to speak, thought better of it, then looked at the floor and sighed.

'Mmm. Why do you want to enlist, son?' Carl paused, trying to think of the right response. 'Well?'

'Get some life, sir?' He raised his eyebrows, crinkled his eyes in uncertainty.

'Don't you mean s*erve my country*?' A dry laugh rasped in Sergeant Bush's throat.

'Oh yes, sir. That too.'

'Very admirable, I'm sure.' The sergeant spoke in a practiced voice, beginning to be bored. He rubbed his temples with an outstretched hand, as though he'd rather be somewhere else.

'Can you tell me something about yourself…Here sit down, sit.'

'Yes, sir. Thank you. Well…' Carl couldn't think of a single thing to say.

'Well…? You okay?'

'I'm fine, sir. Well… I'm strong.'

'Can see that for myself.'

'I'm pretty good with machinery, engines and such. I can shoot. I got hold of a Springfield last fall, a 30 calibre M1903. It's a nice piece of metal… I never travelled, sir. I'd kind of like to, you know?'

'Sure, I know. Do you have brothers and sisters?'

'No, sir.'

'What about your parents?'

'Sir?'

'Will they manage the farm without you? We need farmers too, you know.'

'Sure. They'll manage.'

'Do you know what's happening over there, Mr McCullough? It's not like you're being called up yet, if at all.'

'I do, sir. I heard the radio. Those Brits got it tough, the bombing and all. I think I could be useful. I'm not scared of Nazis. Is that an officer's uniform, sir?'

The sergeant scratched his head, sighed.

'There's a lot to learn, son.' Resentment frilled the edges of his words.

'Yes, sir. Do you get proper training? Artillery?'

'All that, if you get in. Tell me some more.'

'Well. There's not a lot to tell. Spent all my life working on the farm. We're wheat farmers mainly. Don't get to meet many folks where I live. Live too far from town to depend on it, you know.'

'A regular cowboy, aren't you, Mr McCullough?'

'I guess.'

'How did you do in school?'

'Not too good, left at fifteen, but I guess you don't have to graduate to get killed. That right, sir?'

'If you're smart, it might help you stay alive.'

'Oh, I'll stay alive. Survival is something I know about. If you knew my father, sir…'

'Okay, son. I'll take your word for it.'

After a brief pause when the sergeant looked at Carl more carefully, a resigned look sagging his face, he crossed the room and picked up some papers. 'You'll need to fill in these here forms. You can do them now or you can take some time, think it over, discuss it with your folks and come back to us. We don't want you to do anything hasty.'

'My folks?'

'As you're a farmer, you could be exempt when the times comes.'

'No need to discuss it, sir. I made up my mind.'

'I'm obliged to recommend you take some time here, this is a serious decision and…'

'I've thought about it, sir, no time like the present.'

'In that case, just fill these in. If you're successful at this stage, we'll need to conduct some physical examinations, IQ…that sort of thing, get you fitted up for Government Issue and suchlike. In the meantime, you make yourself comfortable. Here's a pen. Just ignore me.'

'Thank you, sir.'

Sergeant Bush faced the window. With his peripheral vision, he surveyed this hunk of a man who scribbled away his life. His shoulders sank in a huge sigh. He closed his eyes tightly, clenched his jaw and played with a ring on his wedding finger, turning it round and round while he waited. Wished *he* were twenty-three.

Carl got home so late he had to sleep on the porch. The door was bolted against him, he knew better than to knock. No matter, the sky was jet, the stars a fog of sparklers and for the first time in years, he felt light-headed, something akin to pleasure. A quiver of youthful vigour vibrated through him; a surge of yearning so strong he was almost nauseated; the closed door on his future was suddenly ajar, and through the aperture he could see people, places, life. There was music, dancing, everyone was laughing. He was the popular one, the one they all wanted to be with. There were foreign voices, bright colours, smart uniforms and women…

He was glad to be on the porch, felt he could think more clearly out there breathing the night air, watching the falling stars, unpolluted by the stench and taint of life indoors.

Next morning, a searing pain shot through his head bringing tears.

'You been down with those whores? Have you? Have you? You're just no good…plain no good.'

A fist gripped around his throat, pulled him up, pushed him down, up, down, thudding his head against the floor of the porch, choking him out of sleep.

'No Pop, honest. I enlisted, in the army…' Carl coughed out.

'You what? Tell me that's a lie and do it quick, boy.'

He saw a woman standing back from the upstairs window watching while he lay cowering, his hands at his face in defence, knees curling in protection. Leaning over him, slapping him hard with the back, front, back of his hand was a much smaller, wiry man. The woman's face was impassive, resigned, her body stiff as iron. What she saw was a small boy and a bully: snarling, dangerous, unpredictable; fragile as ice in sun, rigid as clay after a hot summer.

She scraped her forearms with her fingernails, opening old scars, stroking the wounds with her palms and staring at the whispers of blood in a kind of daze. She put her hands to her face, wiping a faint smear of it onto her cheeks, across her lips.

Carl saw the marks later: the blood on her face, dark, crusted.

Felt like a rat on a sinking ship.

Chapter Seven

Tobruk
19 June '42

Dear Mr and Mrs Conroy,

It is with regret that I write to inform you that on 13 June, your son, Private Edward 'Ned' Conroy, 1st Armoured Division, Eighth Army, was seriously injured in fighting at a desert area called Knightsbridge. He was driving a petrol supply lorry when he was hit.

At present he is undergoing treatment in a field hospital in Tobruk. He has broken both legs, has shrapnel wounds and has burns to the hands and face.

As soon as is practicable, he will be removed to a hospital that can better cater to his needs. I am very sorry to be the bearer of distressing news. I enclose a bundle of letters from his family together with his personal belongings that will be safer in your possession until such time as he is sufficiently recovered to reclaim them.

Please be assured that everything that can be done to help him, shall be done.

Yours sincerely,
Harry Forster. Major. Eighth Army.

Chapter Eight

England
October 1942

I smiled as I watched him across the room: animated, convivial, laughing with his friends. It felt so good to see him: Vincent—my little brother, broad now, like Ned, stocky, just a hint of boyhood lingering in the way he moved. When he saw me, he rushed through the arriving crowd and flung his arms around me. We hugged, rocking back and forth in the kind of adult embrace we had never really shared before—the war did that kind of thing.

I breathed in his scent: shaving cream, cigarettes and a sweet milky-ness I had known around him since he was born. The pale sing-song voice people had often mistaken for Welsh, had deepened, acquired a gravely texture. His face was wider, like Dad's, his cheeks rough, dark, a throwback to the Celts in the family line. He had grown into himself: Vincent Conroy, Rear gunner, RAF.

'Wow! Our little Ali's grown up. Look at you. What a dress. You look a million dollars, our kid, that red with your dark hair…' He wet his finger, touched my arm and hissed.

'It's old now. Lily gave it to me,' I twirled around. A shard of bittersweet memory, mingled with longing, and still I had heard nothing from Walter since that day, save the brief, tender note sent from his barracks before he left for overseas, *I regret nothing, Ali dearest. We are one…always have been, always will be…Be safe—my girl with the cornflower blue eyes…*Yet. An uneasy sense lurked at the base of things—time changed things, changed feelings, if he had wanted to write since, surely, he would have, and the fact that he had not done so augured badly.

I checked myself; there was too much misery around already. I would not think about it tonight. Not after the ongoing news about Ned. Not tonight. *Not tonight.* I flicked back my hair, took a deep breath.

'Nice. Very nice.' Vincent hugged me again; allowed his hand, in a gesture of tenderness, so unlike him, to rest on my back. 'Any more news of Ned?'

'Yes, he's been moved a fourth time…to the 53rd South African hospital, wherever that is. But he's going to be transferred to an English hospital in Basingstoke, Hampshire, on home ground at least. We're going to go and see him as soon as he gets there. I know you won't be able to come too but it would be so good to get the family back together. We know at least he's doing well, but…he must be lonely…' I trailed off.

Ned: tolerant, open-hearted, perceptive Ned. My Ned. My big brother. The gentle one, the one that always thinks of others before himself—how I missed him. It was a subject we couldn't discuss at length, to do so would be to acknowledge his mortality, a perception too terrible. Instead, we the family, held ourselves together by believing in the best outcome. To do otherwise was to risk being overwhelmed.

'We'll talk later, yes?' Vincent rubbed his hand across his mouth, his edited emotion betrayed by eyes that looked away from me into the crowd, seeing only the images inside his head.

I nodded. We were young. Death didn't visit the young. Ned would be fine; he would be home. A sudden vacuum was filled by voices and the small intimate laughter of hope and expectation peppered the silence. After some moments, I brought myself into the present. No Walter, no Ned, just here and now. Instead, I watched my other brother staring at Lily who, for the first time since I had known her, looked rather cheerless and was gazing unfocussed across the hangar.

'Are you all right, Lily?' I nudged.

''Course, Nelly.' Lily flashed a smile, but not before she threw a sliding glance at Vincent's arm around me. She was alone, no family. Lily always put on a show; laughed off anything that got too close. We are all somewhere else I thought, or alone, being brave, whatever that amounted to. It's why we're all here. I put my arm about her shoulders.

'This is Lily,' I said to Vincent, pulling her forward like a prize, as though I should take some credit for the blonde glamorous new friend I had managed to acquire.

'Hiya Lily, welcome to Mary Ann Site, Burtonwood.' Vincent made a flourish with his arm, his face askew at its dubious attractions, clearly delighted at the bonus of me having a gorgeous friend in tow. Lily lit up.

'So…one of your *big* brothers? Charmed I'm sure. *Mary Ann* site. You're having me on?'

'Nope.'

'That doesn't say much for its inmates, now does it?' she flirted, tapping a finger on his sleeve.

Vincent raised his eyebrows.

'Take no notice. She's outrageous, practising to be Mae West, aren't you, Lily?' I said quickly.

'No practice required!' Lily smiled sideways at Vincent as though sizing him up, then flashed her eyes at the men who were forming a cluster around us. 'Something tells me we're going to have a grand time.'

Vincent nodded. 'We did all right. Sent a truck over to the Ringway base to ferry over a few of the girls that wanted to come. Show these Yanks a thing or two!'

'Yanks? My God, are they here already?' Lily's eyes widened.

'Are they here? I'll say,' Vincent blustered. 'Arrived two days ago. They're already lording it over us. Our lads are a bit put out. Rumour is they intend to take over the base eventually. I suppose we have to be hospitable…Anyway, we've got a great band set up: Benny Nelson, down from the North-East, look. C'mon, I'll introduce you to some of the lads. They're dying to meet you.'

'C'mon Lily…' I pulled my friend away from the group that hovered like midges.

'I tell you, girl, we're going to do all right tonight,' Lily leered as she pursed her mouth and reapplied lipstick.

Teetering on red borrowed heels, I click-clacked over the concrete floor of the hangar, conscious of being watched, enjoying the frisson of reflected glory, following as I did in Lily's sashaying wake. We kicked up small clouds of red iron dust as we edged along to a makeshift bar at the far end of the room. Trestle tables were precariously loaded with bottles of ale and spirits.

In front, glasses were stacked in boxes like a party in someone's parlour. Half-barrels of beer were 'settling' on another trestle at right angles to the first, the floor around it already wet with spillage. A waiting group of around ten people shouted orders at a flustered barman that was alone trying to issue drinks.

I tried to quell my quivering hands and thighs, moisten my dry mouth as I mustered courage to look properly about me at the shifting crowd. More than one low greedy whistle reached me, which made me smile inside. I felt the silkiness on my thighs of my new and only pair of nylons, suspenders catching my hipbones. I smoothed my dress, self-conscious, coy. I wasn't alone.

Women, bunched around the edges of the hangar, colourful flowers in an herbaceous border. They seemed caught in a breeze, thick with scent and tobacco, as they nodded and swayed within groups, all of them turning their faces toward soldiers, touching up red lips, crimping curls, clinking glasses, their eyes glittering, mouths pouting. Women were more beautiful, men more handsome in the heady atmosphere of rootless strangers. There was almost, amongst the cluttered laughter and urgent greetings, a measure of desperation, as though communal happiness for the future depended on what happened that night. The room was charged with possibility.

'What'll you have to drink, Ali, Lily?'

'Port and lemonade.' Lily smiled, pulling me towards her, turning her back on a rather garrulous soldier who'd clearly been sampling the ale for some time.

'Port it is. Ali?'

'I don't know, what shall I have? I don't really drink.'

'Two ports please.' Lily preened. 'Where have you *been*, Ali? Didn't they teach you anything where you grew up?'

There were things Lily knew, I didn't want to know.

'Proper Miss Goody Two Shoes is our Ali. Aren't you, love?' Vincent winked, nudged my arm, but it was Lily he was watching.

'True. All that convent training, don't you know.' I put on my superior look; enjoyed my 'proper' reputation, though not the idea of being prim.

'Mind, you know what they say about convent girls...dark horses,' Lily laughed, raising her eyebrows. 'I left school at fourteen. Couldn't get out quick enough,' she continued in her flat Salford issue.

'Me too,' Vincent added. 'Our Ali here can quote Shakespeare but can't order a drink. Now what sort of education is that? I ask you, Lily?'

'A ruddy boring one,' she laughed, dipping her head provocatively and stroking her hair, exposing her bare underarm. I had never realised how easily manipulated my baby brother could be.

'Watch it, you two,' I said, trying not to feel left out.

'When are we going to meet these Yanks then?' Lily said suddenly, looking past us into the crowd.

'Just about now, by the look of it.'

There was a scuffle at the door. Raised voices.

A Cary Grant look-alike in an immaculate khaki uniform swaggered forward, hands in his pockets, taking in the whole room. He looked like he'd just walked off a film set. Hoots of derision echoed from the entrance hall, as immaculately clad soldiers poured in behind him like golden syrup. Twenty or thirty of them sauntered over the dance-floor, evidently a group used to getting what they wanted.

'How much beer you got?' I overheard one of them shout as they jostled for space at the bar.

Another walked up to me, closed my open mouth with his fingers. 'Catching flies, honey?' I blushed, wanting to make a snappy retort but nothing came out. I shrugged instead and felt foolish as he winked and moved away. 'Pardon me, ma'am, can I get through here?'

'About eight half barrels,' the barman shouted.

'You're gonna need it. Is it cold?' the American said loudly, nodding, anticipating the answer.

'Cold...?'

'Jeez. Warm beer again,' he shouted over his shoulder. 'We're gonna have to teach you guys about a little thing called...ice. And you're gonna need some help, buddy.'

'Not backwards in coming forward, are they?' I whispered to Vincent, giving a haughty look as the men surrounded the bar, making us stand back to accommodate them. I shook my hair from my face, tried to be tall.

A few perfunctory squeaks from the 'stage' made our heads turn to the band whose members were arranging chairs, shuffling through sheet music, adjusting stands and one by one trying to find C. After a pause, the musicians looked to the conductor, who, with a sudden wave of the baton, struck up *Twelfth Street Rag*, magically breathing life into the dingy hangar.

A small clatter of sound accompanied the large overhead lights being extinguished and smaller ones around the hall being lit. A mirrored mosaic globe like a shy moon was slowly lowered, suspended from a steel ceiling joist. A beam of light was focussed on it, which, as the globe turned in the heat, sent flurries of snow lights across every face in the room giving the odd sensation of everything being slowed down. I had never seen anything like it.

It had begun.

'Wanna dance, Miss?' Lily's face lit in surprise as *Cary Grant* walked straight up to her, looked her in the eye, her chest, her eye again. 'C'mon, I'm taking root here!'

'Yes, all right, why not.' She shrugged her shoulders at me, left Vincent holding her drink and was the first girl on the dance floor with an American. She walked with an exaggerated wiggle of her hips, at which the group of Americans close by whistled, while I watched in awe, just a little peeved that it wasn't me.

'Bloody cheek,' Vincent smarted.

'Jealous? Some of them do seem a bit…forward.'

'I'll say. They don't hang around. Look at them, they're like flies around jam. C'mon, our kid, the first one's for you, let's show them a thing or two.'

I smiled, complicit. As a dancer Vincent always had the edge on Ned and Dad. When he coaxed me into the swing of the dance, it was as though someone had switched on a light. I laughed aloud, unselfconsciously. While I danced, there was no sick brother lying in a hospital somewhere. No Walter sleeping in a bivvy in no man's land. No grease and grime of the factory. No long, lonely nights in a house of dubious repute. No war.

Vincent and I were just moving back to the bar after a waltz when the music changed, the band upped the volume, started to play *Jitterbug*. Americans cheered and hooted, put down their drinks and moved confidently toward the women that framed the edges of the dance-floor. They tried to cajole girls but most resisted, nervous, laughing and shaking their heads, so men started grabbing other men, pouting their lips, putting on female mannerisms, hugely exaggerated.

Shimmying together, hips locked, making cow eyes, holding each other close, they broke out, as though they had rehearsed. Great hunks of men cavorted around with each other. Looping under arms, swirling around, even jumping into the air to be caught and thrown back by the other, the iron dust rising from the concrete floor in a fine mist that settled like a red stain on ankles, calves and cavalry twill.

When a lively, laughing American, not much taller than I, grabbed my arm, I couldn't resist. His movements were sleek and agile. I learned fast. Exposed knickers and thighs flew as girls, increasingly, were thrown and caught clumsily, moving to a wild beat by an army of men who smelled of surplus, cheap hair oil and, increasingly, sweat. I felt feral. That night I could see that Americans knew how to live; it was a dangerous perception.

I was having a rest, having danced almost every dance for what seemed like hours, searching for somewhere to sit down for a few minutes, when a huge man, moved up behind me.

'I apologise on behalf of my fellow soldiers, Ma'am,' he said, over my shoulder.

'What…Sorry?' I wasn't sure I'd heard properly.

'It's a bad show,' he continued as though I had.

'Well, at least one of them can see it,' a very young British soldier standing next to me remarked irritably into his beer.

'Yeah, sorry,' the giant of a man responded airily over his shoulder.

The young soldier looked put out.

'But it's such fun,' I volunteered, still catching my breath.

'We're supposed to be here to help, not take over.'

'Took you long enough, mate,' was just discernible from the young soldier. The big man bit his lip and ignored it.

'I don't know why you're apologising. Frankly, I think everyone needs a bit of cheering up.' I wished he would go away.

Peripherally, I saw him sigh, smiling, looking about him as though trying to decide how to initiate a conversation, aware that his opening line clearly had had the wrong effect. Hesitantly, and stooping to speak at my level, as I continued to gaze ahead of me at the moving 'snow-covered' dance floor, he tried again.

'Your boys have put up a good show for us.'

'Well, it wasn't just for you, you know,' I laughed, wishing he'd make up his mind. The faint mewling of 'hear, hear' came from the soldier behind.

The big man, clearly irritated, turned his height and bulk around to the soldier.

'I'm not looking for trouble here. Are you?'

The soldier put two hands up, palms outwards, shrugged his shoulders, backing off.

'So,' he said, leaning back to me, 'you having fun?'

'Yes. I'm having fun, aren't you?'

'Sure. It's just…'

'Good. I'd hate to think Americans were wet blankets,' I said haughtily.

'Never been called that before,' he said, after the briefest of pauses.

He moved around beside me and without waiting for a response began to ask me about myself:

'So, where you from? You live local?'

Conversation, strained and difficult because of the volume of the music, was intermittent. Without taking much interest, I answered his questions blandly. My interest perked up, however, when I turned and looked at him properly. Were all Americans this handsome?

There was the slightest feeling that he was acting out a part, on his best behaviour, or so like a film star I couldn't tell the difference; white teeth and creases in his trousers like a razor's edge. He was a bit serious, kept on with his questions, my family, my work, did I, for God's sake, *come here often*? Was he being ironic? I couldn't read him. He looked me up and down, down and up, as though he couldn't decide what kind of girl I was.

I took another gulp of the port that kept appearing from random hands and stared out over the heaving bodies that seemed to have acquired a mass momentum, my body rocking from side to side. All around us girls were enjoined in mayhem. I felt heady, intoxicated, Port was nice. The more of it I drank, the more it tasted like fruit juice.

Suddenly, I wanted to dance again, but felt held back. I could see a rather sweet-looking Brit making his way towards me and I out-stretched my hand to meet his, shouting back to the big man: 'I'm twenty, the world is turning upside down. If you'll excuse me, I'm going to dance', whereupon the American neatly stepped between us, took hold of my hand instead and pulled me onto the dance floor.

'Well, if I can't beat 'em, I'll have to join 'em?'

He wasn't a dancer; held me too tight, made me feel clumsy, trod on my feet a few times and once, as I tottered off balance on Lily's heels, tripped me up. 'Always dreamed of having a girl like you fall for me,' he said as he pulled me up with such ease I felt like a feather in his hands.

He wanted to know where I lived. Could he *call by?* I laughed; told him it was the other side of the city. Told him I was *spoken for*. I made polite conversation, broken by the crescendo of what seemed like the band's finale, all the while scanning the room searching for Lily and wondering where she could be. The last time I saw her, she and *Cary* were getting a little close.

Suddenly, Vincent pushed through the crowd looking flushed and hot, said he'd been looking for me and the truck was leaving soon. I told the big man who stood just a little too close that I'd 'better make tracks'.

'And you are?'

'Alice. Alice Conroy.'

'And you work at A. V. Roes factory, right?'

'That's right,' I laughed, flattered at his attention.

'Carl McCullough. Pleased, ma'am, to have almost met you.' He picked up my limp hand and kissed it, whilst I, trying to subdue a hiccough, smiled sweetly in appreciation of his gentlemanliness.

Starting to feel rather unwell, I said goodbye to my American rather abruptly before I began to feel worse. As we stepped apart, the brooch in my dress got caught in his sleeve. 'I guess we're hooked,' he smiled, and I hesitated, feeling the heat of his body against me. When he said nothing, I moved away, feeling I had missed an opportunity. Why had I hesitated? Why had I used Walter as an excuse? It was just a dance, a conversation; there was no harm in it.

I moved through the crowd of bodies toward the door, looking for Vincent, suddenly hemmed in by people shoving and pushing. Announcements were being made about transport. Musical instruments were being packed away along with the fantasy of the dance, extinguished by the crack of the illumination of the huge overhead lights exposing the grim reality of the aircraft hangar once again. The dancehall became factory-like, grey, colour-washed.

I looked about me, blinking in the brightness. The women seemed ugly suddenly: lipstick had worn to a smudged redness, mouths looked like sores. Curls had dropped and were hanging limply like tails. White sweaty skin highlighted blemishes. Dresses were too tight to be flattering. The men, transformed from suitors to predators, racehorses to stray dogs, as their faces winced with unsatisfied lust, were still hunting, steely eyed for any opportunity before the night should end…or perhaps it was me…perhaps, the way I was feeling, I was just seeing things differently.

When I finally pushed through the jam by the door, I saw a transformation from a few hours before. Outside, girls who had been archly reticent were scribbling addresses, or smooching, huddled in shadows, hands pushing, pulling at clothing. Shameless.

As I watched them, a sudden longing clawed at me. I was lonely…more than lonely. Walter had not written, and what we had just a year ago, became, in that moment, something that belonged to another life. Everything was changing so fast, things that had seemed permanent became transient. Men were here one day, drinking and dancing as if their survival depended on it, the next week they were fighting in foreign countries where their lives really did depend on it. Everyone wanted to live in the moment, and it was not just the men.

I was no longer the naïve girl that grew up on the moors; I loved Walter more than myself, but life was passing us by. I just wanted to live a little but didn't know how not to feel guilt. I almost wished I had become pregnant with Walter's child, as his mother had done with his father. At least something in my life would be certain, part of Walter would be here with me, something real to wait for instead of pinning my hopes on shadows.

I looked back into the hangar, but the tall American had disappeared.

I leaned against the wall, trying to feel separate from what I perceived. Saw aircraft hangars, rows and rows of Nissen huts, storage sheds, the Mess Hall. Autumn cold and perspiration made my dress feel wet. It was a perfect clear night with stars like sequins on black velvet. I thought about Ned and felt mournful suddenly. Hated the war, hated the person that had hurt him. Then Walter—where was he? What was he doing? What was *I* doing? What were we all doing? Laughing, kissing, and now pulling at each other like animals in a feeding frenzy, when people we loved were out there somewhere, under this sky.

I looked up, trying to focus then glanced around at the swelling ooze of people whilst looking for Vincent, listening to the trip and drawl of loud American voices filling the night air, their phrases upturned at the end like questions. Then I spied him, pressed against the perimeter fence, locked in an embrace with a tall woman, almost his height, his face buried in her hair, his hands tucked up somewhere. Even him.

Tears ran hot down my cheeks. I longed suddenly to kick off Lily's ridiculous shoes and put on my boots, my windjammer. Longed to be high up, walking with Walter, all the rest of it just scribbled out.

I would write to Walter again tomorrow. It was time, more than time.

I turned towards the grinding gears of the trucks as they turned off the road and down the slope toward the hangar. I began to walk toward one of them and felt a sudden involuntary retching. So ugly. Over and over. People stepped around me laughing, grimacing, glad it wasn't them. My nose dripped. I felt cheap.

I wrote that night.

Middleton.
Oct '42

Dear Walter,

    I wanted to write and tell you how I need to hear from you. How could you leave it all this time? It is so very long since I saw you. We are older…there is temptation…

God no!

Dearest Walter,
Have you changed your feelings towards me…?

No.

Dear Walter,
    I have had no letter from you and stupid pride has prevented me from writing again. I know there must be a good reason, but please if you can, write. I miss you. Tell me you are doing all right. Tell me we are fine.
    I want you.
    I love you.
    Be safe.

Ali XXXX

    The next morning, I posted it to the address he had given me for overseas troops before I had a chance to change my mind.

Chapter Nine

England
December 1942

Servicemen and women, parents, friends, wives and babies, huddled together, smoking, laughing, surrounded by Forces holdalls; names printed on them like those of schoolchildren going on a trip. Happy chatter diluted the vacant stares of some and ebullient swagger of others.

When the train wheezed into Manchester's London Road Station, its slow dull brake-screech drowned all conversation. Groups surged forward enveloped in steam that billowed like a dense fog momentarily draining them of colour and lending a somewhat spectral aspect to the scene. Dad shuffled through to climb up and bag some seats, squeezing through kissing couples and families saying their goodbyes.

'Sorry, excuse me, sorry love, if I could just come through…' almost falling over the jungle of kit in his haste.

In our compartment, we were the only civilians. Two of the soldiers jostled one another to help me with my small overnight bag, and almost as an afterthought, helped Mam. Dad scowled through knitted brows as though he both knew their game, and because they were treading on his territory. Mam laughed at him, 'Get off with you, Bernard,' while he huffed like a dog trying to decide whether he should bark.

Mam smiled while she bustled, making herself and everyone else comfortable. I felt myself blush at her behaviour. 'Nice to be back with the boys, eh Alice?' she cooed in her upturned voice.

I smiled my embarrassment, discreetly sneaking coy glances at the soldiers, while they talked amongst themselves. I could see by the way they caught my eye that I was meant to be listening too.

'…aye, that sun was so hot I felt like Lawrence of bloody Arabia…Oh sorry, Miss.'

'Yeh, can't say I'm sorry that that little scrap is done and dusted,' a sun-tanned soldier said, rolling a cigarette. 'Mind if I light up, ladies?'

'No, no, of course not,' Mam said, slightly po-faced, as I could tell she was secretly wishing Dad got a non-smoking compartment. 'You boys must have your pleasures, where you're going.'

Dad and I gave her a withering look.

'Where to this time?' one soldier said to no one in particular.

'God knows,' another soldier answered. 'All I know is, I've to make my way to Romsey Barracks and await orders.'

'And what about you, Miss? Having a little holiday?' the sun-tanned soldier asked. I smiled, opened my mouth to reply.

'We're travelling to visit our son in Park Prewett Hospital in Basingstoke,' Dad cut in.

'My brother,' I nodded, looking at Dad, then back at the soldier.

'Wounded in the desert,' Dad added curtly.

'Bad, was it?' one of the sailors asked.

'Bad enough,' he replied and looked out of the window.

'He's going to be fine though. He's home…well, in England at any rate, that's the main thing,' Mam said, trying to assuage the insensitivity of her husband, aware that the same could happen to any one of them.

The sailor nodded, staring absently first at the ceiling then the floor, while the movement of the train with its clickety-clack rhythm rocked us in unison. Sitting by the window, I stared at the faint reflection of myself, set against the steam that flew by, thinking of nothing in particular, and was able to look more closely at the others in the carriage by the same means. One of the soldiers surreptitiously stared at my legs and nudged the soldier beside him who raised his eyebrows and smirked, unaware that I watched him. I had to turn my head to hide my smile.

Mam, as usual, brought so much food we ended up sharing it with two sailors who hadn't any. When we'd eaten our picnics and conversation had died down, we settled into our own internal space, stared out at the countryside, untouched by war for the most part.

I wondered where Walter was at that moment, what he was doing, whether he had received my letter. Hard to imagine how he was getting through his day somewhere, whatever that entailed. But I'd got used to missing him. I was bored with missing him.

I stared at the disappearing landscape until my breath made the window foggy, I wiped it with my sleeve, felt a sudden sinking feeling.

When the train slowed and passed through a town, the war was evident once more. There were troops. Army wagons. A woman pushed a pram full of coal, while two toddlers whinged and tugged at her coat. As the train pulled into Derby Station, another woman, about Mam's age, in a black hat and coat, stood shivering on the platform, as though not knowing which train to take. She looked at us in the carriage, her raw eyes darting from one to another, searching for someone. There was an expression of such complete desolation about her pallid, sunken face that it played on my mind for days afterwards. That night, I would dream about her.

'It's lovely to spend some time with you, love. I miss you,' Mam said quietly, sensing my mood.

'It's grand for me too, Mam.'

'I wish you didn't have to work in that horrid factory. When I think of your school reports…you could have gone on…you know. Oh Ali, I could spit.' Mam shook her head, turned her wedding ring round and round on her finger.

'Steady on, Mam, I'm only twenty. Anyway, it's not so bad. I like the independence.'

'Aye,' Dad said, a little loudly, 'you're all right, girl. Got the right attitude. Plenty of time to plough your own furrow after the war.'

He looked around him, as though addressing the soldiers, who were, for the most part, involved in conversations of their own or playing cards. He added quietly, leaning into me, 'Besides, you'll marry one day, so it won't make no difference, love.'

'Not necessarily, Dad,' I said, as though an alternative had just suggested itself.

'For heaven's sake, Bernard, let the poor girl have a life first.' Mam's loud whisper made me cringe.

'Don't be so nowty, woman.'

Dad put both hands to his face for a long moment then brushed them back through his thinning hair, his eyes closed tight, a soft, resigned sigh escaping. He looked worn. I realised I hadn't given much thought to how he missed male company, how he bore the burden of Mam's anxiety, as well as his own. I was always too busy trying to placate Mam. She must have seen my pensive look and glanced sideways, her face angled, as though trying to see Dad through my eyes, then back at me to show she understood.

She smiled, put her hand over his. He placed his other hand over hers and squeezed, giving her a wan smile. She inhaled sharply, stared at the floor where I imagine she saw her husband's fears written .

About half an hour before our arrival into London, I decided to have a walk to stretch my legs. I headed down toward the rear of the train where the corridor wasn't so crowded, bobbing and sliding around those standing or sitting on kit bags, holding on as the carriage swayed. Almost all the way down, I heard the drone of German planes. I felt the blood drain from my face, my legs go weak. A soldier grabbed my arm.

'Quick hen, into the guards' van.'

I rushed in with him, heard the sirens, the whine. He shut the door.

'S'alright hen, we'll be safe in here.' His voice modulated up at the end like a question.

'You're Scotch,' I said.

'Aye, well, last time I looked anyhow. But it's Scottish, hen, nae Scotch, though I wouldna say nae to one, if you get ma drift.'

The train continued swaying to and fro while we hung onto the bars on the wall, listening. As the noise outside abated, I looked about me and saw amongst the baggage, crates of Victoria plums packed in stacks in the back of the van.

'Plums!' I exclaimed. It was so rare to see fresh fruit and in December—how could it be possible?

'Don't mind if I do,' the soldier said, as he steadied himself and wandered over to begin opening one of the crates. 'Here hen, fill your pockets. You'll no have a better chance.'

'But we can't just…can we?'

'Look love, if I can be called up to fight, maybe pop my clogs for my country, I'm damn sure it can afford a few measly plums to make the going easier.'

Laughing conspiratorially, we took as many as we could carry and ate until we had plum juice dripping from our chins.

'Evidence!' he laughed.

As I left to go back to the compartment, my cardigan pockets bulging, I thanked him.

'What's your name?' he shouted after me.

'Alice.'

'Aye right…Alice in plunderland.'

What's yours?' I shouted.

'Hamish. The mad Hatter.'

'Bye, Hamish.'

'Bye, hen. Every time I eat plums from now on, I'll think of our little tea party.'

Funny the things you remember. I often wonder what happened to Hamish.

Discouraged from seeing Ned until the morning after our journey—*he's better in the mornings*—we decided to spend two hours in London on the way through—a distraction—before taking another train onto Basingstoke.

There were posters, like wallpaper, pasted on every available surface, on windows, buses and buildings. Posters about 'National Security', about how to 'Increase Production', recruitment posters for the Forces and those of Churchill smiling: 'Let us go forward together'. I counted thirty-two posters in a five-minute stretch: How to 'Save for Victory', to 'Register for Civil Defence Duties', to eat 'National Wholemeal Bread', to 'Carry Your Gas Mask' and so on. One poster caught my eye particularly: 'Women of Britain, Come into the Factories'.

We got up early next morning; none of us slept. The room was cold, the sheets damp and clammy. The landlady of the small hotel was used to visitors whose reason for staying was a hospital visit. At eight she served breakfast, such as it was: powdered eggs and toast, wearing a thin skin of marmalade. Pale tea. I wondered how many times the tea leaves had been used. In the background *I'll be seeing you* played tinnily on the radio; mam couldn't speak. No one was hungry.

At the hospital, a sister greeted us at the entrance to the ward like a pallid nun, hands linked together in front, face pious.

'He'll be so happy to see you. Sir Harold Gillies, his specialist, is very pleased with him. He's doing very well really. A word though…' her voice was sharp, a knife through soft butter, 'he still has a long way to go. There *will* be more operations.' Mam stood stone-like, staring at the sister's face. Dad, hands in his pockets, looked at his shoes, shuffled his feet, avoided eye contact.

'I don't mean to alarm you…' Mam closed her eyes, 'but the burns…and he has, sadly, lost an eye.' *Oh God, oh God.* 'The doctors at the field hospital fought to save it but it became infected. His other eye is perfect.'

We exchanged looks. I blinked back tears, blew my nose. 'There's something else. He has lost the fingers on his left hand. I'm sorry. He's been very brave throughout; he needs you to be brave now.'

'Thank you. Can we see him?' Dad barked, his voice leaden.

The sister turned; her shoes squeaking on the linoleum floor. We followed on behind. I noticed my parents holding hands. Turning into the Burns Unit and then the ward, a smell like warm cheese hit us. Airless. The high windows were all closed. Shafts of sunlight contrasted with the greyness of everything. The ward was small, eight beds. They were all young men with missing limbs, eyes or a sense of what or who they were. I felt a rising panic. Most stared. One, swathed in bandages, smiled at me. I smiled back.

'Come and visit *me*, love,' he called after me in a northern accent I recognised. Liverpool?

One bed had curtains around. I could hear the groans of a man having dressings removed. His pain churned my stomach. I could smell iodine.

'Nearly there now…well done. That wasn't too bad, eh?' a female voice soothed from behind the curtain.

There was a young man, perhaps twenty years old, who had no ears, no hands and only one arm. He was covered in burns, red weeping sores. None of us had ever seen anything so distressing. He stared as though from behind a screen, invisible. By the next bed, the sister stopped.

'Ned…your family is here.'

I hardly recognised my brother; he was so thin.

'Mam…Dad…Ali love…' Ned stretched out his right hand. His smile, like an old crone, was wide, open. He had no top teeth. He wore a patch over his left eye. His face was mostly clear of burns, but the scarring crept up on his neck from under his hospital gown like patterns on a frosted windowpane. Both legs were in plaster. Mam went straight to him on the left of the bed. She took his hand in her right hand and bent down, placing her cheek beside his and stayed there, her body rocking. Dad stood at the foot of the bed holding on to the iron stead.

'Son, son. How wonderful, wonderful.'

I went to the right of the bed and sat on a stool, put both of my hands over Ned's other hand, what was left of it. I couldn't speak.

When Mam stood, her face glistening, she was smiling.

'Ned love, how we've missed you.'

Chapter Ten

England
February 1943

Every day I expected things to be different; changes at the *front* to filter down to the factory floor; the war to take a dramatic turn, to be over even. But every day, except for those where there had to be an extra *push*, things were the same. War changed everything, but at Avie Rose it was always the same: hard, monotonous and boring.

Hearing from Walter would have been the one bright light, but nothing. He had had a change of heart—that was it. His feelings had altered in some way, and I must have seemed a small consideration, a remnant of childhood, in the light of where he was now. He just couldn't bring himself to say it was over, that was why he hadn't written. Yes, that is how it would be. Life must be hard, I thought, wherever he is, but it is hard also for those at home, waiting, always waiting....

I had no idea.

And on my rare weekends home, it was no longer the refuge it had been, it seemed there was only ever bad news when I got there. Mam and Dad forever pre-occupied; affection and laughter replaced by far-eyed forgetfulness, heavy silences, and an edginess that made it difficult to be around them. There was occasionally a forced jollity, but it seemed that all conversation eventually led to the same grim subject, and to give it voice made it more real, so we just slid away from it.

And there were fewer friends when I got there.

Daniel Donnelly—*Dirty Danny Boy*—my dream partner at the Catholic dances, Hebden's Fred Astaire. Predatory instincts of an alley cat. Joined the Irish rifles in '41. I remember his excitement when he left: *I'll come back full of stories for you, Ali Conroy, so I will...You'll not turn your nose up at me when I'm a hero...* Blown up by a landmine in Egypt. He was nineteen.

Georgie Black from Heptonstall, one of Ned's best friends, died in a blanket of tank and artillery fire at El Alamein. I saw him in my dreams, running blind, sand in his eyes, screaming. His body was picked up in pieces by the light of flares. Twenty-one.

Maria Henderson with her mane of red ringlets, a year ahead of me at school. Played *Fur Elise* for me on the piano once, at break time. I can see it so clearly still: the sun drifting in through a lazy afternoon like a moving, living thing that took comfort in the notes she played with such skill, curling in a haze of yellow light around her, through her hair. I, just a young girl, uncertain where to put my incumbent affections, had a crush on her.

Maria went out with the Army Pay Corps to Cairo. Her ship was attacked by U boats in the Bay of Biscay en route to Alexandria. All lost.

I was tired.

Tired of rations. Watery stew, dumplings, if you were lucky. I hated dumplings. Tired of building bombs to kill people. Tired of worrying when Ned and Walter would come home, and every time Vincent went. Tired of air-raid sirens, the smell of brick-dust and burning, coffins in the street.

I was tired of Percy and Ida digging me out of bed to 'entertain' Yanks who came around looking for fun while the 'boys' were away. Lily and I would sit trying to smile between yawns and watery eyes. Lipstick skew-whiff, smelling of unchanged sheets, watching Percy stuff his face with whatever sweet things the men brought with them as bribery while the gramophone scratched out Glenn Miller. Sometimes the Americans were nice, just wanted the company. They offered stockings and chewing gum, missed their families. Sometimes they made assumptions.

However, one day, the man I had nicknamed *Mr Gorgeous*, the big American from the dance at Burtonwood the previous October, turned up out of the blue at Oscar Street. He stood in pale pristine khaki towering on our doorstep looking as though he had lost his way on a film set. He'd been to A. V. Roes, he said, to find out my address. He'd lied, told them he knew my brother, had news for me. I was just in from work, hair scrunched into a snood, face matt-white like early morning, still in my overalls and smelling of the factory. The house stank of cabbage and onion and a faint hiss of steam issued from the kitchen, giving a lisp to everything.

Invited in by Ida, he walked into the parlour looking like a bison in a birdcage; his uniform made the room and everything in it look dingy. The radio was blaring, crackling its midweek blah, while Ida fell over herself, wringing her hands around a dishcloth, couldn't do enough.

'Turn that racket down, Perce,' she bellowed over the din, then with a bashful attempt at grace that sounded like Joyce Grenfell, 'P'raps we could offer the gentleman some form of refreshment?'

'I'm fine, ma'am. Thanks.' Carl looked awkward, unsure whether he should sit down. He remained standing.

'I'm listening to it,' Percy whinged, '…besides,' he muttered, looking up and down at the mighty beast that had just deposited itself in his parlour, leaning back in his chair to do so, 'this isn't the time or place to entertain doughboys.'
That is rich, I thought.

I felt Carl *had* taken a liberty; how dare he use my brother? I was irritated at being caught looking my worst but liked the randomness of his visit. Flattered too. There was the merest frisson that, perhaps, things may not turn out to be so dreary after all? Life had been so very dull, spending every night alone in a miserable boarding house with no one for company. Lily was no use; she was always at the pictures or the ice rink with *Cary Grant.*

While I stood trying to think what to do with him, desperately pulling off the snood, pressing my hair into some kind of shape, biting my lips to bring some colour into them, it made me smile to see the effect he had on Ida, whose obsequious fawning, sniffing profit in it somewhere: free cigarettes, nylons, was getting short shrift.

'I'm real sorry to butt in on you like this, I know it's been a long time…I've been kinda busy. I thought about you though…Alice…and so I decided, hey, there's a new movie on at the Odeon, *Casablanca*, I think it's called, anyhow, it has Humphrey Bogart in it. An' I thought, why don't I mosey on across town and ask her, you know?'

Carl's face was worried eager, like a child in a sweet shop with no money in his pocket. One hand fiddled with the cuff of his jacket. I stood waiting, smug at his discomfort, enjoying the tease.

'I like him, don't you? Like him? Humphrey Bogart.'

'Yes…I like him,' I said after a while. Percy had turned down the radio and moved around in his chair, squinting at the proceedings, an expression on his pocked, seedy face resembling awe. Ida hovered near the door, narrow-eyed and thin-lipped from curling wisps of cigarette smoke, afraid to miss anything.

'Ahem…What I mean is…would you like to go? With me, I mean…tonight.'

'That would be nice…yes. Thank you. I'll need to change though.' I had to suppress a joyful squeak as I leapt up the stairs two by two, at the change of events and the idea of dating an exotic American. After all, there was no harm in it; I just wanted a bit of fun and a change of scenery.

'What about your dinner…' Ida trailed in a flaccid tone as I disappeared behind the slam of my bedroom door.

Carl waited in the parlour attempting small talk, his muscled bulk settled in an easy chair that looked anything but, by the weight deposited upon it, which creaked and groaned every time Carl moved, making Percy's eyes dart and mouth twitch. Ida, fluffed up, assumed a mock maternal role: '…and when will she be back? She's got work in the morning; you know…' as if I hadn't arrived back in the room.

As I walked down the street beside him, I wished I had borrowed Lily's red shoes with the high heels. Carl was gentlemanly, in an awkward sort of way. He made sure he walked on the outside of the pavement, or 'sidewalk' as he called it, held onto my elbow across the road and made a project out of buying the tickets and presenting an ice cream cone to me. I felt protected. I did. Enjoyed the fuss. Enjoyed him taking charge.

All around us at the picture-house, even before the organist had finished playing his 'intro', arms were creeping around girls' necks or over their laps. I heard more than one slap and a lot of giggling. I hadn't been to the pictures much as a child, the nearest picture-house being too far away, and it made me feel a little uneasy.

When the curtain drew back, the dramatic overture began, lights went down, and I felt the fresh thrill of make-believe. I looked at the profile of the man beside me reflected by the screen: *so* good-looking: thick black hair slicked back from his face, a square jaw jutting forward slightly and dark eyes. I was aware of the bulging bicep through his sleeve, the smell of his uniform, cigarettes and something sweet, peppermint. His hands on his lap, huge worker's hands, scrubbed pink clean.

At the end of the film, he handed over a huge hanky, never said a word. I got the impression he didn't do this much; take girls out. Perhaps he was shy; he had certainly seemed too engrossed in the film to notice me, which was a relief. I liked his deference and smiled to myself in the darkness.

With no moon, it was hard to see our way back in the blackout, so we walked gingerly, wide-eyed in the darkness, talking all the while. His accent was soft and drawling, nasal, but not unpleasant and, by contrast, I was conscious of my own northern flat vowels. I enjoyed the *newness* of him; had never met anyone from America before, at least not properly. We were so different and yet, in a way, the film had followed us onto the street; I was Bergman, he Bogart. Both caught up in wartime, both away from home.

Reality dribbled into the drains with the light rain that had started to fall; I began to enjoy the fantasy of it. Walter and me? We were 'friends', I said. There was an *understanding*, nothing promised. I don't know why I lied. Carl suddenly stepped in front of me, stopped me walking and bent down.

'D'you mind if I kiss you…I've been wanting to all night.'

Any other time, I'd have laughed at the cheek, remembered who I was: Alice Conroy: good Catholic girl with a boyfriend away fighting. But there, in that space and time, I became the limp heroine. I hadn't seen Walter for so long, I was angry with him for not writing and Carl *had* travelled an awful long way to find me.

He kissed me awkwardly, not unpleasantly, then again, more firmly, his upper lip and chin scratchy against my skin. He smelt of tobacco. Hands crept around my waist, lifting me slightly and my neck hurt, straining up to him, but I was determined to make it a *romantic* experience. I had never kissed anyone properly other than Walter and I felt I was breaking some sacred law, intimacy with a stranger. But I was Bergman, he Bogart.

Suddenly, the light drizzle became a heavy downpour. We ran for cover, giggling because it was fun, different, two characters playing a part. He pulled me along by the hand, slipping and sliding on a shiny rink of rain.

'Slow down,' I laughed. 'Slow down.'

I didn't see the raised paving stone in the dark and tripped and fell sideways heavily. I curled half in the road, half out, hugging my arm, immobile, my silence betraying my pain; also, my annoyance—why had he let slip my hand? Then slowly, I allowed him to help me up.

'You okay? Damn it…' He kicked the curb in anger.

'I'm all right…really…ouch, no don't touch it.'

The crepe dress, for which I had saved my coupons, was ruined: the rain made the front of it stiffen and lose shape. I had torn the seam of my only coat as I fell. Nothing was romantic anymore.

Back at the digs, Ida put on a show:

'Poor thing, what was you thinking of in all that rain? Come here, love, c'mon, set yourself down. You'll need to see the doctor. I'm sure this kind gentleman will give you half a crown. Perce, you'll need to run and get Dr Hines.' Made it clear to Carl, if it was broken, I would have to go home.

'I'm not a nurse, after all, though I think I'm a bit of a mum to her, don't you know.'

Carl had to go. Had to somehow make his way to the other side of Manchester and it was already ten-thirty. He left in a flurry of apologies. Could he come over again?

'And break the other arm?' I joked through a wince of pain, feeling a pale waxiness, as though I might faint. He didn't smile. A whisper of frustration hung about his face.

He pushed a ten-shilling note into Percy's hand, 'for the doctor'. Percy examined it carefully before closing his hand over it. Carl leaned forward as though to kiss me, thought better of it and eased himself away.

I was left lean with wet clothes, a painful arm and a mouth that tingled from five o'clock shadow. Ida stood over me blowing smoke rings.

'…well, that's what we're here for, love.'
And Percy fussing. I was making the anaglypta damp, leaning against it.

*

Sent home to Mam and Dad, Doctor Jackson ordered rest; apart from my arm, I was *run down*. The foreman at Avie Rose wasn't happy and Lily begged me not to leave her alone at the digs for longer than was absolutely necessary, whingeing that a fracture was no excuse. Percy and Ida let me know that there would be no rent reduction, '…and be sure to give our best to your parents. Let them know how well we look after you.'

Mam couldn't disguise her pleasure at having me back in Hebden for a few weeks, secretly glad I was *ill*. She tried hard to restore what, to her, seemed to have been lost between us. Small acts of maternal love: combing my hair, straightening my clothes, plumping cushions for me to sit on. Watching. Exchanging worried looks with Dad, that I tolerated, knowing she needed to be needed. She said repeatedly: I was *too quiet, too thin*. Dad wanted to know about the American, wanting someone to blame for my injury.

I began eating properly again; Mam gave me corned beef, despite rationing. Apple pie and custard on Sundays was back on the menu, thanks to the Bramleys from the garden kept in the apple store and I slowly began to put some weight back on. I read a lot, smothered myself in the luxury of words, of time. Dad went to the library and brought home all sorts of odd books for me and watched my face as I perused them, waiting for reassurance that he had chosen well. I told him it wasn't my leg that was broken, but he wanted to do it and I let him.
He seemed frailer.

I was shocked to learn that Vincent was on an overseas mission, based abroad. He'd had a weekend pass, then left. Mam said he had no idea where he was going; it was all very secret. She had seen him off at Huddersfield Station. That was all she knew.

I could picture the scene, it wasn't difficult. Mam would be stoical, her mouth pulled tight, her back stretched tall as she organised his departure, like a child going on a school trip. She would be dressed in her Sunday best, smelling of April Violets, her patent handbag on her arm. She would make him take his hands out of his pockets, straighten his collar and tell him to remember his manners, then pile him up with food he couldn't carry.

The crease of worry on her forehead would deepen as she reached up on tiptoes, best shoes polished, holding onto his shoulders to kiss him. She wouldn't look him in the eye, instead she would brush away a speck of something from his collar, blinking rapidly, silent. He would kiss her back then laugh as the train issued, sneezing into the station, slicing through the moment. Dad would have said his goodbyes at home, wouldn't trust himself.

She told me she made him promise not to get hurt. He replied he wasn't sure about that: 'I've heard about these continental women…'

He said he would write. She said he was excited to be going, laughed as he got onto the train; didn't look back.

While I was settling into the life there, with all its echoes of childhood, I had a letter from Walter; well…four letters bundled together, forwarded from my digs. I ran up to my bedroom while I unravelled his history of the last two years. But before I opened them, I smelt them, trying to discern Walter's scent, then held them a moment against my heart, closing my eyes and praying there would be no bad news. I read each, in order of when they were sent, with increasing realisation and horror at the danger he had been in, was still in.

Of course, it was war—I knew that, but names spoken on the radio, names that appeared on newsreels with increasing frequency, all told or shown in a blur of battle, was where Walter had been with the Eighth army: Tobruk, near where Ned was injured. Cairo. Tobruk again. Benghazi. Now Tripoli.

Walter had been busy. The losses, he said, had been terrible; he was alive still—remarkably. There were gaps where the letter had been censored, but I was able to read between the blacked-out lines and I shuddered to know what my *angular Saxon* had been through. *I* was worried about boredom and a fractured arm while *he* was out there, in all that. Shame on me… shame on me.

Reading between tears, I could sense his gradual disaffection with the life he was leading, and to a point, with the faith that remained in us, as a couple, lamenting, in one of the letters, that he had not heard from me for so long. The fourth and most recent seeming resigned, accepting that perhaps life had moved on for me.

I read with an increasing alarm of how very separate our wartime experiences were, I guessed that life had perhaps moved on for him too. How easily misunderstandings happen when contact is so infrequent, when there is no voice, no facial expression to accompany the words, so that the words themselves seem to shift and change their shape like chameleons.

*

The postmark of the last letter was a month old.

Tripoli
Jan '43

Dear Alice,

I know my letters are infrequent but until your note, which I admit I received about a month ago (I have been a little occupied…), I have heard nothing from you. Have you written and they have gone astray? Are you all right? I must say it was so good to receive it, it told me more than you know… My God, it is so long since that day in Heaton Park—can it really have been almost two years? How much we have both seen since then, my dearest Ali.

We have had some fighting here and it goes on, we are making good, if slow, progress. But what do we know really? We just follow orders. As you have probably realised, it is not always easy to get mail out, so this will probably be the last letter for a while. I don't know how life is for you at home. We hear stories of course, but we don't really know.

What I want to say to you though, is this: I want you to live your life Ali love. Don't wait around being unhappy. Trust me, I understand what you feel—sometimes I think I know you better than you know yourself. But who knows when we'll meet again? It's hard to believe you are real sometimes. There's so much I'd like to tell you, but to do so, under the circumstances, would be unfair. I don't want to put a noose around you. Don't be bound by promises made in the heat of the moment; you must be free love—no one knows that better than I.

I am all right, really, but I don't want to have to worry about you. I need to believe you are getting on with living. I often think about what Dad did to Mam. I am not him, but still, anything could happen. I may not be the same man when I return; at least a man that you would want. No one will ever give these years back to us. Even if we both make it through this, we may be very different people at the end of it.

Don't punish yourself. I know you, Ali—you are impulsive, and things may happen that you didn't plan. No one can take all of this out of our heads. War messes with us; makes us do things we wouldn't normally contemplate. I will not judge you and I hope you will not judge me. Do you understand?

I think of you often and remember everything. I hope your family is okay (I know about Ned—tell him I think of him).

Please give them my love.

*Love, always,
Walter xxx*

Book Two

Chapter Eleven

England
1944

Wiping my floury hands on my pinny, I rushed, smiling, to answer the door where I stared into a chest of khaki.

'Hi honey. Surprise, surprise!'

'Carl...?'

'Hope you don't mind my showing up like this. Your landlady gave me your address. It was kind of nice to get out of the city for a few hours.'

He stooped on the step, avoiding the porch lantern, which swung to and fro to the side of his head, a scrappy bunch of flowers and two packets of nylons in his hands.

'Er, these are for your mom, if she wears them. Hey, is this okay? You look kind of mad.'

I felt the smile drain from my face, my jaw tighten. He was out of context; too big, all teeth and brass buttons. I felt a creeping over my skin as I mumbled a lacklustre greeting, wished he wouldn't call me honey. I wasn't his honey.

'Aren't you going to invite the young man in? Where are your manners?'

Hovering, curious, behind me in the hallway, Mam pushed past and beckoned him. She shot a look at me; her mouth set in a thin line.

'We don't meet many Americans up here. Goodness me, I thought my sons were tall but you're a giant.'

'Six five, ma'am.'

'Well, well! You're welcome, I'm sure. You must be the friend Alice has told us about. Come on, come in, I'll put the kettle on.'

Again, that look. What was it exactly?

'I'm sorry, Carl, forgive me,' I brushed aside his kiss, looking behind to be sure Mam hadn't seen. 'I just didn't expect you; you know.'

'Couldn't wait for you to come back. I know it's your brother's homecoming an' all, but I'm leaving next week. Going into action.' He said it like he'd just eaten the last piece of cheesecake in the shop. But there was an awkwardness, his head hung, childlike. I warmed.

'You've been here so long; I suppose I just thought…Where are you going?'

Carl laughed, raised his eyebrows and shoulders, shook his head. Big things were happening. All leave cancelled. Training curtailed. No-one knew what or where.

'I expected to see the war out at Burtonwood now I'm trained up for groundwork, but it's all hands on deck, as you Brits say. It's kind of exciting, I guess.'

'Here, I've brought you a sandwich, cheese and tomato, I'm sure you haven't eaten. We've had our lunch.'

'Thanks Mam.'

'That's very kind, ma'am. Appreciate it.'

Normally, she would have stayed, had tea with us. Been nosy. But I suspected that Carl's uniform unnerved her; Carol Gratton from the town had upped and gone two weeks since. Exchanged Hebden for Florida and her new husband wasn't even there yet. The town talked of nothing else. It was, in its way, a scandal.

There was something else. She was prepared for Ned's homecoming; nothing should dilute that. He would be arriving with his dad anytime. It was only for a few days before he returned to hospital for more operations. The first time home since before he left for war. By some miracle Vincent was already home, the family complete. What was this stranger doing turning up now? *He* had never seen action. Turning up with nylons… I think Mam wanted to throw them at him.

'They must have missed the one o'clock train, they'll not be here now before four. When…Carl, is it? When Carl has had his sandwich, why don't you go for a walk? I'll finish off in the kitchen, it's all done anyway.'

It was sunny yet cool. As we rounded the hill and headed up the bridleway a sharp wind snapped at our clothes, shortened our breath. I felt the neighbours' eyes, even though we saw no one. When Carl tried to put his arm around me, I spun away.

'Not here; are you mad?'

Carl didn't understand. I knew what he was thinking: last time we were together, I hadn't pulled away, on the contrary. He pushed up his bottom lip and shrugged with a slight shake of the head walking on. He had told me once: 'there are places you can go for easy women...' I didn't ask him how he knew. 'You're different, Alice, a tease, sure, but there's an animal in you just itching to get out. You just don't know it yet...'

I bridled at what he said, but for all the wrong reasons. I even secretly liked the fact that he'd taken the trouble to think about it, even if he was wrong. But that day at Hebden, I was quiet, stiff. Walter hung around in the air, solid as a wall between us. *Our* relationship. *Our* future. *His* territory, marked on every hill, every bend in the lane.

I hadn't seen him for three years, but we were here, together, etched in the landscape, letters or no letters. It had always been just a question of time. Carl belonged to the city, to my other life. He had been merely filling a void. Hard to believe I'd known him for more than a year. Friends though. That's all it had been. The occasional kiss. Harmless. I seemed to have been able to separate him from my relationship with Walter, until, that is, last week in Manchester.

Carl knew about Walter, but *he* was here and Walter wasn't. That gave him a clear run. The last thing I had wanted was to bring Carl to this place. That's the trouble with fire: it spreads.

Yet as we walked further up the path and the houses petered away into the distance, I relaxed, felt a rush, a bending in the wind. All this way to see me. I was flattered. Part of me wanted to parade him: *Look what I've got...a good-looking American soldier wants me. Put that in your parochial pipe.* And he was leaving for the front; there was no danger in a relationship with a man whose days in England were numbered. I felt a sudden warming and linked my arm through his. He smiled so warmly I began to be glad he was there.

The last few months *had* been fun. The American soldiers made me laugh, though Carl was quiet in a mixed group, especially when Lily and *Cary Grant* made up a foursome. Lily's man, an urbane New Yorker, would make small jokes at Carl's expense, imitate his accent, call him *country boy*. Most of the time, I felt defensive of Carl, considered the others boorish and unkind.

Burgeoning maternal instincts would come into play as I sought to protect him, the way Mam had with us kids when one of us was left out of the group. Other times though, it made me look at Carl in a new light and I was glad we were not...a couple. In those moments I could hear the slowness in Carl's voice; his American drawl petered into dullness when in company with the sharp, slick banter of the others. Then I would look at his magnificent face, his body, and he would transmute, shift into something faintly bovine; the roundness of his shoulder, the curve of his jaw as he slowly chewed his gum, the glassiness in his eyes, emotionless, empty.

Then *Cary*, perceiving my discomfiture, would slap Carl on the back and buy him another beer, break the moment. Carl would smile; try to join in. Afterwards, Carl would brood, snap, so that I, complicit in his awkwardness, would feel guilty, pamper him, talk to him like a small boy. That's when he would melt, hold me, soak me up like a dry sponge, take away my breath, want me. That's when it happened.

Eight of us, three English women including Lily and I, and five G.I.'s had gone out together dancing at the Ritz. Carl was territorial as usual, but the men had other ideas.

'Hey buddy, c'mon now, share and share alike.'

Two of the men were very good dancers, but other men in the frame was like putting more than one bull into a field. Halfway through the evening, Carl got up and stood by the bar. Part of me wished him *good riddance*. Part of me noticed women watching him, liking what they saw.

After jiving a dance or two, drawing breath, I walked over to him. He stood stony, chin dipped, staring at me through his eyebrows.

'Are you all right?' I slipped one arm through the crook of his elbow.

'I'm going. You coming?' He lifted his eyes from me, poured them over a tall, attractive blond standing beside him, who reciprocated with a duplicitous smile and a look that implied her amusement at what she had overheard. 'I've had enough of dancing.'

The blond raised her eyebrows in a suggestive way, then giggled with her girlfriends. I raised my heels to look taller. Perspiration beaded my forehead and upper lip.

'Why can't you join in? Why the moodiness?' I gave the blond a *hands-off* glower while looking her up and down.

'Bye.' Carl picked up his beer, drained it and began to walk away, unhooking my arm as he did so. He threw a mock salute and a wink to the blond.

'I wouldn't let that one off the hook, deary,' the blond said loudly.

I ignored her, walked after him.

'Wait. Carl, wait.' I caught up with him at the cloakroom. He handed me the ticket.

'Want your coat or are you staying?'

I took the ticket and handed it to the attendant. Pulling my coat about me, I ran out after him, angry but exhilarated in the drama of it; that I, little Ali Conroy, could make a man like Carl jealous.

Once outside in the black night, we walked for a while. I was having to half run to keep up, when, as we turned into Oxford Road, Carl suddenly pushed me into a doorway and began kissing me, quite aggressively, pushing his body at me, holding my hips against him, talking all the time:

'I can't bear to see you with the others. I want you to myself... you understand, all to myself. I want you to want *me*, to take you away with me where no one else can have you. I want you...understand?'

Though muted fury hung about me like a smell of burning, I reciprocated as he pressed tobacco-kisses on me. The smell of beer and cigarettes disgusted me but I was excited too. I wanted him; like an animal feeling only need. His hands were pushing at me, moulding my body into the shape he wanted, wrapping my legs around him. He lifted my buttocks so that my feet left the ground. I made no effort to stop him. I felt light and airy, as though I were weightless, felt the cold wall on my back, saw my absurd, washed-out reflection in the shop window. I clutched onto his neck and closed my eyes.

He stopped for a moment and growled softly like an engine idling, then made a decision. I did nothing to stop him. Even though it hurt, I wanted to be taken.

'Oh God. I love you, honey...you know that.'

When it was over, he lowered me to the ground.

'I'm sorry, I'm so sorry. Are you all right, are you?'

'I don't know...'

'Was that the first time for you? I could kinda tell. Jeez, that feels good, you know?'

I stood silent, awkwardly straightening my clothes, confused, still in the moment. I was still aroused, disappointed. Was that it? I hadn't enough time for guilt to set in. I wondered how we got to this point; we were friends, just friends, weren't we? He looked at me, eager, nervous, waiting for me to speak. When I didn't, he sighed, the look was replaced by a cold glare. It wasn't the reaction he hoped for and cursorily handed me a handkerchief from his pocket.

'Here, use this.' He lit a cigarette and turned and stared out into the darkness. A detached expression settled on him like a dusting of snow. I did not move. My vacant stare, like the translucent eye of a waxwork figure, stared back at me from the shop window, across which was emblazoned: *William Mason, family butcher. Best quality cuts.*

And today, at home, I was being forced to realise what I had done. I could no longer call myself Walter's girl. I had waited for him for three years and I had ended that with heartless mechanical pumping against a cold stone wall in a shop doorway. What kind of 'nice girl' had I turned out to be?

Though dry, there were patches of cloud coming in, threatening rain. The early spring sun intermittently spattered light coloured patches onto the green and ochre folds of the landscape. I wandered off the path, clambered over the granite outcrop on the collar of a hill and onto a level promontory where the view opened up. This was a favourite secret place. Carl lagged behind. I looked back, waiting.

'Call yourself a country boy?' I shouted.

'I am. Don't get much more country than where I live. Americans don't walk much. Not for pleasure anyhow.'

I noticed how he didn't look around, instead his eyes crept over the ground, choosing his steps. He lifted his head and saw me standing on the rock.

'You're so…goddamn flimsy, look at you, I wonder you don't just blow away.'

'Perhaps I shall.'

His eyes changed, looked darker. The open country with its far-reaching views held no pleasure for him. He wanted what was in his immediate space. I knew it and liked it.

'So, this is home.' Obeying my distant gaze, he looked down the hill toward the basin that was Hebden, across the valley and up to the square tower of Heptonstall Church on the opposite hill. 'It's so different, you know, from mine. Your mom's nice. I think she likes me. Couldn't stop thinking about last week. You're my girl now. Does your mom know you're my girl? Have you told her?'

'Not really, no.'

'Why? Why haven't you told her?'

'I don't know…I…'

'Hell Alice?'

'I'll tell her after you've gone, all right?' I lied, staring over towards the church, twirling a strand of hair around my finger. I hadn't thought about this relationship as something to share with my family.

'Today?'

'Yes, if you want.'

'I want. Now come here, sit. Here, the ground's dry.' He took off his jacket and lay it down for me. 'Come on.'

I sat awkwardly, felt the wind drop. Felt his breath on my cheek.

'You know, I've been here all this time and now we've got something going, I'm leaving. I'll be back for you; you know that don't you?'

'That's what Walter said.' It was out before I could stop myself. 'I mean when he left, he and I…'

'Why did you have to mention him?' A deep frown sliced between his eyebrows. He took a breath, thought about it a moment then smiled. 'Besides, you're my girl now, I told you. That's way gone. In the past. Don't you think in three years he hasn't been…you know, kicking up his heels a little?'

'I don't know…' Suddenly, that letter last year began to make sense.

'C'mon Alice, he's not fighting all the time, you know. Besides, you and him…well, you were just kids, not like you and me. Hell, I'm serious, Alice. I want you to come visit me at home, see my country.' He lay back on the ground, looked at the sky. 'I never had much, you know. Family life wasn't…well, like yours. But I've got *you* now.'

I felt his thoughts settle in my mind. He looked at me in such a tender loving way as though I, little Ali Conroy, was worth something. I didn't want to disappoint. Walter had always shrunk from telling me what was in his mind, afraid of making promises he couldn't keep. Even after we made love and he had asked me to be his. What exactly did he mean by that? Carl forced the pace, perhaps pushed me into actions I wouldn't normally take. Or just maybe, he brought out the real me.

'I need you, honey, I do.'

I bent my head to him, pecked him lightly, maternally, on the forehead. He pulled me toward him, kissed me on the mouth, pushed his hand into my blouse, sighed when he felt me.

'I love your breasts, they're so…surprising.' His mouth curled in a salacious smile.

'Slow down. Not here.' I tried to pull myself away, looking around, making sure we couldn't be seen.

'I brought some rubbers, you know, in case.'

He fumbled in his pocket and pulled one out and started to tear off the packaging with his teeth.

'What! You came here expecting this? To my home?'

'Hey hey…steady on. It's just I'm going away and well, it's not as if we haven't, you know, done it, is it? C'mon honey, I just thought, better be safe?'

He pulled me back down to him, gently. I could taste metal in my mouth, I tried to swallow but somehow couldn't. I felt a kind of recoil, the way I felt when I came upon a ravaged sheep on the moors that some errant fox had taken. When he started to kiss me, moving down my neck to my breasts, further… I didn't resist. I didn't want to resist. I was both revolted and aroused.

The more he touched me, the more I needed him not to stop. I heard myself whimpering in lust. When I came to a climax, salt tears marked my face as I lay silent, stilled but rigid with new reserve. Afterwards, it wasn't so much that we'd had sex again that troubled me; but that I had wanted it so much. Women weren't supposed to feel that way unless they were in love. Was it possible to love two men? Was I in love with Carl? Perhaps I was.

'Are you all right, love? You look peaky. Is it getting cold out? Where's the American? Has he gone?'

'Yes Mam.'

'Long way to come for a walk, he must be keen. You need to watch it, young lady, men like that always want something, especially Yanks.'

I wanted to go and wash, felt smeared with Carl. Thought Mam would smell my guilt, the way you can smell a dead rat under the floorboards. And yet…each time I thought of him, I felt newly aroused. Forbidden fruit.

But Mam turned to the job in hand, singing along with Lena Horne on the radio…*since he went away, there's no sun up in the sky, stormy weather…*

'Help me set the table, love, they'll be here any minute.'

Chapter Twelve

England
1944

Walter's Mam shouted a lot, it was her way of coping. She had the sort of home that held secrets; grief bound up in old letters, postcards, a curl of hair, an old pipe. Anger. Although I couldn't know beyond what Walter had told me as I was never invited in. Walter said she was always apologising for the state of the house that she never stopped cleaning. She would look at people's shoes when they knocked, then keep them on the doorstep.

'Walter…Walter…can you hear me? Alice is here,' she would yell up the stairs. Then when he appeared, she would whisper to him behind the door: 'What do you hang around with *her* for? Why don't you go off and play football?' I think she thought he was soft.

'She doesn't like me,' I remarked once, meaning I didn't like her.

'She does really, just can't show it. You're a girl. She's jealous because she didn't have any. She's used to it now. Besides, you're posh; probably thinks you look down on us.'

'I couldn't be posh if I tried.'

'I know that.'

'Hey…steady on.'

'You've got trees. Better address. She'd look down on you if the boot was on the other foot. She's like that; thinks she married beneath herself. She's very balanced, my Mam, got a chip on both shoulders.'

No love lost. Still, I decided to call at the house to try to glean any news of Walter before I went back to Manchester. It was about time. More than time. No matter that I had done what I'd done, he was still someone I loved—would always love. Since Ned had been home, I had become fixated by the things he told us of the actuality of living each day just trying to survive. And by his injuries: the scarring on his neck, shoulders and chest pervaded my dreams, making me, each time on waking, understand the pain that was *out there*.

I had started to be afraid.

I began to fear that the war was madness, a huge mistake, out of control, that the men in charge had no idea what they were doing or how it would end. Soldiers and civilians were caught up in its vortex like matchsticks tossed into a tornado.

And it was being home. The landscape, incomplete somehow without Walter in it. Everywhere I looked, there he was, and it was not just what I could see. The scent of him, still in my head: Pears soap and wood-smoke, bicycle oil, swimming pools. I knew I had let him down but, I told myself, three years was a long time. I was young and I craved affection.

If there had been letters, it might have been easier, but silence made for uncertainty; moral boundaries became blurred, people did things that in peacetime would have been unthinkable. There was also the nagging doubt that Walter and I may not feel the same after all this time, that our love may have transmuted into something altogether more fraternal and that it would be foolish to trust to a childhood dream.

I was trying to justify myself.

So, here I was, on my way to remind myself that he existed. Since the four letters I'd heard nothing. Although I had replied, each letter telling him everything about my work at the factory, the situation at home, about family and life in general in a country during wartime, I did not mention Carl, nor my confusion.

There was no point adding to his feeling of isolation—something Ned told us was part of a soldier's daily life—but he probably guessed. If he no longer regarded us as *together*, then it made no difference. Since then, I had tried to push him out of my mind so that I didn't have to feel bad about enjoying myself. I hadn't succeeded. Infatuated with Carl, I reasoned, I was caught up in my own tornado.

Being in Manchester, with Lily and Carl had made me throw caution and my true nature to the breeze, as if I had begun again as someone else. Yet still I missed him. This vacillation, I reasoned, was inevitable in a vacillating world.

At home though, everything was real. I suppose at the heart of my self-deception had been the hope that, despite everything, Walter may still want me, would one day come home and rescue me from myself. Hoped even, that when he did, *he* might have something to expiate, something to make him want to forgive me as I would forgive him. But on home turf I saw the delusion for what it was. I simply hadn't been strong enough to wait.

I walked awkwardly down the steep cobbled lane towards Fairford where Walter lived, biting on the soft sides of my mouth and blinking to prevent the moisture in my eyes turning to tears. I knocked on the door. The peeling, bottle-green council paint, just the same. There was a nervous twitch of the lace curtain. My heart throbbed; fingers tingled. The door opened. Mrs Bradshaw smiled a loose smile.

'Alice Conroy well, well, well…how are you? I hear you live in Manchester now?'

'Hello Mrs Bradshaw. I'm fine, thank you. Yes, I've been living in Middleton Junction for a while now. How are you?'

'Fine I'm sure.' There was a Lancashire burr in her voice I had never detected before. She looked older. Smelled of bleach.

'What can I do for you?' She looked me up and down. One hand on the door, the other on the doorframe.

'I've come about Walter. I haven't heard from him for some time. I wondered if you had any news.'

'Don't you write to one another?' She looked genuinely surprised.

'Well yes, of course. But not for a while. He said it was difficult. I think we've sort of lost touch.'

'Thought you two lived in each other's pockets.' She folded her arms, a hint of smugness creeping over her posture. She gave a crooked smile, raised an eyebrow. ''Course, it's difficult to get the letters through. I've had only two in six months. He's had a rough time of it by all accounts. Though not injured like your Ned, thank God, leastways not that I know of…and we all know how fast bad news travels. How *is* he, by the way?' She leaned forward, her voice hushed, as though she were speaking of the dead.

'Oh Ned. Yes, poor Ned. He's doing well. Very well actually, under the circumstances. It was lovely to have him home for a few days.' I smiled mock-brightly, desperate to return to the subject of Walter.

'I'm glad, give him my best, you know.'

'Yes, thank you. Tell me, please, how has Walter had a rough time? I mean, I know it's all awful, but is there something I don't know? Where is he?' I leaned in to catch what she was saying, afraid to miss a vital detail.

'Well, that's anyone's guess, love, at the moment. He never tells me where he is. He knows I worry.'

'But…'

'I'm just reading between the lines, so to speak. Our Walt…he's so…well you know him. Cheerful. But his last letter was, how shall I put it? Morose. Yes morose.' She looked down at her feet, paused. I noticed the way she held herself in with her folded arms, her cardigan crossed over at the front like a shawl, shoulders hunched like an old lady. There was a slight break in her voice, she swallowed to collect herself.

For perhaps the first time, I could see the mother in her: helpless, trapped in her worry by her love for her son. Why hadn't I seen it before?

'Not surprising really. He seems to be wondering why he's fighting. I think he's lost a lot of friends; you know.' She nodded, eyes closed, then sniffed, paused, collected herself. 'Anyhow, I'm writing to him this week. I write every week, though I don't know if he gets them. I'll tell him I've seen you.'

The door began ever so slightly to close.

'Thanks Mrs Bradshaw, send him my love.' Mrs Bradshaw stopped closing the door and stared incomprehensively at me.

'Why don't you send it yourself? Not meaning to be rude or 'owt.'

'I…yes, of course…I'll do that.'

'He's a long way from home, easy to forget the danger he's in. It might cheer him up. Usual address.'

'You're right. I will. Thanks.'

'Well then. Thanks for calling. Give my best to your family. Tarra.'

'Goodbye.'

The door closed six inches from my face. I turned and walked stiffly back up the hill, wishing I hadn't gone. *Mea culpa, mea maxima culpa.*

*

Next day, when I returned to my digs, there was a note waiting for me in large unwieldy handwriting.

25 March 1944

Dear Alice,

I hope the family get together was good and your brother is doing fine. By now your back at Ida's (lucky you), hope thats okay. I thought maybe we could meet up. I got hold of a jeep again this weekend, if your free, we could take a ride. It's my last pass. Everyones confined to barracks from now until I go. We'll be training big time.

How about it? You can telefone and get a message to me. Just say yes or no. If yes, give me a time and I'll pick you up Saterday.

Looking forward to it,

Love, Carl

It made me squirm, the spelling, the grammar. I was pretty sure the letter had been opened; Ida looked furtive. I was embarrassed; soiled by association. Then checked my childish snobbery. Who the hell did I think *I* was? But it wasn't only that. Being with Ned and hearing about Walter had made up my mind. It was time for me to grow up.

'For God's sake, you don't even know Walter anymore,' Lily moaned as she filed her nails in our lunch break. 'No one's perfect. Walter wasn't, was he? And Carl *is* bloody gorgeous.'

It was true. And Carl *had* been distracting, but like a new and dangerous hobby that you realise isn't worth the risk, it was time to stop before I injured both of us. I preferred safer, more familiar territory; my instinct would always return me to nest in those things that I knew. Walter was inseparable from that.

If he still wanted me…even if he didn't, and in my heart I knew he wouldn't, it wasn't fair to lead on Carl any longer. I was also worried that what I felt for Carl was beginning to be more than affection. There couldn't be two soldiers sent abroad that I yearned for.

*

It was a fine morning; the still, warm air filled with birdsong and scents of early blossom. Trees were spangled with pale green shoots encouraged by unusually warm weather. It was a day to be happy in.

Pedestrians shook their heads and tutted as we squealed around corners and bumped and skidded over tramlines in the open jeep on our way out of the city. We could feel the cold and warm draughts of air wash over us from the hedgerows and woodland, as we flew fast and young down country lanes.

When we screeched to a stop in a Cheshire village, windblown and laughing, it wasn't the time to tell Carl of my decision. Better later.

It wasn't right either in the pub, full of servicemen and women, couples. I wanted to fit in, be part of things. Besides there was nowhere quiet to sit and talk, too many people, wrong atmosphere. I would tell him in the evening when the laughter had gone out of the day.

When, after lunch, we wandered through the village toward open countryside, Carl took my hand, looking sideways at me, his head tilted, as though looking at me in a new, almost reverential light, as I rambled on about something inconsequential. We cut away from the road, crossed a stile and walked along an overgrown footpath, through a meadow dotted with huge bare oaks, covered in buds, laughing and teasing all the while.

I procrastinated with myself; it seemed a shame to spoil the mood. We had become…familiar. He was going away soon anyhow. I was overcome by a sense of well-being and burgeoning affection for this unlikely hunk of a man. I'd had a beer at the pub, but it wasn't that. I felt the sun sink into me, smelled the Spring growth, felt the burst of new life, allowed the tiniest acknowledgement to slip into my head, despite myself, how dull life would be again, with no dancing partner; with no Carl.

When he lifted my petticoat, his face absorbed, concentrated, I felt a kind of power, and the rush of lust that ran through me quite took away my resolve. Being wanted was no small thing. I leant back, let him unbutton my blouse, lay with my hands by my sides, in a separate world, smiling at the erotic pleasure. I stared at the sky, not a wisp of cloud, tuned into the tap of a distant woodpecker, felt the grass damp under my neck. I made no effort; I wanted him to have me.

Afterwards, I felt sick. What was I doing? Would I never learn? Was I completely out of control? The heavens scowled disapproval. Guilt, manifested as anger, chewed at me as we walked back to the car in our own shadows, the setting sun cooling at our backs. I would be punished; I was not worthy.

Carl, oblivious to my change of mood, whistled *I'm a yankee doodle dandy…* while I festered. It wasn't fair, I told myself, it was the war, it changed everything. Made me into this. War took people out of their little lives, flung them into something much bigger until they were left breathless, gasping, less or more than they would have been. I didn't know who or what I was anymore. The end began.

I turned on him as though he had tuned into my dilemma.

'…and they all love Walter. I love Walter. I know you don't like me to say it.'

'What the hell…?'

'You don't understand…you can never understand.' I flapped my hands in frustration.

'What are you talking about? I swear to God you are one complicated broad.'

'My family. My family,' I screamed.

'*They* are not you,' Carl shouted back. 'And Walter's in the past. Jeez, you haven't seen him for years. Your mom liked me. What about us, our future?' His voice had a rising pitch, unravelled at the edges.

I continued as though he hadn't spoken, but calmly, my hands fanned out in front of me.

'It's a kind of pressure. Makes me, in a way, want to rebel. Maybe that's what I'm doing. Vincent thinks I'm…well I don't know what he thinks, but I'm sure he wonders how I could gallivant around Manchester, while the man I love is away. But if I really loved him, I'd have waited, wouldn't I? That's what nice girls do.' I spoke to the darkening air, trying to understand the muddle that was in my head. I felt cold suddenly.

'Alice, listen to me. I want you. You're mine now. Jeez honey, what are you saying to me? What about today? That wasn't just sex.' He blocked my way, compressed his voice, articulated each syllable.

'No it wasn't…you're right…but…oh, I don't know. It's not you…I feel so wretched.' I began to shiver. 'What a Catholic I turned out to be.' I leaned over and tried to retch into the ditch, riddled with self-hate.

'Stop, Alice.'

'I've been weak. I don't think I love you, Carl. I just don't know. I don't think I know what love is. I can't remember Walter anymore…' I fought the hard sobs that lodged like knots in my throat, my voice thick with misery and shame. 'I'm a woman…I'm not supposed to…feel what I feel…I'm the moth in the flame… you know. Oh God.'

'Crazy talk…crazy girl…Come here.'

Carl held me while I let go, wept into his chest. Despite myself, I wanted him to hold me, wanted him to comfort me, take away my indecision, my remorse.

'I'm so sorry, Carl.'

'It's being home with your family, they've confused you. That and your goddamned religion. This is not a confessional, for Chrissake. Hear? I don't want to know. You do love me, Alice, and I love you, a man can tell these things. You're mine, I told you. God, Alice I want to marry you, be with you forever.' His voice rose an octave, panic in it.

I stopped crying, held my breath, looked at him in a kind of daze.

'It's true, look.'

He grabbed my left hand, fumbling in his trouser pocket for a small box. Then tried clumsily to push a ring from inside onto my wedding finger. There was a tiny diamond between two smaller rubies. I laughed hysterically through my sobs; felt I was being buried between the leaves of some cheap romantic novel.

'A ring?' I took a deep breath, controlled myself.

'Too small,' he said calmly, a strange smile emerging. 'You know I thought it might be, still, no matter, you can wear it on another finger till we get it fixed. It's not much I know. I'll get a better one when I can.' Nonetheless, he forced it onto my finger as he spoke, leaving no void for objection. My hand was white where he held it tight.

I continued to laugh as I wept; wanted to laugh *with* him, but he wouldn't see the comedy, only the slight. I felt myself being drawn into someone else's dream, someone else's idea of love, my resistance weakened by the ironic pleasure of being wanted so much, and because I genuinely felt sorry for him. Nonetheless I loved the boldness of it, the risk. He made me doubt myself. Like a fire out of control, he sucked in all my air until I could no longer breathe.

Three days later, screwing bolts into the cockpit of a Lancaster bomber, I grazed my fingers repeatedly as I lost concentration, gripping the screwdriver with both hands trying to maintain control. The din of the factory drowned out the necessity to talk to Lily, who, during each break wouldn't leave the subject of Carl alone.

'Aw c'mon, our kid, we could have a double wedding, wouldn't that be great? We could meet up in America. Imagine that, leaving this dump. There's nothing here for us…aw c'mon…where's your sense of adventure?' Lily's large diamond flashed in the arc lights. It was the subject of much talk at the digs.

'Must be bleedin' loaded, your Yank,' Percy bleated, scratching his head and looking at Lily in a new light. I didn't show them my ring, which I had been unable to remove. Instead, I turned it around on my finger so that the gems faced my palm; a thin gold band was all that showed, which, I joked, was a curtain ring bought to keep the boys at bay. It signified nothing, yet, I resented the fact that Lily's was in a different class.

The tender note that arrived from Carl, posted before he left, 'looking forward to our future together', finally made me act.

April 1944
Middleton J.

Dear Carl,
When you are back, we must talk. You are a good man and do not deserve to be messed around, so I'll get straight to the point. I cannot do as you wish much as I do not want to hurt you. I shall return your ring to you when I can.
Life is complicated, is it not? My instinct however has always been that we were never meant to be more than friends. I thank you for the great compliment you have paid me. I am truly sorry for everything.
Keep safe,

Alice

I wrote to Walter on the same day.

April 1944
Middleton J.

My dear, dear Walter,
Where are you? Are you all right? Why haven't you written? I need to hear from you, need so much to see you. Your last letter, so long ago, was beautiful. I shall keep it always. Then nothing. This wretched war has changed everything.
Write to me, Walter. Tell me about your war, even the awful bits. Your Mam told me it's been bad for you. I pray for you every night. We used to share everything, remember? Can you share with me what's happening? Can you bear

to do that? I'm not a child anymore and I know you're not either. Tell me what you're feeling inside. Is there still a place for us?

I miss you. Without you, I am not a good person. I need you to help me with this. That is, if you can forgive what I have become. I have done things I should never have done and I don't know who I am anymore.

How selfish of me to go on about how I need rescuing when you are in so much danger. Somehow, I never imagine anything bad happening to you. Not to you, though I know it's happening to so many others. I imagine a guardian angel forever behind you, just on your left shoulder. I hope I'm right.

I love you, Walter. I'm lost. Come home to me.

Your Ali XXXX

I posted the letters the next morning. When Carl came back, I would return his ring, which I would have cut off as soon as possible. Maybe he was right. Maybe I *was* beginning to love him, whatever love was. Maybe there were different kinds of love. But I knew whatever it was that precipitated my feelings of yearning, I felt it for Walter more.

Chapter Thirteen

Italy
July 1944

Lake Trasimeno spread out before him, its oily calm, pink in the evening light. Walter removed his clothes slowly, methodically, to reveal a body that was wiry, athletic, stained by antique dirt and dried sweat. He removed his dog-tags and lay them on top of his uniform, scratching at the lice in his groin. The air was still, the heat of the day beginning to wane and on the west shore, early lights twinkled pale through bushes, the reflection of the vermilion sky undulating on the water.

Italian voices drifted across the water, distant; the faint *meow* of animated derision, laughter that sounded like peacetime. He listened for a while then waded into the shallows, felt the tingle of cool run up his body, goose-bumps spreading in patches like waves. The ground was stony, but further in, silky mud oozed between his toes and with barely a ripple, Walter slid his body into the sun-warmed lake, a fanning chevron marking momentarily that he was there and then not.

After a few exploratory strokes, he found his rhythm and pushed into deeper, darker water, feeling a sense of coming home, returning to his natural element. He emptied his mind and allowed the cool of the deeper water to absorb him and stop him thinking.

After Monte Cassino, he had begun to measure his life in abstracts. The tangled mess of shifting memories and sensory impressions that filled him with both longing and despair made him feel he was losing his grip. Tedium, horror, frustration, anger and grief manifested in a deep weariness and feeling of helplessness.

He had been grateful for the respite Kesselring had given them after ordering the German retreat from Cassino, nonetheless it allowed time to think. Arriving at Trasimeno had been comparatively easy. Foot-rot had become an issue again.

Boots. Blisters. Wet socks. And food. The boredom of it: bully beef again, and again. But, he thought, it's only when you stop that it hits you.

On the march North through Rome, he had pondered the innocence of the girls and women as they rushed forward with posies and kisses; the desire they ignited, the soft rise in their breathing revealing the sensuality beneath their clothes; the jiggling of their perfect bodies. The memory of their playful caresses stayed on his lips and cheeks to be savoured later. As he marched, he practised smiling through an etched weather-torn face. When he wasn't marching, he was drunk when he could get it.

The fantasy of Alice came into his mind from time to time, a dream from an impossibly lovely childhood. She didn't fit into his world now, leastways not in daytime. And yet, still, he wrote his journal, recording everything for her so that one day she would know, one day she would see that he thought of her, wanted her, but did not want to bind her to him with letters, promises he may not be able to keep, the way his father had done with his mother. His life was not his to control. Besides, he was ashamed of what he had become.

He thought how none of those in authority seemed to know what they were doing. So little filtered down to the ranks that orders were like Chinese whispers and most of it seemed like a cock up; a battle won came more of a surprise than relief. Reasons for fighting had become perfunctory, mechanical, but he wasn't sure he wanted to go home either.

It was best not to think about it. He had no illusions; he knew he would die—he didn't want to, it just seemed inevitable. His mother would have called it a premonition. It was just a question of time. It wasn't death he feared, but the discomfort of existence; routinely doing stuff that in peacetime would be considered heinous.

This knowledge made him brave, though he didn't think he deserved the decoration they were foisting upon him; he hadn't consciously put himself at risk when he jumped into the Rapido River. The guy was drowning and being shot at. It just needed to be done, so he did it. The most difficult part had been getting both of them out of the water in full kit. He had seen real feats of bravery that had gone unnoticed. It was merely symbolic, they needed heroes, give the rest something to fight for: their moment of glory. It meant nothing.

So dark was the space he occupied in his mind, that a few hours before he entered the lake to try to forget, he forced himself to recall it all one more time, as the premonition, whose shadow was ever present, informed him that he could not wait. It could be the final chapter of the journey of his life, recorded so that someone, somewhere would know what it was like. To bear witness. But also, because by writing it, he could let it go. He left the journal in camp with instructions, as always, in the event of his death, to whom it must be given:

February '44
Just above Inferno Valley
Italy

It's bitter cold, rain like rods. The big guns and tanks can't move for the mud, avalanches of the stuff. And the strangest thing, when they dig out the corpses, they're stripped. Shoes and shirts gone. Just men, naked as babes, no telling what side they were on.

The slit trenches fill with water till our feet are rotten with it. Stukas dive-bomb us, screaming like Furies. On the hill, big guns stare down; impossible to move without them seeing. Behind are more soldiers trying to come up, scrambling like rats on scree. Smoke screens don't last long; it drifts, rolls like smog, stinging eyes.

It's all there, on their faces. A quietness: a resignation, something you can't explain. Then out of the chaos, Jim, with Bill on the forward slope, shout, in high falsetto, clear as a choirboy:

'Get over here...for Chrissake, get down.'

But I can't make it to the mortar hole. Trip on a hump of grey rock shaped like an elbow rising from the earth. I fall flat, exposed, clinging to the wet scrub, as an old 'moaner' whines its way toward me and explodes with a force that lifts me clean off the ground.

Missed.

Seconds later, new rain falls as I crouch trying to breathe in the thin air. A shower of bloody bits. The mortar-hole now twice the size, empty space where Jim and Bill should be. The pink rain dribbles down my cheeks, into my mouth.

Christ. Christ.

Still the lice scratch in my groin. Still, I feet life crawling through me while a God somewhere plays His game, sets up the next shot.

But I'm alone, deaf, save the ringing in my ears. I edge forward, heavy with pack and wet dirt, feet strangely passive. Absent. Think about the shop, the sound of the till ringing up. Then a voice:

'Bradshaw, get your arse down here. What the fuck're you doing, man? Where are Taylor and Hamilton?'

We could see the monastery up above. Untouched in a vast wasteland of mud and mortar-holes. A palace in Passchendaele, the officer called it. On the slope ahead, a farm.

'It's heavily fortified, Kraut machine guns line the banks. The big guns'll shell it, then acting infantry follow in when I tell you. B Company first. And for fuck's sake, keep your heads down.'

Soldiers all over the hill. Unclear whose. Poles mostly now, a tough bunch. Good lads. Then, a barrage of pounding; dull heavy thuds whose sound seems to disappear into the earth, leaving only tremors.

'Go, go.'

B Company tries it.

Cut down from the sides to a man.

'A Company, wait for tank support.' The officer wears an old man on his thirty-year face.

Eventually, the tanks heave their way up, shifting from side to side like bag ladies, eliminating the Germans in the ditch.

'A Company, go. Go!'

I weave my way through the smoking turrets. A gunner ahead of me charges up the hill with a heavy American 'Thompson', almost as big as himself. Stumbling over the bodies of B Company, we expect to die at any second.

I separate, go around to the left, sense life. Carefully placing every footstep, skirting the holes, smell last year's lavender, thyme, something like that. There falls a quiet—unnatural, as I push open the barn door.

The roof is gone. Dust smarts my eyes, fills my lungs. Inside, a weak sun noses its way through cloud, falls over open rafters. A fog of blasted particles floats undecided, up, down, in ribbons of disturbed rain-filled air.

I'll remember it for the rest of my life; the saddest thing I've ever seen. The main beam, intact, out of place at shoulder level, is held up, not by stone walls which lay tumbled, scattered, but by the broken backs of four huge, magnificent, dray horses, still tethered, alive, eye-wild with pain, stilled into unnatural shapes.

I am in hell.

Tears dribble warm over my grit-spattered face as I pointed my rifle at the head of the nearest. I'm used to guns, loading, firing. Big guns that can wipe out a village. *Killing horses, one by one at close range is something else. As I fire the last shot, two soldiers from* A *Company run in, rifles cocked.*

'Will anyone remember this?' I say, as they shuffle through the debris toward me.

'Monte Cassino? Probably not. We certainly won't if we don't get off this fucking hill', said a young soldier, looked about fifteen. 'C'mon, it's all clear. We're moving out.'

I've had no leave for nearly three years. Three years living like a rat. But I can't go home yet. Not with this in my head. I'm all fucked up.

That evening, we are ordered to bury our comrades. First collect personal possessions, then put the bodies onto stretchers and carry them down the hill. Identity discs from lads I'd shared everything with, jangled in my pocket.

As I pick through, lifting stiff heads, I think about the night before with Jim and Bill. We couldn't dig in, too stony and scrubby. Built sangars instead from loose rocks. No cover, just a slit trench that we lay in listening for noises, waiting for dawn, unable to fire in case we hit one of our own patrols. Whispers of Polish, from other divisions, wafted through the night like gifts from strangers.

'Got a letter last week, finally,' Jim said smokily, cupping his cigarette.

'Yeh? What's in it? She's not going to leave him for you?'

'Complicated. I dunno,' Jim replied. ''Course, she married too young, it was what the families wanted.'

'What did she say?' I asked, hungry for news of anything that wasn't here and now.

'Och, she said she loved me, you know…' Bill and I made crooning noises. 'Says she yearns for me. Imagine that.' A small smile curled the edges of his mouth. 'Don't laugh or I'll tell you no more, so I bloody won't.'

Bill wrinkled his face, shook his head. Didn't believe in 'love'. Said it was like religion: 'opium of the masses'. He was a Communist; had left university to fight in Spain before this.

'No really though…' Jim's voice notched up an octave, 'how can any woman yearn for me?' Bill sniggered into his blanket at his friend's doleful eyes and filthy face.

'Och, you're such a soulless arse, so y'are,' Jim elbowed Bill in the ribs.

'Do you yearn for her?' I asked.

'Hell fire! Why complicate a good fuck with all this?'

'Shut up, Bill. Do you?'

'I do. Aye, I do that. There's something else though…' He sucked deeply on the butt of his dying cigarette, stubbed it out heavily into the earth, then covered his mouth with his palm, pressing his fingers and thumb into the hollows beneath his cheekbones.

'Go on, what?' I pressed.

Jim took a deep breath and sighed. He looked back at me and shrugged his shoulders.

'Well, you know I had that leave six months since? She's pregnant, not sure if it's his or mine.'

There was just a whisper of 'Christ' from Bill. Jim smiled, pulled off his tin hat. Scratched his head.

Now, it doesn't matter.

I wrestle with the idea of non-existence. Not even a corpse. Like getting lost in infinite space. Thoughts, memories, plans, all that we are. Atoms. Exploding atoms.

Fight for your country they keep saying, but on that hill, I fought for myself, scared all the time, we all were.

And there's the monastery. Still. Taunting. Holding up our lives. I hate it. That whole fucking hill is covered in blood.

Two days later, a warming sun nudges us into life. Out of the silence, a drone. From the mist, a ghostly armada of Flying Fortresses drifts, diffused, decorating the sky like migrating birds. I shield my eyes, stared. Ours. Wonder where they are headed, when things start to drop from them, hundreds, hailing down onto the monastery.

Whistles, cries and roaring began to reverberate over the mountain. We duck and run. And run. The barrage catching our tail-end. Sweat scalds my eyes, my uniform soaked, chest moving like bellows; I push forward until the shells start breaking amongst us. I feel euphoric. Charged. Like I've seen God; forked lightning at His fingertips. Then it stops. Drifting gun-fog moves over the hill like a veil, giving everything a grey-white hue.

For some minutes an eerie silence, then I hear cheering. The men are cheering. Me too. We grab one another, hug and shout. When the ballyhoo subsides, I hear a Welshman shout in the near distance:

'Why the hell are you cheerin'? It's a bloody church. What are we doin' on this God-forsaken hill? What the hell are we fightin' for?'

The mood changes from elation to confusion. Bathed in smoke, man looks to man, boy to boy, behind us a trail of mangled soldiers. A strange, filled silence falls amongst us.

I stand breathing hard. One hand, white-fingered, clutching my rifle, the other clinking the identity discs in my pocket. I become aware of my bodily stink, sweat running down my belly into my groin.

And now tonight, as usual, I am recording it. All of it. Perhaps the last of it…I never want to forget what I've seen in this war.

To you, Alice, my Alice, my friend and lover, as always, just in case… I hope you never have to read it. You belong to a different world now. Or I do.

I don't like what I've become. Seen things. Done what no man should.

*

But, as he swam into a darkening sky leaving the shores far behind him, his mind was empty, clear of the detritus accumulated over the last three years. Occasionally, things brushed against his legs, flotsam or curious fish. After an hour or so he stopped, trod water and looked about him. The land was now black, the water pale and deep. A near full moon hovered low on the horizon like a footlight on a stage.

Sensing something around his feet, he looped and dived, felt about him. There was nothing. He swam down further, pulled against the heavy water, deeper and deeper still. Breathing did not occur to him, he sensed only a ripple of ecstasy running through his body like electricity. He felt himself compressed as though sucked through a narrow tube. There was a rush in his ears. It seemed he was floating, not in the water but in the air just above it, the moonlit lake a pool of white. Nothing seemed to matter. It was all right now.

'Di chi e'sta roba? Puzza pure. Hey, Marco, prendila. Dai, tirala indietro a me. Guardatemi ragazzi. A chi assomiglio? A uno di quei Crauti!'

The gaggle of boys that found his uniform kicked it around the beach on their way to school, mimicking a soldier goose-stepping, unsure what army this was. They smelt the clothes, threw them down in disgust and continued kicking them as they roved along the beach, until little bits of Walter were spread over thirty metres of shoreline. The dog-tags slithered into the shallows.

The day after his disappearance, soldiers in his division, back in camp, had notice of their forthcoming home leave. The first for his division in over three years.

The letter from Alice lay in the mail, waiting.

Chapter Fourteen

England
Hebden Bridge
July '44

Dearest Ali,

I don't know how to tell you this, love. Last night Walter's mother came around with a letter from the War Office, which I enclose, asking us to forward it to you. We don't know anything more at this stage. Darling, we are so, so sorry. Can you come home? Don't be on your own. I'm so sad to send you such distressing news but you need to know.

Your ever-loving Mam,
God bless XXX

N0 3/RA/1/2 Army Form B. 104-83
Record Office

Sir or Madam,

I regret to inform you that a report has been received from the War Office to the effect that (No.) 997968 (Rank) Private

(Name) Bradshaw Walter George.

(Regiment) Royal Artillery

was posted as "missing" on 17 July 1944 in Southern Europe.

The report that he is missing does not necessarily mean that he has been killed, as he may be a prisoner of war or temporarily separated from his regiment.

Official reports that men are prisoners of war take some time to reach this country, and if he has been captured by the enemy it is probable that unofficial news will reach you first. In that case, I am to ask you to forward any postcard or letter received at once to this office, and it will be returned to you as soon as possible.

Should any further official information be received, it will be at once communicated to you.

I am,

Sir or Madam,
Your Obedient Servant,
J. M. Turnbull.
Major.
Officer in charge of Records.

August 1944
Middleton Junction

It was not true. Walter could not be dead. Some instinct told me it wasn't possible.

Two weeks later, another letter arrived from the war office confirming that it was so, *due to overwhelming evidence.*

Still, I could not believe it. I would have felt something, had some sense of his passing. They told me I was in denial. No one ever believed, unless they had seen it for themselves. He was twenty-two years old…ten years ago, he had been twelve. How could it be?

They had his dog-tags, found at the water's edge of Lake Trasimeno. His clothes. There was the decomposed body washed up on the western shore. Unidentifiable. Unimaginable. Already buried.

Beautiful, sandy-haired, green-eyed Walter. His wide mouth and easy smile. How could it be? How could he exist and then not? Always he had been somewhere when I was not with him, like some affirmation of my own existence; without him in the world, who was I?

Walter was dead, they said.

Walter *was* dead.

He had gone for a swim and had drowned.

On the bed in my grubby digs, behind a locked door, I lay like a small bird having been hit by a truck: folded in, flat, as though most of me had been sucked out. A huge immoveable weight lay on my chest that threatened to stop my heart from beating. Breathing came in snatches, each inhalation a supreme effort. Several times I tried to let myself give in to what seemed inevitable, then I would gasp, disappointed by my own weakness; my inability to simply stop.

I couldn't go home to Hebden, couldn't face the anguish of others, the unendurable grief of his mother. There was something too intimate about my own; to share would have been to dilute it. It had to be pure. Each morning brought the fresh horror of Walter's death, the knowledge that *I* was alive.

There was also guilt.

I couldn't bear to look in the mirror. I didn't want absolution, didn't deserve it and in any case *that,* I could never now get. I wanted to suffer. Knew my life somewhere along the line would punish me for what I had done. Hoped that it would. The only small satisfaction was the knowledge that I had finally made a choice and had, in my own way, told Walter, in my letter to him. I hoped he might have read it. Hoped one day I might convince myself it was better that he never knew of Carl, that what we'd had remained untainted.

At first, at night, when sleep would come suddenly and steal me away from misery, I would dream of him. We were always children in those dreams, innocent, uncorrupted. Details came to me I thought I had forgotten: Walter scrambling for apples, pulling his body along ridged groaning branches, so that he could get for me the best at the top of the tree, throwing them into my skirt one by one whilst I stood beneath, arms outstretched, observing: his tongue in his teeth, his right arm stretched ever higher to grasp the ones just out of reach, his taut frame, balanced precariously, completely handsome. And smiling to myself, that it was I, unbeknown to him, being the lightest and most agile in the family, that did the scrumping when Mam needed apples for a pie.

Or the concentration on his face as he tried to explain to me how to repair the bicycle chain after we had free-wheeled down Horsehold, our legs outstretched yelling, until I swerved and crashed into the hawthorn. I knew all the while how to do it—two older brothers—I just wanted to both watch him and create a hero—in my mind and his. And I wondered, even in my abject state, why women are content not to be heroes too.

I would turn over on waking, drying my face in the pillow, trying to stop my mind. But then, as I lay in half sleep, I would think of him on long simmering summer days, in shorts, pumps and nothing else until his skin took on a freckled tan. Saw the pale skin that crept out of the rim around his shorts when he stretched and moved, that at ten embarrassed me, but at fifteen provoked an entirely different reaction.

There were moments when I even laughed, almost hysterically, at the images in my head; my past—so much part of the person I had become, before inwardly folding in renewed wretchedness with the realisation of all that had happened since.

Nothing mattered. I took to walking the city streets at the heart of night, just to be alone. Imagined Walter's face in dark shop windows standing behind me. I would turn quickly, longing to catch his shadow in the rain-soaked streets, strain to hear his voice reaching me from wherever he was, but all I heard was a gust of wind, a creaking door sign, the rain pattering. I begged a benign God to give me one last glimpse of him; allow me one last word.

Night after night when everyone was sleeping, I would do this; search out his spectre, hold up my face to the rain, smell the beginnings of autumn decay, feel the sharp prickle of cold down my neck, allow the wind to push at me until I drifted like a leaf, torn prematurely from the branch, until settling on the pavement edge I would curl into myself.

There, I would wail like a wild creature, wallowing in the sensuous self-indulgence of abject sorrow, feeling the instinct to go to ground; find a foxhole and crawl deep inside, as though at some other stage in my existence I had indeed been a wild thing.

No one saw all of this. No one knew. When men approached me in the early hours looking for sex, I laughed at them, crossed the street. I had no fear.

There were two levels to my existence. At work with Lily, at the digs, as the months wore on, they thought I was strong, that time was healing. I slept, ate, worked. Wanted nothing, was self-contained. It was clear to those that loved me, that my *quiet*; my ability to continue with life, was an act. I was a woman walking in shadow.

When I opened Walter's journal, sent to his mother with his *effects*, and passed on to me, I was confused. I opened the cover and on the first blank page it said: *For Alice*. I turned it over in my hands. Smelled it. Ran my fingers along the spine. Flicked through the wrinkled pages. This was all that had come back to me; a paper notebook that smelt of the sea and stale sweat. Most of it had to wait until I had the strength. But at that moment, I opened it randomly in the middle:

...Bobby Fynes from Dorset. Smokes and reads all the time. Told me that Dickens' David Copperfield had saved his life. Camped on the beach in Southern Italy, behind enemy lines, he'd done his watch and, off duty, had rigged up a torch and was reading by it in the night.

In the early hours, Gerry discovered their position, came at them from the sea with knives. They killed the sentries and two sleeping soldiers in bivvies beside his, before the alarm was raised, and they were killed. The officer in charge supposed Fynes' torchlight had prevented Gerry from killing him; being awake he could have raised the alarm. Best book he'd ever read. Barmy, the whole shooting match is barmy...

I turned the page.

...most of the blokes don't want to kill anyone. Everyone all over bloody Europe is doing as they are told. Why? Why can't some German see what's happening and bump off that crazy bugger Hitler? Why do we let half the world kill one another because one man has an idea?

Some blokes enjoy it, of course; they had nothing at home, you can always tell. This whole shebang gives them a kind of credibility, a power. They're quite happy killing Gerry, the more the better. At home they'd be kicking up stink in the pubs, causing trouble. Then there are those who put your life at risk...

Here was a Walter I didn't know. Had he known that his journal would be a way of giving me back part of his life? I opened a page near the end and read of Jim and Bill at Monte Cassino: *I am in hell...*

I closed the book. Enough. Walter would not have forgiven me. All I'd had to do was wait, keep faith, *keep the home-fires burning.* That was what women did, wasn't it? The comparison of his strength and my weakness would be held before me always. I would have suffocated under the weight of it. I looked in the mirror. What did I see there? Was this the girl with whom I had grown up? Calamitously, seeking any kind of solace, I fell back to what I knew.

Come to me all of you who are heavily laden and I shall refresh you...

'Forgive me, Father, for I have sinned. It has been...a long time since my last confession.'

'And what is it that you need to confess? Are you there, my child?' I could hear the priest shuffling, getting comfortable, as though it had been a long day and he became aware it was about to get longer.

'Yes Father…I just don't know how to start.' I tried not to see the shadowy profile through the grille, the tired eyes. The sweet musty smell of incense heightened my sense of doom. I felt claustrophobic in that small dark space.

'Well, surely the beginning is the best place now. Take your time, my dear, God is listening.' He coughed and waited.

In fits and starts, I told Father Molloy, the priest of Oldham and Middleton parish, the most intimate story of my life. Of my family, of Walter, of my relationship with Carl, of Walter's death. There was a long pause before he spoke. He cleared his throat.

'Clearly, none of this has been easy. For your poor brother to be injured so, and the other still away fighting. Dear, dear. And to lose your…your childhood sweetheart is surely a terrible thing? A most terrible thing. Mmm. And you say, my child, that you have…given yourself to this man? This American?'

'Yes Father.' I was barely audible.

'And you say that you don't think you love him. Yes, I see. But how can you be sure?'

'Since Walter died—'

'Ah my dear, grief plays terrible tricks on us, don't you know? It's a funny thing; we only remember the good things; put halos around the departed. Halos that would weigh them down if they were alive. You tell me one thing, but your actions suggest another. I think perhaps you have more feeling for this young man, this Carl, than you realise. Hmmm? You feel guilt about Walter and maybe that distorts things just a little. What I'm trying to say…is that in the eyes of God, you have given yourself to Carl and that must mean something. Isn't that right?'

'I suppose…'

'Yes indeed. It could be that Walter was stopping you from loving Carl. It *is* possible to love more than one person…People bring out different sides of us you know…But you owe it to yourself, to your personal happiness and your everlasting soul to find that love, to make it work with this man.'

'But I can't Father, he—'

'Is it that he doesn't want *you*, my dear?'

'No no, not at all,' I protested in a rising cadence, affronted. I felt as though I was walking backwards, a wall behind me. 'He wants to marry me…' a dash of pride in my voice.

Father Molloy sounded euphoric, even laughed a little.

'Well then, my dear, as I see it, your dilemma is solved. Yes indeed.' He paused, returned to his sombre tone. 'You can put right your sin of fornication by taking this man unto yourself, when you are ready, in the sacrament of holy matrimony and taking unto yourself no other.'

'But Father—'

'Love will come, my dear. Trust me, love will come.'

As I knelt on the hard rail in the pew, head in my hands, I offered up my *Hail Marys*, *Our Fathers* and *Glory be's,* in penance and relief. A statue of Saint Jude loomed large above me with outstretched hands.

I was surprised at the comfort I felt, as though Father Molloy had made possible that which wasn't before; provided, in a way, a catharsis. Could it be that he was right? Being with Carl might assuage my guilt; I could perhaps make *him* happy, now that I had failed Walter? Going to live in another country would remove me from all the memories, the problems. Start again. It would be a kind of good sacrifice. I could love Carl, I knew that. He deserved some happiness too. I *could* make it better. Couldn't I?

It was only later I realised that religion…God…was just an excuse. I needed a way out of my misery and Father Malloy seemed to provide it.

I rubbed my aching eyes, stifled an exhausted yawn. Even if I couldn't find true happiness, I could, perhaps, atone.

I folded away this knowledge, made the sign of the cross slowly, deliberately, then raised myself with a conscious sense of renewed devotion, genuflected and walked out of the church, shielding my eyes from the scalding sunlight.

Chapter Fifteen

Then Carl came back.

Injured at Falaise. *Operation Tractable.* Shot in the shoulder by a fellow American soldier: *friendly fire.*

He seemed changed. Had been away only a few months but sharp edges were worn smooth, and he seemed less sure of the world around him, like a drunk waking up in the morning; tired, subdued. I didn't refuse to see him; it made no difference now. Despite the advice of Father Molloy, I couldn't stop myself resenting his return when Walter could not. Worse than that, my guilt subverted my instincts; made me cruel.

Yet the only person I really hated was myself. I asked him how he could live and not Walter? I blamed him for my weakness and told *him* alone all that I was feeling, confided my grief and my anger, emptied myself. Gave him no sympathy. Used him.

'Walter and I were different,' I spat. 'I wish I'd never met you. Wish I'd written to him; told him that no one else…*no one* could be to me what he was.'

'I can see that,' Carl mumbled, nodding acceptance. 'He was a soldier. I know what he was. I respect him. Jesus, he's got medals. An' I know, I know, he was a decent guy and you loved him. When I got your letter…you know…breaking it off. Well, I knew. Suppose I always knew.' He looked up at my thin face, blotched with misery, my hair damp against my cheeks, veins standing rigid on my neck, whispered as he looked away. 'Christ, I envy him, all of it.'

'But *he's* dead, and you're alive,' I screamed.

'I know…that too.'

I had wanted a fight. But he told me that self-hatred was something he understood; I had lost Walter, Carl had lost me. I yearned to be kind in response; tell him I was happy he was back; that he was safe, but every good thing I wanted to say made me feel I was replacing one love with another; continuing in my faithlessness; each comment another nail. It was all too soon, so I remained silent. Passive. I returned his ring, which, curiously, had slipped off my finger when I was washing.

He was gentle and kind and loving. Briefly, a lid loosened from a jar...

'I didn't understand before, you know? Half the time you're crazy scared, the rest, you just hope you do the right thing.' His face was open, his eyes faraway. 'That first night...Jeez...'

He rubbed his hands through his hair, elbows on his knees. It seemed he needed to talk, I didn't interrupt while he told me the story of his life in France.

'...it was somethin' else, y'know? I was separated from my 'stick' of infantrymen, they were kind of scattered in pockets, all over the show. Boy, I can tell you, I sure felt alone. We were a completely mixed bunch: different companies, battalions, regiments, even divisions. Strangers. But crouching there without them in the dark...well, if I'm honest, I felt a kind of panic. 'Course, at the last minute our unit's orders had been changed, I didn't know what the hell I was supposed to be doing, had no idea where I was; what I should do.

'I hesitated before I jumped. Well hell, I thought—am I really gonna do this? The plane had been dippin' and reelin', avoiding a wall of tracer fire. An' all the while a popping sound as bullets whizzed through the fuselage. My God, the view through the open doors of the C-47 was like the fucking fourth of July: coloured lights and the crackle an' bangs just like fireworks.

'When I had to stand and hook up, I could feel the press of men behind me, most of them desperate to get out, whatever. Men were throwing up. One refused to go altogether. A shove in my back pushed me out, everyone afraid of going too far and landing in the sea. It's a strange feeling you know, you can't breathe, like there's a wall of wind coming at you. Anyhow, jerked by the ring, my chute opened, pulled me swaying and bucking on my risers. I was too high, and I knew it, just had to hope the krauts couldn't fire straight.'

'I never realised you—'

'When I landed, I pulled in my chute, turned off the red light, realised I was okay and fumbled with the buckles to release the straps. I heard movement close to me so clicked my cricket and waited for a two-click response. Nothing. I froze and waited. Then I heard it again very close, a soft tread and a sound of ripping grass, heavy breathing. As my eyes adjusted, I saw their black outlines against the sky. Huge. Close. Cows. They were just cows, Alice!' He laughed almost hysterically, shaking his head. I didn't stop him or comment, just let him ramble on. 'They'd gathered around me and were just staring like cows do, chewing the cud.

'I crawled a bit and looked around. Ditches and high hedgerows, couldn't see a damn thing Entangled roots in the banks were ten feet thick in places. I wondered how the hell the tanks, if they ever turned up, would get through. I had no radio, not even a walkie-talkie. My rifle and two grenades, which had scared the shit out of me on landing, was all…Gee, sorry, Alice. Soldier talk.'

I smiled limply, shaking my head. 'I can't believe they sent you into battle so unprepared. Was it always like that?'

'Alice…you have no idea…'

He put his head in his hands, shaking it, his knuckles white with pressure. I touched his knee. 'It's all right, Carl…go on.'

'Have you ever been afraid? You know, so your mouth gets real dry? I pushed my chute deep into the tangled roots, hunkered in against the bank and waited. And waited. God, I was hungry. I was dirty; smelled of cowpat, was dog-tired and needed to, you know…shit…sorry…Gee, what am I saying?'

'You're telling me how it was. It's all right.'

'I could hear the far-off sound of artillery, the big guns vibrating in the earth, a slight delay in the sound that followed, like the flat boom of thunder on a summer's night, y'know? I watched the path of tracer fire arcing in the distance, like multicoloured falling stars. Real pretty.

'It felt like a screw-up. Worse, most of those I jumped with were from airborne divisions. They knew what the hell they were doing. Jumping out of an airplane in the dead of night; that was some crazy son-of-a-bitch thing to do. You got to remember; I'd spent the last couple of months sharing a small area of the South coast of England with upwards of two million other servicemen. Sitting in this field alone, in the dark, was…well it was lonely.'

'Did no one tell you what to do if that should happen?' I asked, trying to understand the sheer mess of the whole thing, but he didn't hear me.

'The training had been a fucking shambles from the outset, made worse by the endless rain. Mud, shit-loads of it. During the day, we marched all over Southwest of England, at night slept in foxholes. "Feel the terrain," our officer would shout, a jumped-up West Pointer who wouldn't know a kraut if he kicked him in the ass. "Look for the dips and gullies in the landscape that no civilian would notice. It may save your life." Yeh, right.

'We crawled under barbed wire, ammo whistling inches above our heads. Explosions going off all over the place. Bayonet practice, hours on the firing range, poison gas drills, airplane and tank identification, how to use explosives, all of it. But no-one, not one single goddamned son of a bitch seemed to know exactly what each unit would be doing on the day. I kept asking when we were going to learn to jump? "Soon," was the reply. Always "soon".

'Eisenhower came to see us, y'know, cheerleading the troops. "Men…you are like a big family, your units must be tough, cohesive, well trained, well equipped and ready to go."

'I was impressed. Then reality kicked in. None of that was true. When they started using live ammo, commanders panicked, we ran, accidents happened. It was all about getting us ashore on the big day. No one mentioned what the airborne troops should do when they found themselves off target in fields with hedges thick as goddamned houses.'

'I can hardly believe that they would send you into battle so unprepared. Who oversaw the people in charge?' I asked when he paused long enough for me to speak. He glanced up as though taking in what I said but somehow looking through me, then pressed on regardless.

'Jeez, I remember the three thousand residents that were moved out of their homes and farms at Slapton Sands so's we could use it for manoeuvres: target practice. At home we'd have made such a goddamned stink over such a bum deal. I watched as one old folk's house was bulldozed to rubble to make the road wider for the tanks. They didn't say a word, just watched in silence.

'We did as we were told. One gigantic balls up.'

'My God!' I felt myself suddenly taking sides against the Americans on behalf of the people of Slapton Sands. 'Who gave you the right to do that to ordinary people? That could have been my parents—'

'It's war, Alice. Anything goes. Better than a German tank. Forget civilised behaviour…that gets sacrificed on the altar of *expediency,* as my officer called it.

Anyhow, there I am in this field, when, at last, dawn started to push up, birds started singing an' stuff, I felt better. I knew at least which way was East. Seemed so strange, brown and white cows grazing peacefully an' me squatting in battledress. I wanted to laugh. Felt ridiculous. Then I saw figures through the hedge. Voices. Kraut voices. I felt the blood drain from my face and realised that light was no ally; I could be seen.

'I pressed myself into the side of the bank, saw four German soldiers walking on the other side. Just boys, fourteen or fifteen, loping, long-legged, rifles slung on their backs, hands in their pockets. I held my breath, my heart pounding. One looked over, I was sure he'd seen me. "Schaut her, Kuehe! Veilleicht koennen wir sie melken?"

'"Uuu…Ich bin todmuede…"

'I felt for my M-1 and remembered that I'd failed to load it. I could've killed 'em all. One of the boys smiled, I was sure it was at me. Told myself I'd left so-called 'civilisation' six hours before, couldn't just arrive and start shooting kids.

'Suddenly, there was a burst of machine-gun fire nearby, like the sound of tearing cardboard. The German boys ran, and I rolled down the slope of the bank, into a ditch. "Fancy meeting you here, buddy," came an American voice.

'Jeez, I can't tell you how good that felt; like I could feel blood surging around my body, heart pounding. Pressed flat into the ditch were three of the men I jumped with. "Boy, am I glad to see yous."

'"Likewise, safety in numbers and all that. Well, we're not gonna go thataway. We need to find our rendezvous point, or at least some of our unit, a senior officer, someone." He looked nervous as a jack-rabbit. "Christ, they don't pay us enough to make the friggin' decisions."

'We scraped ourselves through the hedgerow after going every which way. Then stopped, had a breather, listened. "We can't dig in, the Krauts got the whole goddamned shooting match over here: tanks, artillery, communications…" The shortest of the troopers said, breathing hard between words. "We been moving for hours, they're everywhere. They know we're here, we heard guns popping off all night. If they spot us, we're done for. They're not being polite; there'll be bits of us all over the friggin' peninsula."

'So, we spent almost an hour going one way, looking for bumps in the earth that could be mines, hitting Germans and running like hell. Because it was flat, we had no sense of direction. One of the guys had a compass, but kept shaking and tapping it, as the arrow swung this way and that, never settling. "Goddamned equipment."

'We were going round in fucking circles. Then we heard the click of a machine gun fixing on us. Before we could get down, one of the guys was hit in the head. The gun kept firing but couldn't depress low enough to hit us again. By the time the firing stopped, the trooper was dead. We just ran.

'Unit cohesion they talked about, what a joke. No unit, no fucking cohesion. "We need to locate the Command Post," one of the guys, who looked like an eleventh grader, said. The others looked at him as though he were crazy.

'Yeh, like we just follow the fucking signposts.'

'Just before sunrise, we met up with a larger group near a farm outside a small village. They had no mortars, few machine guns or bazookas, one radio which had been banged up in the jump and hardly any medical supplies. No one was in control of anything, so we just stood around. We didn't even have a map between us.' He stopped speaking, shaking his head again, staring at the floor. He then pushed two fingers into his eyes to stem tears.'

'You don't need to go through this again, Carl, it's all right.' I put my hand on his arm and squeezed. 'It's enough.'

'Yes, I do, Alice, I want you to know this…I want to tell you so's you understand, okay?'

'Okay.' I nodded, looking down so as not to embarrass him while tears streamed down his face.

'After twenty minutes or so, a force of around seventy men arrived. With them a Lieutenant Colonel, who looked like he meant business. He spread a map on the ground. "Let's hope he's not the hero type, huh?" one of the men whispered. "Hi guys, good to see you," he said, like he was going to the fair or somethin'. "I'm Lieutenant Colonel Hope."

'"Christ, that's all we need," the same trooper said. "We're a little fragmented I know. Some of you have failed to meet up with your units. Still, we have a job to do. Forget your previous orders for now. This is what we're going to do. As I see it, we must split into two groups. We just came through a village, Saint Martin de Varreville, we had some trouble there…"

'My jaw fell open as I looked at the shabby group of German soldiers that suddenly appeared encircled by the officer's men. "As you can see, we have prisoners with us; a lot of their friends are dead. I don't want any accidents. Clear?" We eyed them up. They looked like darned schoolboys about to take an exam. One of them was shuffling rosary beads in his hand, the front of his trousers was wet. So, this was the enemy. Jeez… "I've located our position here," the officer yelled. He pointed to a speck on the map. "We need to secure the exits from Utah, so that our boys coming in from the sea can get off the beach."

'I noticed one of the men that came in with the officer. He carried his rifle upside down, butt forward over his shoulder, as though he'd been hunting rabbits in the backwoods. Had a German belt slung across his tunic. When I moved closer to take a look, the trooper pointed to the inscription on the flying eagle buckle: *Gott Mit Uns.* "*God is with us*…Like hell He was," he said as he chewed his gum, a big smile pasted across his ugly face.

'"This group, exit three, the other exit four," the officer carried on. "This is Sergeant Winter; he'll go with the first group. I'll go with the second. Any questions?"'

'So, you went? With this Sergeant Winter?' I prompted when Carl fell silent again—he was there, near that farm, listening to instructions, fear oozing out of him like sweat.

'My group moved forward, close to a small village. We could see the church steeple, a spindly crucifix, kind of black against the rising sun. We could smell baking. "Nothing like falling out of an airplane, running across half of France, and killing a few Krauts to give you an appetite, now, is there," the trooper with the German belt whispered to me as he crouched. "How d'you fancy croysants and coffee in the square?"

'"They're gonna have one helluva surprise anytime now," one of them said, looking at the peaceful village.

'Suddenly, krauts appeared on the causeway retreating from the beach. At the signal from Sergeant Winter, we opened fire. Christ, we was firing all over the show, surprised we hit anyone, but they all fell down screeching and crying. I laughed out loud, kind of weird, you know?

'We moved down the causeway towards the shore, each of us behind the one in front, as big guns blasted the beach. Seasoned paratroopers, with blackened faces ran past us, slick, like they knew what they was doing and surrounded a German bunker. A single cannon had been returning fire offshore. A jittering white flag almost instantly appeared from a hole in the wall. On the sergeant's nod one of the paratroopers, using the barrel of his gun, beckoned them out in small groups.

'Several of the men were instructed to enclose them in a makeshift prison of their own barbed wire; I was so close I could smell their breath, feel their fear, sense their relief. When they stood exposed, their hands joined behind their heads, and saw how they'd outnumbered us two to one they looked pretty shame faced. Jeez, I thought, all krauts are either kids or old men.

'Then we had to climb up the dunes and wait for the Fourth Infantry Division to land on the beach. But holy fucking Mahony, you should've seen it. It was…well…it was an ocean black with boats; hundreds of L.C.I.'s, pitchin' and reelin', packed with infantry, just offshore. Behind them, warships, hundreds of 'em. Then all fucking hell let loose. Dainty smoke-rings appeared all over the sky from the destroyers in the distance, while craters the size of trucks began to appear all around us. We just covered our ears and ducked…'

Increasingly, he had become animated, his hands flying about as he relived that day in June on the sand dunes of Utah Beach, emotions threading through his face like the patterns of light and shade on an undulating ocean. But he stopped suddenly as though he had become aware of a loss of control. I didn't speak, just sat with my head low, listening but somewhere else, in my own space. He went quiet for a moment. Stared at the floor shaking his head once more, his lips drawn in. Then he brought himself back, smiled, inhaled and continued in another tone altogether; less excited, more resigned. Reverential.

'There were good moments. Cherbourg. You should have seen their faces.' His crooked smiled waned. 'Falaise, when we linked up with the Brits, was terrible. Stuck on the banks of the Orne, waiting to cross. It was real heavy going… Brits hand to hand fighting with bayonets. Jeez…there were some real heroes that day. It was…something else, medieval.

'What I remember most is the digging; slit trenches. Hundreds of 'em. Sometimes they were too shallow, rocks and stones. You had to lie flat in them, couldn't see what anyone was doing without risking getting your head blown off, or getting shrapnel full on from the shelling.

'Patrols were sent out to capture krauts, bring them in for interrogation. They all shouted as they came in, their hands over their heads: *'Ich bin nicht ein Deutscher'*. To hear them, they were Hungarian, Romanian, none of them were fucking Germans…sorry Alice.

'Dead Krauts everywhere. It was carnage. Rotting horses and cows bloated with their legs stuck up in the air like waxwork figures, the smell of rotting bodies… Jeez, the destruction. That country is stained with so much blood. How the hell are they gonna rebuild all of that when it's over? Makes me glad I'm an American, I can go back, and everything will be the same. The war is over for me now.'

I'd never heard Carl say so much. He didn't need me to respond. It was a release of pressure, an unburdening. I don't know…perhaps there was no one else that would listen. Everything I heard, I related to Walter; he'd had three years of it.

Chapter Sixteen

England
April 1945

'I don't understand, Ali. Why? So soon after Walter's...after Walter.' Mam dabbed her eyes, blew her nose loudly, shook her head.

'Don't bring Walter into this. I've tortured myself enough. He was away three years, Mam...he hardly wrote. I loved him. You know I did, I always will—that will never go away. All the 'what ifs' in the world can't bring him back to me and I have to salvage what I can in my life. Can't you see that?'

'Your life? You're not yet twenty-three, Ali, your *life* has barely begun—'

'Things change. Everything around us is changed; we're none of us the same as we were. I'm not a child anymore and despite what you think, despite...you know...everything, I do love him. I didn't think I did. He was just a...well, a friend really. But since he came back from France...I don't know...Is there a problem with me trying to be happy?'

'He's a yank, *that's* the problem,' Dad snapped, wiping his beaded forehead with a handkerchief. 'A bloody great yank. Flashing his money around while our boys are being shot to pieces. Leeching off the kindness of ordinary folk, stealing their daughters from under their noses. It makes me sick.' He stopped, breathless, put his head in his hands. 'I don't know what the hell you think you're playing at, young lady. Why do you want to give up everything...your home, your family? For *love*? I don't think so.' He paced the floor, smacking the back of his hand repeatedly onto the unturned palm of his other. His face was blotchy, the tips of his ears red.

'It's my decision. I'm not a child. I'm only twenty-three, yes—but old enough to fight for my country, old enough to die for it, like Walter,' I replied. 'And Carl was in France. A lot of Americans were killed in France, as if you didn't know.'

'Pity he wasn't.'

'Bernard!' Mam shouted.

'Better him than her, which if she goes, she'll be as good as, to us.'

'Don't…don't,' she dissolved again, groaning.

Dad leaned his forehead against the pane, stared unseeing out of the window before turning red-eyed towards me. He took hold of my limp hand, pressed it to his face kissing my fingers, hesitating, swallowing before he spoke.

'Oh…Ali, Ali.' He smiled wanly. His voice was subdued. He pulled me to him, wrapped his arms around me, one hand in my hair. I stood stiff, lost in the largeness of his embrace, my face pressed on his chest, arms folded in like closed wings. 'I love you, Ali, *we* love you. You're our baby…You know, war distorts things, magnifies feelings, what you feel now may not be a true measure of things. Even though you wouldn't share it with us, we know how Walter's death affected you; you're emotionally vulnerable, love.

'Don't leave, not with Vincent still in France. I'm begging you, Ali. You mean…everything.' He paused, released me, pulled his arm across his eyes. 'Please Ali, give up this whole idea.' His voice was nasal, soft. 'The war is almost over. Let Carl go home, wait a year, if you still feel the same then I shall give you my blessing. You have my word.'

'Please Ali, do as your dad says. He's right love…*please,*' Mam said gently, an upbeat edge elevating her voice.

They stared at me, wide-eyed, expectant. There was silence when it seemed things could go either way. All that I had been before Walter's death wanted to run to them, be held, forget all about Carl, America, just be Ali Conroy again: the girl who loved wild places, her family, her home, her country. The girl with the cornflower blue eyes. The girl that didn't give a fig for her religion with all its stuffy rules, or even God for that matter, until the corrosive effect of its preaching forced a guilt on her so deep that she couldn't separate it out from reality.

'I'm so sorry, Dad…Mam, I can't,' I said finally. 'I…I can't explain.' It was true, I couldn't. What would I say? That I knew they were right? I seemed to have spent my life swerving to avoid good fortune. 'I'd like you to come to my wedding.'

'Over my dead body,' Dad finally whispered, his shoulders shrunk like an old man, his face pink and swollen. Mam, pale, trembling, wailed into her hands.

'That's your choice, Dad. Mam?' I answered firmly. Mam's breath caught in her throat.

'If you go ahead with this, Alice…' Dad hesitated, then continued in the saddest voice I had ever heard, '…we're finished. I'll not come to your wedding, nor will your Mam and you'll not come back to this house.'

'Stop it, Bernard, don't say those things,' Mam screamed.

'Go now, Alice. I can't bear to look at you anymore. Go.'

A line had been crossed. I looked out of the window at the apple tree, the young leaves fluttering, their velvet undersides, the tiny young green fruit. When the apples fell, red and bruised, I would be far from here. I closed my mind. It would be a relief. Everything here was damaged.

*

Father Molloy said we couldn't have flowers in the church. Nor music. Carl was not *of the faith*. It could not therefore be a celebration, in the Roman Catholic sense of the word. Though he was happy to marry us, he said, *put things right*.

Carl was sailing home on 16 April, ten days' time, told me his commanding officer had tried to dissuade him from a hasty marriage:

'Uncle Sam doesn't like it. Thinks these local *ladies* are gold-diggers. D'y'know what I'm saying? Are you sure you don't need time to adjust, a cooling off period…?' Then admitted, with a hint of swagger, that he himself was to *tie the knot*, 'a real winsome girl—y'know—*different…*' and if Carl would not wait then he'd 'better make it snappy'. There would be a lot to do organising US permission for me to immigrate. Once gained, the government would take it from there.

Carl felt uncomfortable about the whole *church thing*. I said we had to be married in the eyes of God, otherwise we wouldn't be married at all. I may not have been a good Catholic, but I *was* a Catholic.

'You must understand, Mr McCullough, it's not that there's anything unconstitutional in your proposed marriage. It is, of course, a very happy event. It's just…we Catholics are a strange breed. A sort of big family. We prefer to…' he bent over as though imparting a secret, rattling his rosary beads in one hand, 'what shall I say…keep the family silver where it belongs? However, if you converted…'

'Maybe this whole damn thing is a bad idea.' Carl banged the church door on his way out, then punched it, full fist.

'Stop it, Carl, calm down.'

'*Calm down*,' he shouted as though to an audience in the street. 'I'm a goddamned American, not some crazy scumbag. He should be grateful.'

'Carl, don't say those things, you don't understand.'

'I don't want to understand, do you hear? When we get back home, it'll be different.'

'What do you mean?'

'Different. Just you and me.' Carl walked on ahead of me. I ran trying to keep up.

He was sullen for days. I found myself persuading *him* that everything would work out. He seemed to be withdrawing from me. When I spoke, he snapped a reply or didn't answer at all. Silent and subdued, he didn't touch me, seemed indifferent. He would knead his shoulder endlessly, but shrug me away if I tried to help, his mind somewhere else. I began to be afraid that he no longer wanted me, that he would change his mind about the wedding. Then I reminded myself that he had had a tough few months, that he needed time.

But still, I became clumsy at work, kept grazing my hands and knocking my shins against the steel sprockets of the caterpillar tracks. I had a feeling of incumbent hopelessness—could I get anything right? Not to mention the *I told you so's* I would get from my family. I knew I had been hard on him of late. What right did I have to do that? Who did I think *I* was?

My family wouldn't acknowledge him, which made him furious; '…who the hell are they to be so goddamned high and mighty.' Now I was forcing him into a Catholic wedding that he neither wanted nor needed. The more he backed away from me, the more I wanted him. The thought of losing him too was almost more than I could bear; I could foresee a scenario where I could be left with nothing: no Walter, no family and no Carl. Sleep was impossible.

When he apologised some days later—he'd talked to some of the guys, realised the priest wasn't being personal, I wept with relief in his arms and apologised for the way I had greeted him on his return. I told him, at last, that I knew I loved him and begged his forgiveness. He just held me, told me once we got away from everyone, we could start a new life together. That he would love me always, that he would never let me go. At last, I knew for sure we were doing the right thing.

*

Sanctus Dunstanus Pax. I stood in front of St Dunstan's, unsteady in a pair of Lily's shoes on the cobbled street, and squinted at the red brick edifice towering over me. It looked new, not like a church should look. Not like St Thomas's below Walter's house, its old millstone grit walls buried into the hillside, kind old Father Martin.

Behind me, trams wheeled and clunked, sparks flying from overhead cables. To my left *The Museum Inn*. A couple of old men sitting outside on chairs stared over blankly at a mere wisp of a girl in a white frock carrying a posy of pink flowers. Beside her, an enormous yank in uniform who didn't look very happy.

'Must be up the duff,' one of them muttered, before taking a swig of ale and wiping his white moustache on his sleeve.

A soldier propped up the doorway of the pub. Eyes closed, he smiled into the frail sun that had fought through the low grey cloud, his hand curling protectively around a half-drunk pint of ale that he held close to his chest.

To the right, just visible in the distance was a green curved hilltop, part of the Pennine Chain, pale in the blinking sunlight like a child's painting.

I wished my brothers were there. Vincent, home on leave three weeks ago, had taken me on the long journey south to see Ned; still having fragments of shrapnel removed. His legs had been re-broken and set a second time to allow him to walk again. They had fitted a glass eye. Surgeons were working on his scar tissue. He had new teeth. The operations went on. He had had over thirty.

We had avoided the subject of my marriage even though we all knew the reason I was there was to say goodbye. I watched my brothers animated in their war talk…For them nothing had changed except the subject of their banter. I listened, interested, but distant, already an outsider, my gaze wandering down Ned's neck to his burns. I tried not to stare at his glass eye when he spoke. Wondered where our childhood had gone.

'…then right after D-Day, we flew sorties from a makeshift airfield near Caen, to clear…you know…obstructions, hunting down Gerry.' Vincent, leaned forward, tipping the edge of the wooden hospital chair, apparently untouched by his brush with war. Ned, older by decades, was war-weary, resigned.

'We had the bomb line marked on our map, so anything we saw; guns, tanks, troops, you know…was fair game. Later on when Gerry increased their flak, we got caught out a few times. As soon as we got into a dive, they would open up and we'd have to go through the lot.' He acted out the scene, like a boy in a playground, standing up, arms outstretched, dive-bombing the bed, punctuating the action with ack ack sound effects.

'Tricky stuff for the pilots. Trying to get the sight on what we were attacking…looking at the turn and slip indicator to try to get the skid out—'

'Weren't you frightened?' I interrupted.

'Well, unless the flak was heavy, you just got on with it. We didn't bother looking out for German fighters. In fact, apart from chasing two Fockewulfs over the channel after they'd bombed Brighton, I never saw a German aeroplane in the air through the whole of my tour.' He smiled, slapped his hands on his thighs, waited for his brother to respond. Ned nodded slowly.

'Oh…it was different, you know. *We* just heard the explosions. The lads on the big guns never saw their faces.' He paused, flexing the muscles on his damaged hand. 'How did you feel mowing them down like that?' he asked suddenly.

'Crikey, I don't know,' Vincent replied, oblivious to any implied rebuke. 'The adrenalin was flowing; I don't think we had any feelings about it. I suppose I shouldn't say it but shooting up troops on the roads was bloody good fun; they would fall over like nine-pins. They weren't *people*. We didn't think about it. I didn't *hate* Gerry, if that's what you mean. It was just a job. And…you know…we were getting our own back. That's war.'

As we stood outside the church waiting for Lily and her fiancé, I thought of how Ned had refrained from asking me not to go to America, unlike Vincent who argued with me all the way back on the train; called me a *bloody little fool*. Flat on his back, Ned had held me tight, buried his face in my neck, told me he would write, told me that Dad would come around. If unhappy, I was to let him know, he would get me home. He told me nothing was forever. Told me he loved me, always would.

Vincent left Hebden without telling me.

'Are your witnesses here yet? We need to get started, I have a funeral in an hour…' Father Molloy blustered, his white cassock billowing like a spinnaker.

'They're here, Father, just coming.' I could see the pair queuing to get off the tram that had pulled into the junction on Moston Lane.

'Sorry we're nearly late,' Lily shouted from the door of the tram. Carl looked relieved to see them, walked over and shook *Cary Grant's* hand vigorously.

'He's nervous,' I whispered to Lily.

'Not bleedin' surprised,' she breezed, casting her eye over the priest suspiciously. 'Aren't you?'

'Don't know. I don't feel anything really. Well…that is, happy, of course.'

'Yes, 'course you are, love.' She took out her compact, patted her cheeks with powder, pursed her lips. 'Couldn't Vincent come?'

'He's back in France. It's all over, bar the shouting, he says.'

'Shall we go in?' Father Molloy strode on into the dark interior of St Dunstan's.

I felt foolish at the idea of walking down the aisle alone and tugged on Lily's jacket to stop her going on ahead. Once inside, a musty brown smell assailed me; the usual churchy smell but something mingled in with it—fish and chips? I looked at Father Molloy's fingers. He took Carl to one side to explain what would happen next. Nice. Wedged in between a poke of chips and a funeral.

I looked around the big empty church. Statues with glassy eyes: Mary and Joseph, St Jude, St Veronica and surely, St Dunstan somewhere? 'Spooky,' Lily whispered. And the stations of the cross; icons from childhood.

I stared at the rows of empty pews; *it wasn't meant to be this way*…Imagined all the faces that weren't there. I was to follow Carl to America when everything was sorted out. There was plenty of time to tell them of my marriage before I left. It was too soon after Walter's death to tell them then.

So, there we were: a bride and groom, two witnesses and a priest.

Lily and I shuffled awkwardly down to the altar. Lily turned around, made faces at the men, trying to get Carl to walk with me. Carl shrugged; his hands upturned. Lily raised her eyes and tutted loudly. We all scuffled when we reached the alter rail trying to organise ourselves. Lily stared, transfixed, at the crucifix that hung suspended by heavy chains over the altar, a bloody Jesus nailed onto it.

'Christ,' she muttered.

'Precisely; now sit down and stop gawping, haven't you been in a church before?' I pushed Lily into a seat, after which I knelt, began to cross myself then stood again quickly as the others stared. Father Molloy fussed, making us swap sides. *Cary Grant* began to snigger, asked loudly what he was supposed to do. The priest glared over half-moon spectacles.

'We are gathered in the sight of almighty God to join together this man and this woman in Holy Matrimony…'

When we came out, Lily fumbled in her handbag for rice, which, once thrown, clung to our shoulders and hair, clammy in the drizzle that had been threatening all day. The soldier no longer stood in the doorway of *The Museum*, the two old men had gone, the door closed. The Pennines now shrouded in mist, were invisible behind the sullen buildings. Carl put his arm around my shoulders, bent down, kissed my cheek tenderly, whispering, 'Ali McCullough, I love you. You're all mine now.' Loudly, he said, 'We've done it, let's go celebrate.'

Chapter Seventeen

England
1945

I opened my eyes, looked out over Salisbury plain. No trees. No hills. Just open, undulating, battle-weary green.

I wiped the sleep from my eyes, squinting in the pale morning light from the curtain-less window beside the bed. I was cold. It was raining again. Shuffling onto my other side, I watched the circus, tuned into the sounds of laughter, curses, shouts for shoes, lost in the muddle of luggage under beds. I heard the excitement as though through a megaphone: a distant, distorted clutter. I pulled my blanket up over my face, curled into the foetal position.

Over the week, expectation like a flood had washed through the transit camp, one girl to another, eddying around hopes and fears, creating dreams clear enough to see your face in. Extinguished, for now, was the subterranean, smouldering uncertainty, marking time to explode somewhere along its route, ignited by memory: a photo, a face in a crowd, words.

At night I had dreams: I was in a boat, alone at the helm, but the steering was loose and so I drifted far out to sea. Each time I woke, my face wet with tears, I cursed myself, I had, after all, chosen this life. Dad had been wrong too, hadn't he? How can a father that has watched every awakening emotion on a child's face not understand the one that spells confusion, desperation, guilt? Then, dissolving into half sleep, it would start again: I imagined Dad pulling my fingers from him one by one as I clung on, pushing me out to drift in a rudderless craft. Then each morning, I lay in half sleep with a profound feeling of homesickness. He had sent a message through Vincent: *Keep yourself together*. That was it.

In other dreams, it was Walter that featured: at home standing in the doorway, a silhouette, hardly there but solid as stone. It was as though somehow, I couldn't make the pieces fit in a life that had gone awry.

But in daylight, it was Carl I missed; he was my present and my future. Our wedding day, months before, was the first time we'd spent the night in a bed together and it felt good and right, allowing our bodies to mingle in the comfort of clean sheets and soft pillows. I loved being held while I slept, feeling breath on my neck—being wanted.

Sharing a small double bed with my large husband however had not been luxurious; his large frame and manner of sleeping, legs curled under him, arms stretched out as though swinging a shot-put or splayed on his front across the mattress like a man unused to sharing space was not conducive to a good night's sleep. Beds in the States were huge, he'd said, and promised I would get lost in his.

He was sweet after we married and seemed to leave the detritus of war behind him. This was a new relaxed Carl, a Carl that had lost his *edge*. We didn't have sex, we made love, and I knew in my heart it was going to be all right.

'Hope you're gonna like it, hon…?'

'Like it?'

'Going home. It's not like…not like what you're used to.'

'Well, I like what you've told me. Your mam sounds sweet. Tell me about her again. Is she like mine—always organising and gossiping about the neighbours?'

'No, not really. She's, you know…had a difficult time with Pa, like I told you, but she's a good woman underneath an' he's gone now. She's kind of reserved, you know. An' of course, we have no neighbours…well at least, none so's you'd know it. I'm sure she'll like you.'

'No neighbours? Well, I suppose that means no gossip; a bit lonely though?'

'You're used to the country, you'll be fine.'

'Will I like her?

'Mom? Dunno. Hope so.'

'What's the farm like?

'Kinda solid; built to last the winters and boy are there some winters. Big. It's out you know…a little isolated. Probably needs a lick of paint, some maintenance. Don't know what Mom's done since the old man heaved ho. You can choose stuff, make it pretty.'

'You don't live in a lean-to then?' My neighbour from Hebden: Carol Gratton, had returned from the *Sunshine State* and filed for divorce. Got out there to find her new home was a shack resting on four cornerstones for support, the ground visible through floorboards and wind kept out with cardboard. Surrounded by swamp. Carl laughed.

'No, I don't live in a shack. It's not a palace, but it's okay.'

'I don't suppose we can have our place, you know, on our own?'

'I'm a farmer Alice. It's what I do. How can I farm without a farm?'

'Maybe we could build a little house on the farm?'

'No hon. God knows what shape the farm'll be in. There's no money. Besides, Mom's expecting us. It'll be fine.'

I didn't like the idea of sharing his *mom's* space; room for only one woman in a kitchen. Still, I knew I could change things when I got there, in the meantime, we'd have an in-built babysitter when we eventually needed one. She might even be a second mam to me until such times as my family came out to visit, which I knew, eventually, they would.

Like Ned had said, it was just a question of time. I knew they loved me, and they knew it was reciprocated. Geography wouldn't change that. When Carl spoke of his home, he was honest about its shortcomings, but I heard only what I wanted to hear. The *isolation*, the *winters* I glossed over, imagining that anyone that had grown up on the Yorkshire moors knew all about solitude and hard winters.

The rented room in Salford had been cheap, but clean, private. Walking distance from the city. After being demobbed from Avie Rose it had been easy to leave Oscar Street. Lily's forthcoming wedding in America meant she was also moving out. As we packed our things, we made a pile to give to the Rag and Bone man next time we heard his gravelly street-shout: *rag and boooone*, his horse clodding past, the creaking wheels of his cart. He'd give us a goldfish in return.

Lying in the pile waiting for his weekly visit were the red high-heeled shoes I had borrowed from Lily so many times, scuffed with every dance, every walk home in the rain, worn down with the past three years of living. I almost added the red dress, the one that Walter had loved, the one that made me feel good about myself. It was tired looking, but I demurred, kept it. To add the dress to the shoes was too sad; like throwing away part of my life. Rag and bone.

We gave the fish to Percy—parting gift. Told him not to eat it.

I watched Lily as she folded her things; still street smart and pert, but an inkling of class had crept into her demeanour. A kind of self-conscious Englishness. She no longer dropped her aitches; was more careful and clipped in her enunciation as though keen to set up a contrast to the snappy drawl of her fiancé. She didn't show so much cleavage. Less leg. Was becoming, if truth were told, a bit of a snob. Her wealthy boyfriend was giving her airs; Lily, gilded by association. I felt that there had been some cross over between us, a sense that wafted over me like Lily's new expensive perfume.

Nonetheless, I smiled my goodbye through a blur.

'Safe journey, Lil. Don't speak to any strange men.'

'They're the only ones worth talking to, *you* know that…'

We held each other, made promises we wouldn't keep.

The money that Carl left wasn't going to eke out until his army pay started coming through, while the plans I had to go to college, get a qualification, perhaps become a teacher, were put on hold, as they had been during the six years of war. Now the US government were procrastinating about all of us stranded brides; there was no clear idea of the time frame, it could be months, even years. On the other hand, I could be called to go any week. I couldn't just sit around though.

Now that the war was over, at least in Europe, work was scarce; returning men expected their jobs, wanted wives back in the kitchen and women everywhere, though joyous to have their men back, were quietly lamenting the loss of their newfound freedom. Notwithstanding that, I saw an ad for a 'milliner' with the Raby Hat Company in a small warehouse in Broughton, not too far from where I was living. I had made most of my clothes since I was young; knew my way around a needle and thread and a sewing machine. They could only say no. I wouldn't tell them I was married, about to leave for America.

'Hats,' the manager said, 'everyone wants 'em. We're snowed under now, of course…Well, well. You're very young, what can yer do?' He slouched in his chair; his trousers uncomfortably tight over his groin. He flicked a pencil to and fro. His suit looked as though he'd slept in it, a dark ring around his shirt collar. Lives alone, I thought. A leery twinkle played around his eyes. He spent more time looking at my chest than my letter of application; his face moulded into a permanent grin. Hasn't seen action I thought with relief; there was a pre-war jollity about him.

Women in the background sitting around a large table, pins in their mouths, nudged each other. Hazed by steam from the moulding blocks, they raised their eyebrows as they observed his antics, all the while nodding their heads to Peggy Lee's *Why don't you do Right* that blared from the grill of the gramophone on the wall.

'Well—' I began.

'What d'you think, girls?' he threw over his shoulder at them. 'An' you can stop all that whisperin' an' all...' He winked at me, said loudly, 'Just can't get the staff.' Laughter fractured the silence.

One of them shouted, 'Don't you mind 'im love, he's harmless, one bark an' he'll run off with his tail between his balls.'

Rough as muck, I could hear my mother, but they seemed friendly enough.

'It's true, they keep me in check,' he smiled. 'Bugger it, I don't care if you can make hats or not, we're bloody desperate...got more orders than I can cope with...you can start by watching the blokes polishing crowns and perforating brims, an' so on, learn the difference between your weft and your warp, the trade like. The girls'll train you in trimming. How to feel the ribble, plait with ribbons, make bows, rolls and so forth. It's a skilled job, but you look bright enough. You'll certainly brighten this place up.' He raised his eyebrows, sucked his pencil.

The women cooed in unison.

'Job's yours if you want it, love. Six bob a week. When you get some experience, there'll be a bit of commission for output.'

I hadn't spoken a word. I laughed, nodded.

'When can you start?' He banged down his pencil, placed his fingertips together, elbows on the chair arms, tried not to slouch, look boss-like.

'Now?'

'Done. Find her a chair, ladies, and for God's sake, stop gassing long enough to teach the girl sommat, will yer. And be nice to her...' he leered, 'I can see she's a lady...'

It was like war work. Each day I took the bus to Broughton thinking: this is something I do until life turns the next corner. The only difference being that instead of building the paraphernalia of war, I was making the paraphernalia of peace: hats that made people pretty again, hats to entice and impress. I made buckets, bonnets and berets, fedoras and cloche hats. Some were moulded on blocks, others pleated and stitched. There were buttons, ribbons and bows, feathers and flowers. I became like the women with whom I worked: saucy and silly. I laughed, felt a small sense of family that helped assuage the gulf of homesickness growing like a thing inside me. It was good to feel part of something again.

'You learned in six months what some of this lot took six years! And when you get fed up with your yank and all that sunshine, there'll be a place here for yer, love. Don't you go forgettin' it.'

By the time the letter arrived at the digs in Salford instructing me to report to the transit camp at Tidworth on Salisbury Plain, all of them at Raby's said I could call myself a milliner. As I packed my bags and said my goodbyes, I felt like a soldier being called up.

*

I swept my gaze across the shabby dorm, strewn with *smalls* and stray shoes, then out through the window again, past the barbed wire, over the plain. With my finger, I traced the raindrops that ran down the glass, humming to myself: *I don't want to play in your yard, I don't like you any more…*

At least it wouldn't rain all the time in America. All around me was the excited chatter of young women that had, for the most part, like me, married a man they barely knew.

'Hey! Over there in't bed by the window…yer seen a black shoe?'

It took a moment or two to realise she was looking in my direction.

'Sorry, do you mean me?'

'Yeh sleepyhead. Under yer bed.'

'Oh, I'll look.' I slithered out of my little nest onto the floor and sure enough at the back was a shoe. I pulled it out and held it up. It was a brown brogue.

'God, no thanks, duck, you can keep that' n.'

I smiled and walked over with it.

'Sorry, there's no black one. Does this belong to anyone?' Everyone in the little group that had congregated across two beds shook their heads and stared.

'Must belong to't last lot of flaming idiots, they shifted barracks last week.' Clearly, that was meant to be funny and the girls around her giggled. 'What's your name, duck. Come and join us if yer like. Got any ciggies.'

'Er…Alice. Sorry, I don't smoke and…well, I must wash and dress, but thank you.'

'Suit yerself.'

With that a door closed, she turned her back and started chatting with the women while I padded barefoot back to my bed realising I had both rejected their friendliness in a perceptible assumption of their type and been rejected in a similar vein. Had war taught us nothing? Were we still tribal after all that had happened? Looking back at them, feeling a little sorry that I had appeared aloof, I smiled, but by then their conversation had moved on and there was no reciprocation.

Nevertheless, I found myself tuning into the way they spoke; the language they used, as they sat in tight groups confiding, legs crossed, backs hunched, elbows on knees while outstretched hands with painted fingernails held cigarettes like a gesture to a listening congregation, smoke curling around them like a wall. By the sound of it whatever privations may face them in America, materially they would have more than they had now.

They didn't all cackle when they laughed, or smoke or chew gum. Or swear. I knew what the *nice* girls were thinking, had seen their eyes brush over them, coating them with disdain, their heads drawn back as though avoiding a nasty odour. However, *we* were too reserved initially to get together as a group. Occasionally, two of us would share a glance, raise eyebrows, smile superiorly, away from the frequent type of knee-jerk response:

'What're you smirking at, toffee-nosed cow? We not good enough for you?'

They could be real bitches and they didn't need a crowd to egg them on. Just as loud and nasty alone. I turned from the window, sniffed, tried not to look at them. Still, at least *they* knew how to make friends.

It became embarrassing to undress for inspections in front of these girls, as their eyes grazed over me, looking for something to snigger about. Lucky old Lily had gone to her wedding in New York on an aeroplane. *Cary Grant's* rich family had paid. Funny how things turn out; life can seem pretty random when you think about it.

The jabs and form-filling seemed to fill a part of every day. When I was questioned about relinquishing my British identity pass to begin the process of Americanisation, I had to swallow hard, like taking medicine, holding your breath so the taste does not sicken you. I loved my country and after six years of war, that hitherto ambient patriotism I took for granted had begun to burn its way into my heart and brain.

'Howdy ma'am. Name?'

'You have it on your form there.'

'Just say it please.'

'Alice Con…McCullough.'

'Which is it?'

'Alice McCullough.'

'Why do you wish to enter America?

'The same as everyone here.'

'Just answer the questions, ma'am, be a whole lot quicker that way.

'Disabilities?'

'You've just examined me so—'

'Disabilities?'

'What is your opinion of your new country?'

'I haven't been there yet...'

'Just answer, Ma'am.

'Are you aware of the laws and constitution of your adopted country?'

And so it went on. We felt the whole purpose was designed to catch us out. The tone and smile-less demeanour of the immigration officers seemed to indicate we were somehow trying to get something for nothing. We felt unwelcome, as though, if there had been any choice, we would all have been refused entry just because we were, as they called us *Aliens. Alien Overcomers.*

I couldn't understand the line of questioning that assumed everybody would want to move to America given the chance. I was looking forward to my life in America, wanted to embrace it, love it, but to swear allegiance to a country I knew nothing about? I remained silent, chewed at the soft tissue inside my mouth, and when necessary, lied.

Eventually, I challenged my lethargy, got out of bed and went to the canteen to get lunch, my thoughts a jumble. I would call at the PX after, with its cornucopia of goods still unavailable in England. It always cheered me seeing what I would be able to buy when I finally got there.

I was one of the lucky ones they said, crossing on the Queen Mary at the end of January. The US government was paying for our transportation so long as we went when we were told. Women with children had the highest priority, followed by the pregnant ones, then simply the brides, so I was surprised to find myself one of the first to be going.

Back in the dorm, I threw myself once again upon my bed, fatigued by my lack of endeavour. Still raining. Still cold. I picked up the book I had discovered in the small library, pulled the grey blanket about my feet and began working my way through familiar territory in Gaskell's *North and South*.

Often though, I did not read, but think, the book a screen to deflect conversation. Or eavesdrop. Gaze at the print on the page, my eyes out of focus, whilst listening in to the girls telling their stories of who they were before they married.

Sometimes, silently, involuntarily, I would join in their reverie. This time they were reminiscing about V.E. day, a day that for me signified more than the end of the war in Europe. I remembered so vividly wanting to go home, to share it with my family after all we had been through together. I knew that Ned couldn't be at home for the celebrations, but Vincent was. *Tail-end Charlie*, most dangerous job in the war, survived without a scratch. How like him.
Instead, I spent V.E. day alone with thousands.

It began in the cathedral. Standing by the West door, at the foot of the nave in the only space available, I listened with difficulty through the church's acoustics, to the vicar asking us to *give thanks…never to repeat, never to forget…*

On the steps outside, the Lord Mayor, looking shiny and important in his regalia, smiled broadly between each phrase, as though he were about to make a prize draw. Then later, watching the unfurling of the forty-four flags of the founder members of the United Nations in front of the Town Hall while listening to the relayed broadcast from the King in London, I cried for the first time in months.

Today we give thanks to Almighty God for a great deliverance… Let us remember those who will not come back: their constancy and courage in battle, their sacrifice and endurance in the face of a merciless enemy; let us remember the men in all the services, the women in all the services, who have laid down their lives…

Momentarily, I couldn't breathe. In my head were all the folk I had known and loved who would never come home. And Walter. But more, I *was* home and about to relinquish it.

The streets were crammed but I could hear every crackle in the transmission, every pause and hesitation. People hung onto the king's words as though each was a gift, to be kept, treasured. Locked away. I knew we were a special generation, like those before us in the Great War. Nothing, for us, would ever be the same.

Later, in streets around Manchester, I watched young girls' skirts swirl up around their waists as they flew in jigs, stamping their feet and shouting their joy. An old man laughing and coughing, wiped tears from bleary eyes, a nicotine bliss spread brown-stained over his mouth. And soldiers, not all of whom were yet back, shuffled in slow dances, smiling faces buried in a woman's hair, walking a tightrope between gladness and sorrow. For every warm desperate hello, had been a score of piteously inadequate goodbyes. Men with whom they had spent six years, most of whom they would never meet again.

I wandered from street to street watching, listening; capturing images and sounds I would keep forever. In the parks and squares, bands competed, the bass drum boom reverberating like the dull thud of the big guns. At one point I was pulled into the mayhem by a young boy. I danced, began to feel the excitement trickle down my spine, almost getting the wind of it, then the music stopped. I felt a little silly, drifted on.

In the evening I warmed my hands by the bonfire at St Boniface's near my digs, subdued by collective nostalgia watching the swaying crowd who stood cross-armed, hand in hand, intoxicated by the mood of the moment, faces gold in the firelight. They sang: *There'll be blue birds over, the white cliffs of Dover*...and all the while I kept thinking Walter should have been there, he'd earned it. I knew that somewhere Carl would be celebrating his homecoming; a star-spangled banner rippling in sunlight and an all American band playing a jitterbug somewhere.

When the fireworks lit up the sky with their benign magic, I felt my Englishness; this was my country. Britain my nation. I laughed at the desperate jingoistic nationalism of *Land of Hope and Glory*. Loved and hated it.

Couldn't believe I was leaving. Already married and just a girl. Felt like a traitor.

Suddenly, fingers appeared over the top of my book, pushing it down gently into my lap.

'Are you all right? Here, use this.' A young woman, perhaps a little older than I, handed me a handkerchief, sat down on the edge of my bed.

'My name's Jane, what's yours?'

Chapter Eighteen

England
1946

Laden with luggage we shuffled in sideways through the narrow door into a space no bigger than my bedroom at home. Bunked in the bowels of the ship, in a cabin with no porthole and a humming vibration from the engines, there was an initial silence between us. Our collective apprehension was betrayed through timid gestures: we fiddled with our luggage, bit our lips, the five of us standing, by necessity in a huddle, trying to imagine how we would make room, our bags piled in the middle of the floor, whilst casting anxious glances at each other, wondering how we would get any privacy—where we would undress and so on. Like the naïve teenagers some of us were, we were speechless in the realisation that this was it; we were really going. We were about to cross the Atlantic in the middle of January, in an airless, viewless compartment. One of the girls, the same one that came to my aid at Tidworth, looked around at our sea of faces and said suddenly, in a clear and confident voice:

'Well…shall I start? I'm Jane and no, you'll be relieved to hear, I don't have any children and nor, I believe, do any of you.' The ice cracked a little, warmed by her broad and welcoming smile.

'Thank the Lord, have you seen the mayhem out there? It's all skriking and smelly nappies,' a young girl said shyly, but apparently keen to be friendly.

'There are two thousand three hundred and thirty-three of us according to the boarding list,' Jane responded, already appearing a safe pair of hands; her crisp diction a contrast to the drawn-out Northern vowels of the girl that had just spoken. 'And yup, a lot of babies…my, we have been busy…' She raised her eyebrows, laughed easily as though being on a ship bound for a new life in a new country was the most natural thing in the world.

'That's a lot of cattle to shift to market,' another girl, a Liverpudlian, offered.

Beginning to see the funny side, barriers lowered. Relief was palpable; as a group we appeared to be normal and friendly. The sheer enormity of numbers, giving us, somewhat illogically, a sense of security: *all in it together.*

However, a little later, after we had exchanged brief histories about ourselves, we heard, sooner than we expected, the boom of the siren as the mighty ship began to draw away from Southampton dock. I did not go on deck to wave my goodbyes with the others, instead remained perched on the edge of the nearest bunk, nibbling the soft tissue around my mouth, alone. When the others returned, tear-stained, pale, trembling, as though in shock, I was glad I hadn't gone.

The telegram I sent to Carl a few days beforehand was brief, necessarily bereft of detail or loving addenda. I received a return cable stating simply that he would be in New York to meet me. Kiss kiss. I remember the ruffle of anticipation, the butterflies. I had never been out of England. Except for those on active service, most of the people I knew had never even been to London.

I had feared that life aboard ship would be like the dorm at Tidworth, a world of petty jealousies, territorial liaisons and peer pressure, but from the outset, the five of us began to share confidences, learn about each other's lives, and, inevitably, accord one another some sort of pecking order. Quite spontaneously, age seemed to be the rather arbitrary deciding factor over who would sleep where. As the second oldest I had a choice of bunk and contrary to the others, requested a top one, preferring to be higher and look down on the world rather than up.

It soon became evident that small things in our confined space were important; tidiness, or the lack of, quickly became the main potential for disagreement. Getting along together was paramount. *This is a huge adventure...let's make it fun!* Jane cajoled when tempers frayed, or regret clawed at our edges. She was the peacemaker.

On the cabin wall, she taped a map of America onto which each of us marked where we were going to live, creating a flurry of envy or pride or simply ignorance, especially from the youngest, Elspeth, just seventeen, proud that she alone amongst us would be living in *The Big Apple*. It was an accolade she wore like a badge, other than that, she seemed, to me at least, not to have a clear thought in her head.

During daylight hours, I don't think we seriously pondered whether we had made the right decision. This, even though none of us had seen our partner for months, more than a year in Jane's case. We did not ask the big questions: whether each husband would feel the same about his British bride since returning home and indeed how we would feel also. We'd each of us, ridden the storm of marrying a *yank*. Been accused, however obliquely, of being opportunists, gold-diggers or desperate for a man, any man. Worst of all, guilty of having shown a severe lack of good judgment; deserting our families, friends, even our heritage. We'd felt the thunder of family and public opinion, yet each had stuck to the decision. We were not going to question it now when we most needed to be reassured.

I was at last amongst like-minded people, with whom there was no need to defend my choice. We saw ourselves as having *spunk*, *spirit*, a bit of *go* in us, unlike the *dull girls* we had left behind. All in all, considering some of the women with whom I shared my dorm at Tidworth, I felt content that my fellow travellers, a kind of family for now, were a pretty good bunch.

A week into the voyage, far from land, claustrophobia was a word we used a lot, especially during storms at night; the fact that our cabin was below the water line preyed on our minds. When the sea was rough, the ship, increasingly, pitched like a rowing boat. Instead of clinging to my bunk, keeping my head beneath the blanket as some of the others did, I would get out of the cabin, attempt to get high enough within the ship to see the night sky, surprisingly light against the blackness of the water, and watch the horizon from prow to stern.

We weren't allowed on deck during storms, so I would sit in a lounge area near the fore-part of the ship, sometimes with Jane, watching through the windows, while the prow smacked into waves bigger than houses, juddering as though it would disintegrate, and disappearing under the dark water, seemingly going down and further down still, until our white vacant faces glanced at each other in some doubt as to whether she could come up again.

And then when she did, the opposite sensation, that her prow seemed so high in the air that the stern might simply slip back and be swallowed by the sea. Then the ship would creak and groan and slowly grind back to horizontal and do it all again. Every sigh of relief followed, and was followed by, minutes of controlled terror.

It was an optical illusion, the crew told us; the movement of the sea gave the impression of a see-saw. We were not convinced, nor we noticed as the voyage progressed, were the crew.

Storms were an unknown quantity, no one ever sure when they would abate, or how bad they could get. Despite spending more time praying for safe deliverance than was comforting, I loved them too: that sense of the apocalyptic. Always, it seemed that the real power remained leashed. I felt I'd never seen a storm's ultimate force and something about that appealed to me; the idea of my vulnerability set against something immeasurable, unpredictable. I silently goaded the elements, forced myself to watch the lightning illuminate our isolation, listen to the thunderous boom of the sea and sky, fearful, exhilarated.

On one occasion, a storm blew up quickly, just before supper when the chefs were cooking and waiters preparing the dining room. As the ship began to roll, the middle deck became filled with the sound of smashing crockery and expletives from the kitchen. Whole tables laid for dinner were swept clean by the steepness and severity of the pitching. The more that was smashed, people threw up and babies screamed, the more Jane and I disintegrated into uncontrolled fits of giggles close to hysteria.

Later, when it was calm, just over two weeks into the voyage, I can still remember the distinct sense of wanting to stay just as I was, never arriving, floating like a seagull on a thermal by day, by night mesmerised, perhaps even anaesthetised by the lights of the ship scribbling furiously on the water like a thousand unsaid goodbyes. I had heard the girls sobbing; knew, during the long voyage, inactivity had allowed doubt to creep in.

Some had developed misgivings about the life that awaited them. It shocked me to learn that all of them, except Elspeth and myself, had conducted a great deal of research into the area to which they were going, some even had photos of their new home and in-laws with whom they would be living. Welcoming letters. Information.

Jane had even made enquiries about the requirements for her to take up nursing at Boston General Hospital and had already applied for the necessary permits and retraining courses required by the US authorities. Elspeth, like a frightened cat, arched, looked nonplussed, defensive; trusted that her new husband would take care of everything.

I, hating my parity with Elspeth in this, felt ill equipped. Apart from what Carl had told me, I had conducted no productive enquiries of my own and therefore had no real idea what I was going to. Carl had been characteristically vague, and I, baffling to me now, incurious.

The storms and headwinds we encountered had slowed our progress we learned. As a result, we would be arriving in New York on February 10th, three days late. The ship would deliver its cargo of brides and have much needed repairs to the stabilisers; damage caused by the storms.

As we approached the new continent, the weather calmed, seagulls trailed our wake, and we were able to spend more time on deck, scanning the horizon, hoping always to be the first to view the famous skyline. When I did see it, Manhattan was shrouded in mist like an image in a dream. The statue of liberty that came green and suddenly out of the fog, was smaller than I had imagined, out of proportion, her arms and legs short, her enormous head reminiscent of Christ with his crown of thorns.

As the ship slipped past Ambrose Light the water was still as pond-water. Women jostled with each other crowding the rails, despite the chill, to see the welcoming committee. A tiny Army Transportation Corporation vessel greeted the ship and her cargo, her horn sounding repeatedly, filling the empty air with a sense of urgency and occasion.

The crew of the small boat waved vigorously, shouted hellos that got lost, drowned by the horn and the band on deck that had begun to play *Here comes the Bride.* As the wedding air faded into the cold mist, a woman shouted: 'Welcome to America, girls,' the slow drawl of her accent a winch to our excitement, at which we shouted and waved wildly, registering the shock of actually having arrived, the reality sweet and thick.

I, carried with the tide, *knew* I had made the right decision.

I counted eleven army tugs that brought the great ship into her berth at Pier 90. I scanned the shore for a glimpse of Carl, thinking how different the men waiting by the quayside looked out of uniform, a waving cheering rabble. Others further back, stood awkwardly, bemused, arms folded, rocking on their heels. Overall, more like a bunch of factory workers than the smooth and caramel coloured army they had been. I craned but could not pick Carl out from the crowd keeping my hands on the rail; I couldn't wave to nobody.

Some women, whose new homes would be in New York State and whose husbands were there to meet them, were informed by loudspeaker that they would be allowed to leave the ship that evening. The rest would have to spend another night aboard until the authorities were ready to process us. The only one of our little group that qualified for disembarkation was Elspeth.

Gripping her bags, wide-eyed, pressing her lips together like a child about to go on stage, she confessed to us, her anticipation bubbling into fear and doubt, that her husband had cabled her the day before the voyage, asking that if she could delay her departure a month as it would work out better for him. She had cabled back saying it was too late. The lack of response reassured her that all was well. If it wasn't, she hadn't wanted to know.

Elspeth was halted at the bottom of the gangplank, two steps onto American soil, by the crewmember registering the names of those disembarking, then taken by one of the stewards to one side. After several minutes a man arrived, bustling with an air of authority, clipboard in hand. We had gathered by the rail to get a glimpse of the husband we had heard so much about, and to wave goodbye. We watched instead as the man with the clipboard told Elspeth something that seemed important. We saw his shoulders settle, his head dip, an awkwardness shuffled around his feet.

For a few moments, the two people seemed oblivious to everyone else. Then the man lifted his right hand and placed it on Elspeth's shoulder, whereupon she suddenly crumpled onto the quayside. We learned later that she would be travelling home on the same ship. Her new husband had already begun divorce proceedings.

That evening, as we washed our hair, wrote letters and generally prepared for disembarkation the following day, the mood was subdued. News had filtered back but we had no idea why Elspeth had not come back on board and presumed she had been given accommodation until the ship was repaired and ready to sail again.

The news was that there were six girls in a similar position.

'I can't believe the silly thing would just come on the off-chance that everything would be all right,' one of the girls offered.

'Well, she *is* married. I suppose that if someone married you less than a year ago, it's reasonable to expect that they would still want you.' I felt defensive, vulnerable, especially as I had not spied Carl on the quayside, so tall, I figured, he would be difficult to miss.

We were edgy and, it must be said, titillated by the added drama of Elspeth's predicament. The quietness of the ship, only the faint hum of an auxiliary power unit purring, colluded with an uncomfortable frisson at another's misfortune, and in my case, an increasing sense of foreboding. No-one said how stupid Elspeth had been. All of them thought it.

Later in my bunk lying awake, as I had so many other nights, listening to a sniffling, periodic snoring, I felt that something was slipping away from me. I was surprised by my reluctance to move on. I had begun to know these women well, their most intimate thoughts, life stories. My relief at staying on board ship for another night puzzled me. I had thought I was sure. I knew we needed to get away from one another, from the claustrophobia of life aboard ship; I had been irritated by each of my cabin-mates at one time or another, yet our time together had mattered.

I knew I would look back to this time, suspended between worlds, the die cast, yet somehow with a sense of infinite possibility, of optimism, and that terrible beauty—nostalgia. It had been a purgatory of sorts, a time to be cleansed of the past, before moving on. The voyage out, as I preferred to think of it, as though at some future date there would be a voyage back, had closed a chapter on my childhood.

I turned into my pillow so that the others would not hear the panic in my breathing.

Book Three

Chapter Nineteen

Five Years Later

America
1951

Enter by the narrow gate…the way is hard that leads to life…

As I walk across the yard on my forced return from the Amish house, Sheila, Carl's mother, is sitting on the porch, rocking. She doesn't speak. She knows. Along with the *I told you so* tilt of her head, there's a look. Fear? Anyhow, I walk on by. Don't even get through the door.

'Welcome home.' His face is twitching. There are patches of red on his neck.

He grabs my arm, pulls me through the kitchen into the hall and swings me around so that I fall against the banister rail. I let him. I am limp, resigned to whatever he will do with me. He's mad and my quiescence seems to make him worse. He pushes past and grabs me again, pulls me up the stairs, one by one. I lose my footing, my jaw jams against a stair, teeth sink into my cheek.

Upstairs, he throws me onto the bed. Locks the door. I want to gag. The light from the window highlights one side of his face as he pins down my arms with his knees, straddling me. His eyes are wide, bloodshot. Sweat drips down his temples. He stinks of the barn.

He rips open my bodice, pushes my breasts together, bites in the space between. Leaning back, he snaps off his braces, pulls at his buttons. Yanks up my dress, salivating. Boiling over.

'Don't. Please don't. I beg you, please—'

He swipes the back of his right hand across my face. I feel the jerk on my neck, taste the metal of blood in my mouth.

'Just…shut up. SHUT UP.'

He pulls at my panties so hard they mow my flesh. Gets them as far as my knees and pushes open my legs with his. With his fingers he prods and scrapes, making space and forces himself into me. Dry. He rips against me, catching, friction. Pushes, pushes until he is in as far as he can go. He has one hand on my face, leaning hard on that elbow, pushing fingers into my mouth. I want to bite down hard. Bite till I taste bone, but I lie still.

The other hand holds himself firm, inside. I feel myself suffocating. His chest presses into my cheek, the buttons of his shirt eating into my skin. Stale bourbon sweats out of him as he thrusts. Slowly at first, building up. Warming like an engine. A piston jamming down, indiscriminate. Jam, jam, jam. I see sparks flying from me, hear a sound like grinding metal. He is hard like iron. He jams harder and harder. Grunting, grinding in rhythm, but not coming. Just on and on and on.

After about half an hour, going limp, but trying still, he collapses, putting his full weight onto me, weeping like a child. I am not there, my body, a cold slab of flesh. I am up here, outside, in the clouds, in the sunshine. Somewhere else. I am gone, on my way to England, '...*peace be with you, my child, peace be with you...*' I am flying. One of the geese in formation, a giant chevron across the sky, following an invisible line. My wings beating, beating. I am not there...

And now I am a child again, in my cot, trying to sleep, pushing away the sleep-demons. I hear my father stoking the fire, the jangle of metal on metal, the sudden clang of cutlery from the kitchen, my mother's high-pitched laugh, at something on the radio, slicing the air. Or her anger, raging at my father over some invented misdemeanour because at that moment she is trapped in her life.

Folded into these memories is me, caught in their web. I am looking out at the pleats of upland, rolling like a stormy sea into the Pennines. The blackened houses perched on the tops like breakwaters, mist-filled valleys at their backs, lakes of snow-cloud. I feel, with one hand outstretched from my warm bed, the rattling sash, when the breeze has become a wind and my curtain with its blue fishes blows over my face like a woman's skirt.

I smell the infant scent of fairy stories in their books that sleep in their wooden hammock on my windowsill, each ringed with bedtime drinks; ear-marked, scribbled over, imprints of small jammy fingers still evident as the light picks out *Beauty and the Beast,* her forehead matted with blackcurrant bruises...

Then through the milky light, the jangling and the clattering, beyond The Pike, up above the hills I imagine myself looking down on the world like a freed bird.

'You bitch, you goddamn fucking bitch.'

My body is blood-smeared, torn.

He pulls away, covers his face. Goes out of the room into the bathroom. I can hear the water running, hear Mr Schouten: *...the way is hard that leads to life.*

After washing him from me, I lie here all day and all night. I am overcome. I hear Sheila and her stick going to her room, tap, tap, hear her pause outside the door, sigh. Feel that somewhere along the line of her life, she has been where I am. It is normal. What she knows, what he knows. *Screwed up.* I remember when we met, he told me his family was *screwed up*.

He doesn't come to bed. I am grateful. The next morning it is over. I awake to the smell of breakfast.

'Wake up, honey. There's eggs and hash browns. Coffee? I thought I'd treat you. Coffee in bed. Wakey, wakey.'

I pull myself up, manage a half smile.

'Aren't you gonna say *thank you*?'

'Thank you.'

'That's better. You know…I missed you…I'm sorry about yesterday, I really am, had a few drinks…but you know you mustn't overreact, staying in bed so long, just to make a point.' He sits down on the bed beside me, gently takes hold of my hand. 'You know I love you, and you walked out on me.' His voice almost breaks; if I didn't know better, I'd think he'd been crying. 'I know you'd have come back. But it's not the point, is it? You made me look stupid, honey. Seems there's things we need to talk through. We can talk about things, can't we?'

I am silent. He is penitent, a child wanting forgiveness.

'You know, when I was little, Mom and Pop had some humdingers. There was screaming and crying…but she never left him. Not once…You got nothing to say?'

'Sorry.' I am gazing out at the sky, past him, past this existence.

'That's my girl, come here, let me hold you. No…not like that, not like a rag doll. That's it. You know, marrying you was the best thing I ever did, and when you calm down some, you'll see it. Won't you? Won't you, see it?'

'Yes.' He is shaking. Holding me very tenderly.

'I'm gonna make sure we're happy, happier than ever. I'm so sorry, honey. No man should do what I did. I hate myself. Please forgive me. I'll make you forgive me. And I'll forgive you. I'll be the best husband and you'll be the best wife, won't you?'

'Yes.'

'I'll fix you up with a hobby. Get someone to drive you into town sometimes, give you a break. You'd like that, wouldn't you?'

'Yes…I would like that.'

'Sure, you got the blues here. Mom's not much company for you. I'll fix it, eh?'

Chapter Twenty

America
1953

Yellow, far as the eye can see. And flat. Late summer.

Snakes of wind slither through the grasses, giving it movement, a pulse. I run my hand over my belly, feel the firm flatness of it. The wind is getting up. I sense a change, an increase. The house speaks of it; creaks and whistles echo through the crawl-space under the floor.

Standing at the nursery window, I stare, sigh at the big sky: a moving show of shifting mountains and monsters, make mental notes of the yellows of the earth on this cloud-scudding day. My easel and paints are propped by the window, bought to keep me busy, but the canvas is dry.

I look up, hoping to see the geese pass overhead, feel the thrill of it: North to South, unless they are lost and drifting farther and farther out to sea, carried on the tail of the prevailing wind, until they have gone so far, they cannot turn back. Like me.

The Queen, which brought me here, floats into my mind. There, on the horizon of my imagination, she slices through thirty-foot winter waves, iron grey and foaming, a waterfall of freezing spray suddenly thudding onto the deck. The mighty ship juddering while the Atlantic heaves and shifts its weight. Its surface: sky to a million sea creatures.

I dip below the water line, see great whales, rolling, curving, chasing minnows and myriad tiny creatures, that dart, swerve, and dart again, in rhythm, pushed by the swell. And I there, dandled on the surface with all the other women. Dandled by one government at the behest of another, in rhythm, darting, swerving, going forward to procreate; to live happily ever after.

I sense a line, at the very edge of the earth, where the curvature is sewn with tiny grass stitches onto a finite sky. A line made bolder every time the geese fly over it, a line that leads me from this place.

'Come away from the window, Alice. It's no good you hanging around in there and just staring out the window. You know it sends you half crazy. Come on down now, eh?'

I move my body, though not at first my gaze, into the empty nursery and feel the ache; it was in this room I saw a future, an escape from loneliness.

Soft creamy yellow. I decorated it myself when I was pregnant, sanding the walls, the woodwork, until it was smooth as baby's skin, painting coat after coat until it was perfect. Yellow. A safe colour for all eventualities; the colour of this country in late summer. There was one wall I did not paint in yellow, instead I painted a remembered landscape.

In my mural, below a too-blue sky and fluffy clouds, are green hills dotted with sheep. On the moors, bare, save the wild grasses, are uneven rows of dry-stone walls, where the morning and evening mist rolls and hangs like folds, giving a sensation of rising and falling, like breathing, as though in the moors themselves beats a mighty heart.

The lower slopes are misshapen meadows; at least Carl says they are. Fields here are mostly square, or so large they have no shape. There are oak trees and Friesian cattle. A grey pony grazes, flicking its tail.

In the foreground is a sooty black row of three terraced houses, eighteenth century gritstone, the top end of a small conurbation where a steep town built around a bowl ends, and country begins. The way I remember it. One of the houses has maroon painted window frames. In the backyard, facing open moorland, is a solitary figure. She is tiny with black curls that fall over her face, a stick figure hanging out washing to dry. Lots of men's shirts, trousers. The wind is blowing, whipping the clothes up into empty human shapes...

Hurry up love. You'll be late for your rehearsal. Leave the washing till you get back. There's a pet.

I hear my mother's voice.

I run in, remove my pinny, jump up the narrow stairs two by two. From my bedroom window, the Pennines sprawl, green and empty.

I was not thinking about rehearsals or laundry. But about what had happened the day before, out on the moors above Blackstone Edge.

I am fourteen. His hands tremble on my back, his legs, ramrod straight. He kisses my cheek, then my lips; I'm not sure whether to purse them or not. He puts his tongue in my mouth but doesn't seem sure about it. It feels strange, I want to giggle, wipe my mouth with my sleeve. He smells of chlorine and grass. My legs shiver uncontrollably, I notice the tiny blond hairs in his ears, feel the cold damp of his nose, the rush of blood to my head.

I almost don't want to see him again. I tell no one, blush every time I think of it.

I watch the mirror and smile furtively, see myself looking stupid, give myself an exasperated look that says, 'grow up'. I am pale. I pinch my cheeks, rub red ink from the cover of a book onto my lips. Not too much, the nuns will notice. Girl to woman, easy as that. I get a fluttering in my belly, an unfamiliar sensation in my thighs.

'My Mam says it won't happen. Hitler doesn't want to fight us,' Pat Beagan whispers while Sister Mary Gabrielle rants during music rehearsal.

'From the top, girls. Stand up. Concert performance please. Alice, Pat…when you're ready.'

"The heavens are telling the glory of God…"

I am singing First Soprano. While I teeter on the top notes like a ballerina on points, I think about my brothers. Remember the argument I had with Vincent this morning…

'Alice…Alice. Get down here now.'

I keep sinking into the past; the only place I'm happy but I mustn't rile him, not after last month. I asked him to post yet another letter back to my family, begging them to contact me. When I handed it to him, he just threw it on the side and said he'd do it next time he was in town. Then he asked why I bothered.

'Why? How can you ask me that? I haven't heard from them in seven years. Seven years. Can you begin to imagine what that's like for me? They are my family, I love them.'

'Well, clearly they don't love you, hon. That's one hell of a grudge your Pa is carrying around with him. Live with it. Your family is here now. Forget about them.'

'Forget? You can't possibly imagine that I could do that, do you?'

'You can do anything you set your mind to. You'll have another baby, you'll see. You won't need them.'

'Of course, I'll need them, Carl, and if I did have a baby, they'd be grandparents, my brothers, uncles. I would want to show them my baby. I knew it would be a long time before I saw them again, but seven years? And no contact? I just don't understand it. I'm homesick, Carl…I need to go home…or if that's not possible, ask if they could come here somehow. In fact, I've already asked them…in that letter.'

'Here? They ain't coming here, Alice. That wouldn't work at all.' He walked over to the bureau where he'd thrown the letter and began to rip it up.

'Stop Carl…please…How could you? You have no right. It took me ages to write that letter.'

'No right? I think you'll find, Alice McCullough, that I have every right.'

'Why can't they come? Tell me.'

'Because it's best they don't. It'd unsettle you.'

'So let me go home then.'

'You really are living on the moon. For one thing there's no way on this earth you're leaving here. Understand? You wouldn't come back. You're a married woman, your place is here. Besides, you think I'm about to go down an' rob a bank to pay for it? Think we're fucking Bonnie an' Clyde?'

'But seven years, Carl, is such a very long time, you can't keep me from them all my life, you know. Let's face it, we don't make each other happy—'

'Happy? Enough. Stop the damn tears. You make it sound like a prison sentence—'

'It is. It is a prison sentence,' I yelled back at him, unable to contain it any longer.

With that he took hold of my arm and swung me against the wall then proceeded to slap and punch me. Not on my face—he saved that for special occasions—when he thought I was being *uppity*.

'Think you're in prison, huh? Then here's some penal punishment for you to chew over…'

'Stop…Stop it,' I whimpered. 'I want to go home. Please just let me go home…'

This time he punched me in the stomach and when I keeled over unable to breathe, he kicked me till I couldn't feel my legs and hips.

I didn't walk for four days. He told Sheila I'd fallen down the stairs. Again. But she knew. She always knew and never said a word. Just quietly slipped about the house, silent, invisible, like someone already dead.

I think about that first kiss, soft and young. I met Walter about the same time as I met God. Perhaps, like God, I took him for granted; thought that he would always be there when I decided to believe again, but nothing ever stays the same.

Walter should be in my mural. He was the first person to make me realise that I existed, as distinct from my family. Mam insisting always, when he came calling for the boys, that they take me along because she needed to be alone, and because she understood the sometimes agony of childhood. At night I prayed to him. Then I prayed to God.

...The wonder of His work, displays the firmament...

But the God of my childhood, I muse, was habit: voices raised in unison, sweet melodic supplication. He was the swing of incense that made your eyes water, the murmur of benediction on Wednesday afternoons when you'd rather be playing hop-scotch. He was the hard feel of knees on wood when the hassocks were missing, the monotone of plainsong, the fourteen stations of the cross that never ended, especially when the sun was shining outside and you had a penny in your pocket, enough for a packet of Mo-Jo's.

He was statues and beads, black cassocks and veils. The smell of something long dead in church air. God was the force that may come in the night to take you to hell where you'd burn forever—eternally damned because you missed mass on Sunday or pinched one of Margaret Davies' chocolate biscuits. Twice. With God, you knew where you were.

I have started to dream of Walter, Carl beside me rumbling in heavy sleep, the mattress a hammock in which night is always uphill. I remember the first time, I had to stifle, on waking, a loud cry. We were lying under a tree's canopy, Walter's breath on my face, the imprint of his slender body on mine—a perfectly shaped lid. He pressed his fingers into my neck so hard I thought he would break it and I wanted him to because my dream had always the echo of reality in it, and I deserved punishment.

At first, I pushed away the wound of memory—for that's what it is, but now welcome the pain of it. I build narratives that gather momentum, both in sleep and awake, works of fiction taking me where I really want to be, believing in the nightly visitations—a ghostly fulfilling of a dangerous erotic yearning. Strange that something so long dead can seem so vital. Then I wake, aroused, ashamed, the black crow of the religion of my childhood on my shoulder; remembering who and what I am and what I am not, and try praying to something to take it all away. Until the next time.

If I was happy, perhaps the ghosts of my past could remain at peace, but while I inhabit this living hell, they are troubled and troubling. I know now that

Walter can never be done with. He is a dream that I re-visit, so that he is always a presence in my marriage, tangible, solid as rock. My highly polished secret.

I wonder what will become of me as I stare at the mural of my childhood, mentally recording my feelings to duplicate later in my journal: my furtive, hidden outpouring. The journal started in 1951, given to me by the Amish preacher, that is rapidly becoming a tome, one, for which, I must find ever new devious hiding places. It is, variously, the lump in the sagging mattress, the bulge beneath the loose floor-board, the filled gap behind the dressing table drawer, and most recently: the fugitive in the space between the range and the stone floor in the kitchen so that when Carl goes into town and I retrieve it to write, the top is roast hot, the bottom cold like the earth.

Every dream, memory, overheard conversation, glint of light on a window-pane, every bruise and black eye, all that love and all that hate and all that indifference, has become the significant part of my life: the recording of it. My life is in the writing, in the attempt to make sense of the life I am not living...

The wonder of His work, displays the firmament...

And now, gazing, glassy-eyed, at the painting from the past, planning my next journal entry, I receive from somewhere, a small gift. I recall the day Walter took me by the hand to show me the two nests, not a yard apart, balanced on the beam outside an old shed near his house in Fairford. Blackbirds and swallows. As we tiptoed close, the young swallows began to fly, three of them looped behind their mother as though attached by a waving, whirling string.

And I watched Walter as he watched them. He had one hand raised to shield the light from his eyes, the other in a frozen beckoning gesture, as though half-way through my inclusion in this event, somehow forgotten in the wonder of it. Then I noticed one chick had not flown, instead it teetered on the edge of the beam as though trying to muster the courage to join them. It raised its tiny woolly wings but wavering, plummeted to the ground where it lay on its side, flapping one wing, unable to move. Its mother flew close, looping and wheeling, all dips and swivels, but had her brood strung out behind her and could do nothing.

I picked up the tiny bird and felt its heartbeat. *Walter...Walter...* I whispered, but he was in thrall to the display that had moved higher and higher, silhouetted against the sky. Unsure what to do I stretched up and placed the chick beside the open beaks of the two chicks in the blackbird nest. I knew, even at twelve years old, that I should let it die, but I could feel its pattering heart in my hand.

And now, like the broken swallow in the wrong nest. I turn out toward the light. I close my eyes, think of intimate kisses, soft on my neck, but most of all, of being held. Arms enfolding me, deep in green fern, the hum of insects and shared histories—histories that have marked us out in every feature, every expression, and I am happy. Happiest in a remembered world where everything is safe and known, the pulse of eternity in two heartbeats, and where intimacy, with the only man I could ever love, was just around the corner…

'ALICE. Where the fuck are you? I told you…get down here.'

I breathe in sharply, *Handel* still in my head, exhaling a small moan as I turn away from the painting on the wall, fold away to a safe space the childish fragments and walk downstairs.

I pass the huge bookcase in the hall. Empty except for Sheila's dusty knick-knacks and the one old children's book with pictures from other countries.

'Why are you shouting for me?' Smiling, determined not to carry my nostalgia like a banner, I drift into the large kitchen. Sheila is fiddling with the radio and humming along with Perry Como, *No other love have I.* There is the faint odour of disinfectant. Carl, baggy and sweaty, is washing his hands.

'Give me the towel, Alice. Why do you stand there, day after day, staring like you're going crazy or something? Turn that off, Ma.' Sheila looks up, about to object, thinks better of it and does as he says.

'I've told you. I'm painting…absorbing the view.' I keep smiling, pass him the tea towel.

'No, you ain't, Alice. What's wrong with you? You're miserable as sin and you won't say why. Honestly, sugar, it's been nearly two years, I could shake you.' He pads around the kitchen in his socks where bits of the barn stick out like scarecrow stuffing. One thumb is hooked around the strap of his dungarees, the other he dips in a bowl of ketchup on the table, licks it and does it again. I move over and gently re-cover the bowl with a napkin. He places a gentle hand on my hip.

'You're buggin' me, you know? C'mon now, honey, get me something to eat, will you. My stomach thinks my throat's been cut.'

I can't help it. I know I'm a misery. It's not just this existence, it's losing the baby. A baby conceived that way is not how it should be, but since I lost her, everything feels even darker. If only I could have kept my mouth shut; I was *uppity* just once too often. Losing her was a punishment. *What ye give ye shall receive…*and I give nothing.

I just wanted someone of my own blood family. *Catherine*, after my mam: stillborn. I carried her for eight months, knew every fidget, every time she kicked or stretched, began to know who she would be; loved her like I've never loved anything before. I held her, just for a moment, so light, a bag of feathers, a tiny smile on her puckered blue-pink lips. Black hair, fingernails like mother of pearl, ivory white skin. They took her away in a bag.

There's no point trying to explain any of it to Carl. He is too buried in his own life to be concerned. He didn't even want the child. He said he did, but I knew, I could tell by the look on his face; he was repulsed by my shape, didn't want to share me. I don't think he meant for me to lose her, he just got angry and lashed out the way he does when I retaliate. If I hadn't fallen, perhaps…who knows. Sheila went pale when I told her I was pregnant, said nothing, just stared at her hands, stroked her nails. When I saw the blood running down my legs, I knew it was not just my child's life that was ebbing away.

But it's been too long, I need to get over it. Carl wants me to enjoy my life here and the truth is, even without the fighting, I don't know how. There is nothing here that I want…and I'm tired all the time. I see only empty space. Carl *is* empty space. There is no conversation, no interest in each other's thoughts. Carl sees each day as distinct, to be got through, no sense of addition or achievement, of life leading somewhere, just one full of sensory perceptions, gratifications en route, no empathy or understanding.

He may as well be one of the cattle in the barn. What does that make me? His cow? His barren cow. And I know now that this is all there will ever be. Our lives will not increase, grow together, enlarge and evolve with love, children, plans. We shall not fuse into something whole: *a couple.*

I shall not be able, one day, to see that this is what we have become: something good, like my parents. All we shall have, is what we have now. Like Walter described in his journal: *days of unremitting boredom and drudgery punctuated by abject terror.*

Opening the icebox, I take out some eggs and five slices of ham. One each for Sheila and me. Three for Carl. Potatoes I cooked yesterday for dinner; I'll fry with the ham. Pancakes and syrup.

Late Sunday breakfast. Carl likes it this way and will still expect a roast later. Putting some water on the range to heat, I scoop four heaps of coffee into the pot. He likes his coffee strong, *like my women*. I used to think it was funny. For myself, I put a teaspoon of tea into a small pan that I have warmed. They don't have teapots here. I don't do it if I know Carl is watching, it's one of those things about me that sparks him off:

For Chrissake, why can't you drink coffee like everyone else, and why the friggin' rituals? You only do it to bug me. Don't you, hon? Admit it.

Perhaps I do, I'm not sure. I seem to irritate him a lot. Mam used to say I had it in me to drive people crazy. I think I too must be difficult to live with. I feel so down all the time. Empty. The doctor says it's baby blues without the baby, but I don't know. All I want to do is lie in bed or stare into space. And when I try to make something of myself, I get accused of tarting myself up and end up acquiring a few black bruises to add to the eyeshadow.

Standing by the range turning the bacon, I listen to the wind moaning under the porch. Sounds human somehow. I hope we aren't in for a storm. With the harvest coming up, rain is the last thing we need, guaranteed to put Carl into a frenzy. Leaning against the range, though it is hot, I feel a slight chill run through me. I need to tread carefully. That's how it is with Carl, like walking on broken glass. He says living with me is like bashing his head against the barn door. I don't reply that living with him *is* having your head bashed against the barn door.

My belly presses against the bar on the front of the cooker and my hipbones touch on either side. A test for myself. If they do not touch, if my rounded belly prevents it, then maybe, just maybe everything will change. Maybe worth putting up with the sex. Maybe.

We sit at the table with its plastic lace tablecloth, barely speaking while we eat. Sheila pushes the food around her plate, inspecting every morsel, muttering under her breath. Discreetly, I watch Carl. He holds his fork like a shovel. Talks at me in clipped unfinished sentences: '…barn door's loose…got a stray in the yard…where from, I dunno…' imagining my interest, spitting morsels of food, wiping the grease from around his mouth with the back of his fist and I ask myself: how on God's earth did I end up here?

Chapter Twenty-One

America
January 1954

Sheila is making an effort, showing a modicum of warmth. A weak smile occasionally flits in my direction. She angles her neck in that way of hers, fiddles with her lumpy, brown-specked hands as though pulling off gloves. When she passes me in the kitchen or the hall, she hesitates; perhaps her hand brushes over mine, or she looks at me and I feel she has something important to say. But when she speaks, her voice is weary, her tone flat.

'Time sure is weighing heavy today, la de la…must be something needs doing…'

The clock ticks slowly on the dresser.

Carl and I move around each other, keeping distance. A sun and a moon, moving in our own orbit. When our worlds come too close, he crackles and flares.

'Stop creeping around, for Chrissake. You got nothing to do?' His eyes bulge.

I freeze.

Most of the time he is out working. Saturdays he goes to town. He doesn't like me to do 'man's work', be outdoors; instead, wants me to bake pies, make jam, keep house. Be pretty.

I have begun to know the slip and slither of my footsteps on the stairs, my shadows thrown huge on the walls. I am a ghost. Morning and evening I gaze from an upstairs room at an empty landscape. Flat. Sometimes a yellow-headed blackbird or meadow-lark flies by and I follow it, feel its billow as the wind gives lift, watch as it disappears into infinity. One day a wildcat creeps, head down, across the yard, hunting field mice. Bored, it flops down, stretches its elastic body into a long, sensuous curve, then gets up and pads away, its paws like soft cushions thrown lightly on the dusty clay. Just passing through.

I try to paint the light. A hint of haze or brush of grey. Flat bottomed clouds slide along an invisible glass ceiling, cast shadows that move over the ground; rob the earth of colour. Carl says I paint air. Different kinds of air. *There's no life in your pictures.*

I write home every month still. They do not reply. I thought they would forgive me for leaving them. Eight years. It seems I am out of their minds. Gone. Still, I don't really believe it, so I write. Ordinary letters, hoping one of them will be the spark. Anything would be better than nothing. I tell them about the weather, the scenery. Tell them I am not lonely, that there is so much to do outdoors on the farm. I know they will like that. Tell them how busy I am.

I tell them how I love them, how my heart aches day and night; that I would rather spend a short life with them in it, than a long one without. Tell them to come and get me. Rescue me. I tell them I'm okay. I tell them to write.

With a shrug of his shoulders, Carl takes the letters to town, never asking what I write, just mumbling something like *I don't know why you bother.* Then I wait.

Last August, Carl found a driver to take me to town once a month, for shopping and a change of scenery. Said the guy came into a bar looking for work. There wasn't any. Carl said he looked pretty desperate; thought he'd get him for a decent price. He did.

The first time I went, Carl came too, just to check things out, *look after me.* He said I should choose some things for the farm. Make it *homey.* Said we needed new drapes; bet I could make them if we found some fabric I liked. The driver left us in town for a few hours while Carl and I wandered. It felt good to be around people. I wondered if I could make friends. I smiled a few times, but everyone was too busy; no one seemed to notice me. Besides, there was the distance; even if I made a friend, who would drive over two hours round trip to visit?

I found a few things: lace headcovers for the chairs. A vase. Some pretty paper napkins, and a book: *Of Mice and Men* by a man called John Steinbeck, which I hid in one of the bags so Carl wouldn't make a fuss about the waste of money.

He wouldn't come into the shops, just sort of hung around outside.

As we walked, his eyes followed the scent of stale beer swelling around the entrance to bars. He rubbed his jaw with one hand, shoved the other deep into his pocket. I noticed other couples; watched as a man, around Carl's age, slipped his arm around the waist of his girl, pulling her to him. I saw her smile. I wanted to feel that smile. Carl saw it too. He cleared his throat and spat in the gutter. He wanted what they had.

We ended up at the movies, something I hadn't done since I left England. It was easier to be separate in the darkness. I lost myself in the melodrama, cried easily. Carl slept.

In future, Carl decided we should visit town separately.

In his way, he *is* trying. He does small things to attempt to make me happy. He bought me a kitten that I call 'Blackbird'. He couldn't see that when I held her for the first time, I could think only of Berry, my first cat. He thought I didn't like her. She frightened me; I could feel her heartbeat.

'Stupid name for a cat if you ask me. Cute thing though,' he said as he tickled her throat the day we got her. She purrs whenever he comes close. Funny that… females are so trusting.

He tells me not to worry; I'll have a baby one day. He wants to make it better, wants to make me love him. But there is no longing in me, not for him, not for a long time, not after everything. And I don't, can't, forget. The deep depression I felt after losing the baby has passed, but anger eats at me, consumes my future. I carry it like an internal parasite. I am my own enemy.

His still beautiful body close to me, makes my blood heat till I feel it racing through my veins, the way you feel when your temperature is high and you are fevered. It makes pink spots on my cheeks, which Carl mistakes for desire, but it is revulsion. When he has sex with me, I lie there; focus on the sliver of moon hanging in the black night through the window, see its brown halo, watch the voile drapes fill with air, blowing ghostly into the room.

Jake is the name of the driver. The first few journeys, we travelled more or less in silence, passing the time of day, but that was it. He was distant, preoccupied, and I felt awkward, grown out of the habit of people. Then I got used to the silence and became comfortable with it, began to look forward to the peace of the journeys almost more than the time in town. When he came to pick me up, he would smile, tip his head back in greeting. Notice me.

Now and then he hums strange tunes, a soft vibrato in his voice. Sometimes I doze, cradled by the rocking of the truck and Jake's lullabies. Occasionally, he puts on the radio and we listen to Nelsen Eddy or Ella Fitzgerald or someone. He hangs a small, beaded thing, with a feather attached to the mirror. *A dreamcatcher*, he says.

Jake is getting on. About fifty, fifty-five I'd guess. His skin has deep lines that crease into a circle around his mouth when he smiles. His hair is long, iron grey, tied back in a ponytail. He is an American Indian, from the Crow tribe. His speech is very precise, and he has a habit of saying 'So...?' when we meet, like a question. I'm not sure how he expects me to respond so I usually ignore it and he smiles. He seems to be waiting.

He smells of dust and sweat, of the earth. His clothes are brown and shabby, but clean. Carl said he was glad of the work, wished it was more. I asked Carl why he doesn't use him on the farm. He said he doesn't trust him with the crops: Indian. Trusts him with me though. I don't think Jake cares much for Carl.

Once a month like a new moon, waxing and waning, Jake comes and takes me to and from town.

'So?'

Today, he asks whether I would like to go anywhere else.

'What, you mean other than town?'

'Yes.' He keeps his eyes on the road. He is smiling.

'Is there anywhere else to go?'

'Of course, there is a world out there.'

Such a simple thing to say. I had ceased to think of it. My world has closed down. There is only the farm, the wheat, the plains, and now, town.

'Yes, I suppose...but surely everywhere is too far.'

'If you walk in circles.' He takes his eyes off the road for a moment, looks at me.

'You think I walk in circles?'

'Do you?'

'What do you mean?'

'Like a bird with a broken wing. It has the will to fly but cannot.'

He has not spoken to me this way before. It seems intimate, rude even, but his interest, the fact that he has observed me, is flattering. I feel myself drawn in.

'I tried once. To fly that is.' I flash him a look. 'Anyway, where could we go?'

'Anywhere.'

'Seriously, where is there to go that we could get back today?'

'Well, if you must come back today, that restricts us a little.' He laughs. Is he playing a game with me? 'You know, sometimes you don't have to go very far to find something worth seeing. Just walk.'

A truck coming towards us honks, smoke billows from its exhaust. It passes. Then silence for a while.

'I used to love walking when I lived in England.'

'So?' He nods, waiting.

'Where I grew up, the hills were covered with footpaths and stiles.'

'Stiles?'

'Wooden contraptions that allow you to step over a fence from one field to the next. Not only stiles but kissing gates.' He laughs, baffled. It is strange. Nice. Carl doesn't like me to talk about home.

'A kissing gate is like a stile. It's a swing gate with a curved fence half around. Very cosy. Anyhow, I loved walking.' I go quiet.

'You miss England?'

'Yes…I do.' I gaze at the road ahead.

'Tell me what you miss.'

'You want to know?'

'Yes, I want to know.'

I tell him about Mam and Dad, Ned and Vincent. I tell him stories, watch him nod, smiling. I am back in childhood.

'Our Vincent was a tinker.' He looks puzzled. 'A scoundrel, naughty boy, you know? He would steal apples from the churchyard because it drove the local vicar wild. We had an apple tree in the garden. We didn't need apples, but he would come racing in, arm-deep and hide behind Mam's pinny when she opened the door to Reverend Wallace. She would tell him the Conroys were good Catholic kids, not thieves. Then she'd invite him in for a cup of tea, knowing the miserable sod would choke, rather than drink it. Mam knew. The vicar knew. We all knew.

How can you sleep at night? My Dad would say to her afterwards, then give her a hug for bravery in the field.'

Jake laughed out loud.

'You are so…funny!'

'And it's little things…the sound of foxes at night, the dawn chorus—'

'Dawn chorus?'

'The birdsong in the morning, so loud it wakes you up.'

'Ah yes, I know.' Jake nodded.

'But it's not the same here. And the smells: mown grass…freshly cut privet hedges…'

'That separate the yards?'

'Sort of. We call them gardens. Yards are small concrete spaces behind terraced houses, usually with an outside privy plonked at the bottom and a gate that leads to an alley where the dustbin-men pick up your rubbish.' Jake looked confused.

'Go on,' he said.

'Where was I?'

'Smells,' he smiled. I am not sure he isn't patronising me, but I continue.

'Smells…yes. Damp undergrowth in autumn, fall, as you say. I love that earthy, muddy smell, like the smell of dogs' paws and Wellies. And witch-hazel in the snow, with its spidery yellow flower.'

Jake lifts his head, the inverse of a nod and I hesitate, thinking he wants to say something, but he just looks over quickly 'So?'

'So. It's what I miss. Lived-in countryside and villages whose houses spill their flowers over the garden walls. And spring. One change opening onto another: buds and blossom, snowdrops, crocuses, daffodils, violets, bluebells, cowslips. I love cowslips. Here there is no time for Spring. Everything happens overnight and then no rain for months, just a gradual dying and browning. At home…'

'You mean England?'

'Yes…' I pause a moment, look around outside, '…there are maps that you can follow on foot for miles. Every detail is shown on them, post offices, pubs, ancient churches with steeples or towers. And everything is so accessible. You can set off with a packed lunch, have a wonderful walk, never see a road, and be back for tea or a drink at the pub on the way home.

'Here, there are no footpaths. Walking over a farmer's field is…impossible. A leafy track off a road is not an inviting lane or bridleway, a mystery waiting to be discovered, but a private driveway leading to a farm that says: 'Keep Out' and means it.

'I was so stupid and naïve, we all were. I thought America would be like the films, you know, where everyone is happy and equal. That women like Doris Day baked cakes for each other, men like Gregory Peck brought flowers…'

'I see.' Jake looks mystified.

'I suppose England is like an old shoe, good quality, comfortable, reliable, but worn down, full of scuffs and tears. I thought America would be shiny and new, like a patent leather stiletto you admire in a shop window. But when you get it home, you find it's synthetic, it pinches and was made in China.

'Judging by the television, people here think they can solve everything by spending money, make themselves happy by having the latest this or that. Carl is always telling me to go shopping if I am sad, as though that will put things right. People here have so much, except for those that have nothing. Look at you, forgive me but…the way they treat you. And this is *your* country.'

'Real poverty has little to do with money.' He shakes his head. We are both silent for a while.

'You're angry,' he says suddenly.

'Am I?' I realise he is right.

'Perhaps the things you love are still there, for you to see again one day,' he adds.

'This is my life now.'

'With no love and no hope?'

I remain silent. I can't believe we are discussing this; my whole life summed up that way. 'There you are, walking in circles. Hemming yourself in.' He smiles, lessens the tension. 'The fact you still call England *home* says much. You have not forgotten your birth right.'

He goes quiet, thinking. He is like that. I noticed once when I gave him an apple for the journey, that before he bit into it, he looked at it carefully, one eye on the road, the other on the apple. He stroked the skin with his free hand. Then he smelt it, said, 'this is a good apple', and ate it.

'What else did you do in England that you do not do here?'

'Oh, I don't know…I had a pony, Tara. Nobody wanted her. She'd been badly treated.'

'This was horse country once,' he says wistfully.

It is my turn for silence. I stare at the furrowed lines of ploughed earth stretching to infinity. The earth is grey. Frost sparkles on the ridges in the winter sunshine. The domed sky has creeping cloud moving up, over. It will snow soon.

He pulls into the side of the road. Cuts the engine. Silence makes me awkward. He keeps his hands on the wheel. Large hands. Pale brown, wrinkled. Broad palms, thumbs that look strong.

'I'm sorry. I've talked too much.' I realise I have invited him into my inner world, and I begin to doubt the wisdom of it.

'You know…I think we grow up believing that what we know, is the way things are. It is only when we look outside the circle of our knowledge that we discover a new way of looking at the world… It is the only way to be free. When you compare what you had with what you've got, you feel bad. Even if you had stayed at home, maybe you would have felt the same. Looking back is like that. It is possible that you are looking only for things that support what you feel, that you are trapping yourself within a life of your own making.

'You know…' He shifts in his seat, turns, looking straight at me in a way he hasn't before, '…you imply that both love and hope are missing from your life, but love will be there for you when you are ready. Hope is the important one. It is something you must hold onto. Like happiness, it can slip out of your grasp and be very difficult to regain.'

'What are you saying?'

'Hope is about the future…not the past, but you need it now, here, in the present.'

Without the sound of the motor, it is very quiet. I think suddenly about the war. So distant. The great heart-wrenching waste of it. I look at Jake in profile. When he speaks it always seems significant. He is different from everyone I have known; his brown skin, his Indian-ness. The only comments Carl or Sheila has made about the 'Indians' are that they are *drunken, lazy, better off in reservations*. The single reason I have a measure of freedom with Jake, is because Carl considers him so far beneath us as to be hardly worth his while; on a par with the animals, except that *animals are more useful, you can eat them*.

The people in town are not over friendly towards Indians; second class citizens. Always served last. Why haven't I become angry? Like I did about the 'Snowdrops' who wouldn't let the black soldiers dance with us during the war, or the concentration camps afterwards? I have accepted what I've been told, stopped thinking. I'm not even walking in circles; I've come to a dead stop.

We sit for some minutes in silence.

'Where shall we go then, you decide,' I say eventually.

'Let's start here.' He gets out of the car, walks around to my door. I get out. It is very cold. He breathes in the air, looks at the cloud overhead. Takes his time.

'Father sky…' *Our Father who art in heaven…* He looks at me as though he reads my mind, then down at his feet, stamps the ground. 'Mother earth, your children are we…' I feel uncomfortable, alien.

'Look west.' He tips back his head, indicating with his chin. 'Over there are the Rocky Mountains. You can't see them, but you can sense them, smell them when the Chinook winds blow.' He inhales again deeply, closes his eyes. 'They rise straight up out of the flat earth like awakening giants. When the sun comes up, it's like honey spills over them. You should go there... In the future.

'You know, this is a place full of illusion. You think that because it is flat it is simple—it isn't. You think it is changeless, but each season colours the land in new finery. Only the horizon is the same, only the bones of the land remain untouched by our living upon them. You must allow your mind to expand; inwardly and outwardly; see the whole.'

He takes a step back, turns. Everything he does is slow, deliberate. He raises an arm and points.

'To the north is Canada, it's not far, just think of that...You know Milk River at Wolf Point?' I nod. 'Picks up the flow in the Canadian Rockies, ends up in the Missouri and "Old Misery" at Fort Peck. The colour of milky tea. Sometimes so muddy they say you can see the deer and racoon tracks float by.' He smiles, turns again, casts an eye over the sky, then out over the land. 'Over there the Missouri River flows east, empties into the Mississippi, and over here Clark Fork and Kootenai rivers flow west to the Pacific.' He looks at me. 'There were grizzlies and coyotes, wolves too. Some say they're still around...if you know where to look.

'Here, this land in between, was prairie.' He spreads his arm, palm downwards over the land from East to West '...Buffalo and wild horses roamed in their thousands where we are standing. At night the air was alive with wolf howls. Sometimes still, if you listen on a summer's night you may catch the song of a whippoorwill. I'm sure you have heard the grasshoppers. If you are lucky, you may see glow-worms shining out around you like tiny lanterns...

'On the fringes still, in the summer, you will find clusters of prairie smoke, spiderwort and horsetails, hear upland sandpipers, sedge wren and grasshopper sparrows.' He looks straight at me as though I am a child. I am drawn in by his ability to use nature to subdue my disaffection, but I can't help a feeling that he is assuming control. I resist a small-minded temptation to ask myself who is the paid help here.

'...You see...what you know, is not all there is, nor all there can be... And wherever we are, even if we remain in the land of our birth, always there is something we have lost. Partly it is out of our control, perhaps merely the passing of our youth, or the inability to see things without prejudice that being an adult has taught us. The things we can change though, we should, before regret and age makes us bitter.' Then almost as an afterthought: 'Hope is important, don't let it go.'

Suddenly, I hate myself for what I feel. I *have* learned to be prejudiced. It is as though he reads my mind.

'You're shivering. I think the snow is coming. C'mon, let's go shopping.' He climbs back into the truck and starts the engine.

Chapter Twenty-Two

America
1955

Sheila was bad again last night. Carl decided to get the doctor in. About time. She lies there, big-eyed in her little bed, smelling of stale sheets and yesterday's cabbage. When she stands, her flesh hangs, puckers like chicken skin. Her shoulders droop like an overcoat on a wire hanger. Her belly is swollen, a balloon full of water. Her entire body is metamorphosing.

The weaker she gets, the more I am drawn to her. At first, whenever I entered her room, she glared at me, as though I was circling, weighing her up. Perhaps she expected me to be glad, coming in for the kill. I'm not glad. She is the cartilage between Carl and me; a buffer zone. I want her to be well so that I can be comfortable disliking her again.

Her bedroom smells of carbolic soap and old clothes. She has a hand-mirror and brush on her dressing table, angled, diagonal and I imagine her positioning them each day, slowly, her liver spotted hands trembling in the effort, veins standing proud. There are red marks on her forearms, thin slivers of scars. When she is able, I see her passively observing her reflection in the large dressing-table mirror, touching the lines around her mouth and eyes.
Everything in her space has a dull green feeling.

There is surprising wallpaper in her room, huge swirling patterns in ochre, a red dash at the heart. Staring at that wallpaper day in, day out, would send me crazy.

I think Sheila is beginning to like me; she's grateful at least. So is Carl, he can't bear illness; says the smell makes him want to throw up, so he spends his weekends in town drinking bourbon, trying to pretend it isn't happening.

As I plump her pillows, she leans forward awkwardly, wincing from the deep-seated monster in her belly, looking sideways at me. Wisps of a smile cross her face, her eyes puzzled, like a baby trying to remember something as yet unlearnt. She leans back into the softness, emitting a soft groan of thanks.

She has begun to talk to me, in that clipped way Carl has, random things at first; my trips to town with Jake, the price of groceries, food she doesn't want to eat. Now she talks about Carl. We have strange conversations about him, as though he were dead.

'...could have been a good man, you know. I remember...' she smiles through the fog, 'he was a lovely little boy, *late fall*, you know. Unexpected. Cute in a kind of helpless way. Had a way of sucking his finger and clinging onto the soft underside of my arm like we was connected still. His Daddy would smack his rump, tell him big boys shouldn't hang around their moms so much; jealous. Carl tried to love him...'
She is building up to something.

'Got cancer. I don't need the doctor to tell me that. Mom had cancer, same age as me.'

She is dispassionate and seems resigned to her fate. I don't know what to say to her as she stares at her hands, puts them together, inspects her nails, draws in her lips and sighs.

'Can I get you anything?' I ask limply.

She looks at me again, gives a soft shake of her head; continues with what is in her mind. Her voice is very soft, breaks easily. I strain to hear.

'Nothing is ever simple. I loved his Daddy once.' Her face falls into a scowl as she chews the word over. She flashes a look at me with surprising energy. 'Obsessed with land he was, wanting more and more till there was no one left to be, you know, neighbourly with.' Her eyes search my face. 'Bought one family out; they was desperate for money during the Depression. We had nothing ourselves, what with the bank threatening to for-close on us an' all. We went without food to pay for that farm, Jed found the money somehow...I don't know. Bulldozed it before they'd even driven away. See it was the land he was after. Something got in the way of what he wanted; he just flattened it. Everyone said he was crazy—everyone else was selling, starved out. He was in a way.

'Poor Carl was born clumsy and that always seemed to set him off.' Her features loosened; jaw relaxed. 'His daddy hated me loving him. What I gave, he took away, like there was only so much love to go around. The more Carl's Daddy pushed him away from me, the more I loved him. The more I loved, the more his daddy hated.'

She looked for a reaction, sighed, smoothed the sheets over her swollen belly.

'I wanted to leave, get Carl away where he could grow normal like, but I had no-where to go. So, I stayed, and the best way I could protect my son was to ignore him. Not leaving was the biggest mistake of my life. I want you to remember that…'

'You don't need to tell me—'

'Oh, I do…I do.'

I sense that close to death, she feels some communion with me. She has talked of her mother having had a difficult life. Perhaps she is looking at me and seeing the pattern of generations being repeated, and, safe in the knowledge that life can't hurt her anymore, is beginning to empathise with the fate she knows must be mine. When her breathing becomes laboured, I find a reason to leave, let her recover. But I am driven to hear more.

Each day, I am doing extra chores around her in the hope she will open herself to me. Sometimes there is nothing. If she thinks I want to know, she clams up, plays with the corners of the bedclothes or strokes her hands, stares at the wallpaper, seeing pictures there that reflect in her face. Then she gets agitated, and it starts again. It has been going on for weeks.

The doctor brings the smell of the town with him, his coat wafting fresh air, which I breathe in hungrily, imagining a world out there; people working, travelling, laughing and generally engaged is some productive human activity that does not involve being closeted with the dying as is mine increasingly. I try to smile but he seems disgruntled to have had to come so far. All of his actions seem rehearsed. His manner suggests he is doing us a favour.

'It's not like we're not paying for it…' is all Carl says, but only to me. His face creases, makes him ugly. He looks smaller somehow.

Doctor Ryan is quite young, handsome in a tidy, buttoned up sort of way. He virtually ignores me, I realise I have become invisible.

'Of course, I can't make her come to the hospital, though if she changes her mind, be sure to let me know.' He lowers his voice, casts an eye toward the bed. 'I'm leaving you some pain relief. She'll need it. When it gets worse you contact me, I can give you something stronger. You know she's dying, I assume?' He looks up briefly at Carl. 'Just try to keep her comfortable, there's nothing to be done.' He shuffles the papers into his bag, leaves the medication on the dressing table, pulls his coat about him, buttoning out our world.

'Good day to you.'

I resist the urge to weep. I hear again the words: *you know she's dying, I assume*, as though there was nothing unusual in that. We know it already of course, but just to hear it said aloud so casually is shocking. I realise that over the weeks of tending to her, I have begun to care. I also have the creeping realisation that without Sheila, there is just Carl and me.

'What the heck do they know?' Sheila said when I tried to persuade her to take the doctor's advice and go into hospital. 'People go to these places in the hope they'll be looked after, cured even. Then they get stuck in a bed and ignored. Folks die anyway. Might as well be here. I'll be like my Ma, just accept my fate. I've stayed here all these years I'm not leaving now. If it's my time, so be it.'

Part of me admires her; she scares me too.

I have brought her soup; she has barely eaten since the doctor came two days ago. As I come around the bed to her side, I sense that she has been waiting for me. I slide onto the bed, pick up her limp cold hand between both of mine.

'Soup, Sheila. Can you face it?'

'I need to talk to you.' There is a translucence in her skin. Her eyes are bright. The medication perhaps. 'I want to say…I need to say…sorry. Sorry Alice.' It is the first time she has said this. She clears her throat. I struggle to hear her. 'I know you tried hard with Carl. I know. I didn't make it any easier for you and I'm sorry for that. I guess part of me thought I'd earned him for myself when his father died. Always had to share him, you know? Then he came home from Europe with an *Overcomer*.'

She makes a small sound, an ironic laugh, attempts to ease herself up into a sitting position, winces despite my help and lies back exhausted with the effort. 'But it wasn't only that. The little I knew of Carl's friendships here, before you met him, was that…well, he didn't treat women very well. If you must know, he kind of treated them like something useful when he needed them. Know what I'm saying?'

I nod, uncomfortable. I don't want to hear this.

'Anyways, I knew he had problems. Truth is, I don't think he knows how to love. How should he? Only how to own, to possess, like his Daddy.'

She stops, swallows, waits.

'Sheila…Don't fret, please. Look I'm sure it's not your fault. What you are saying explains a lot, but people have choices too, they can change.' I am trying to let her die easily, but I don't mean what I am saying. It is her fault and her stupid husband. Why didn't she leave? I would have. Then I realise that I have not left either and I ponder this fact.

It is as though life, depending on with whom you share it, can warp you, twist you so out of shape that your younger self would not recognise the person you have become. I shudder in the sure knowledge that the Ali that left England nine years ago is not the Ali that now walks the cusp of death with Sheila, and is, in fact, half dead herself.

'You must rest now, you're too tired for this,' I say, easing myself away, feeling suddenly almost too heavy to move.

'No, no, don't go, please…' I move back to her, lean in as she beckons me closer, put my ear close to her mouth. She whispers: 'Alice…I have some money, quite a lot. Carl got the inheritance from his daddy, such as it was, but this, I want you to have it.'

She is very weak, difficult to understand. I feel impelled to do as she asks.

'Here, under the bedside table. Get it. Take it now please.' I lift the table and find a brown paper bag with two neatly folded rolls of money inside, each with a red rubber band around it. I have no idea how much is there. 'Don't argue. Put it in your pocket now. Hide it. Somewhere very safe.

'I need to know that if you decide to go, it won't be lack of money that stops you. You're young, don't bring a child into this. Go while you can. Carl will never let you go willingly, you know that, but there are ways… Promise me you'll keep the money for that purpose, and don't ever tell Carl what I have done. I love him and I'm doing this for him too. Life would be easier for him alone; he just doesn't know it.'

I hesitate, shocked by her plans for me, by her concern, actively plotting against the son she adores.

'Promise me…now.'

'I promise. I do…Thank you, Sheila…It's a shame you and I—'

'Don't say it. Please don't say it. Don't talk of waste. My whole life is about waste. A person could go mad just thinking about it.'

Six days later Sheila has drifted into coma. Despite increased medication from Doctor Ryan, her pain has been intense. It is a relief to see her relatively peaceful, though I fear she still feels it, for when I attempt to turn her, she stiffens, her hands claw at the air, and when her eyes flicker in puzzlement, her face crumples as though she knows she is about to die.

I decide to leave her still but stay with her, sitting, vacant, my hand resting over hers. Or standing at her window, feeling the immensity of the land, the sky, seeing the barn door swaying slightly against its hinges, hearing the soft call of the cattle, all the while the sweet and sickly scent of death in my nostrils. But all is overlaid with sights and sounds of my own life and what I have done with this precious gift. I find myself praying for the first time in years. I pray for Sheila's painless deliverance. I pray also for mine.

When I turn back to her, I whisper an endearment, tender and kind, knowing it may be the last thing she ever hears, and I watch her face crease with some echo of understanding. Occasionally, she squeezes my hand, even opens her eyes for a moment before returning to her dark world.

Her breathing becomes so slow that I am uncertain exactly when the moment arrives. I shout for Carl when I am sure. He comes into the room, forcing each step. By her bed he picks up her hand, drops his head, cannot look at her face. He looks so large beside her wasted body. I watch him as he tries to think of something suitable to say. Suddenly, blood, bright and thick, oozes from her nose as if from a deep, internal wound. He runs outside, slamming the door behind him.

Chapter Twenty-Three

America
1956

Decorating Sheila's room has given me a project. It can't sit like a shrine but Carl refuses to go in there; thinks it's haunted, which is weird considering he doesn't *believe*. That, however, has given me an idea.

'I want my own room, that's all. We have the space now. I can make it my studio, paint in there.'

'It's just another nail, isn't it? In my goddamn coffin. You want it so you don't have to share with me. Right?'

Right. If it meant no sex, I would sleep in the barn. Better company.

'Let's decorate anyway, then decide.'

The old wallpaper is glued on. I ask Carl if he can help. When he refuses, as I knew he would, I ask whether anyone could help, someone cheap; I am careful to make it look like his idea. He shrugs.

'I suppose Jake could help out. Do what you like, you will anyhow.'

Buying paint and fabric reminds me how I felt when I decorated the nursery. Now I am planning something altogether different. I feel a sense of liberation in this small act. One step.

Jake is surprised on our monthly visit to town when I buy two scrapers and say one is for him. We laugh at what feels like conspiracy. I shall paint the room pale blue and have white curtains with blue fishes. Then I can imagine I am near the sea. I shall fix a bolt on the door.

Strangely, I miss Sheila. It was an odd sort of friendship at the end, but my only one, apart from Jake. Her unselfish act of generosity—not just the money but her compassion—moved me. I realise I have been unfair to her, mirroring her coldness with reciprocation, instead of understanding. And now my relationship with Carl is shown up for what it is. He wants me for what I can give him, and because he would die rather than admit he made a mistake by marrying me. Deep in him, I know he wants things to be as they were in England, but he can't bring himself to be kind; there is no generosity in him. It is as though he would be giving in, showing weakness.

No matter. I wouldn't relent now; there is no generosity in me either. With Carl, there is no understanding.

What I don't give him, he takes. After Sheila died, he told me I was a hypocrite for grieving. I told him someone had to, and to mind his own business.

'Mind your goddamned tongue,' was his response before walking away, stopping, thinking better of it, then turning on his heel and walking back to pull back my head by my hair and striking me hard across the head. I fell against the dresser and blood started to dribble from my forehead. He pushed me to the floor where I lay petrified, knowing what he would do to me but unable to move.

'You fucking bitch. You think you got the monopoly on suffering. You didn't give a damn about my mother. You…' he lifted his leg and kicked me in the belly, '…fucking…' then again on my legs, '…bitch.'

As I lay on the floor screaming, cowering, blood slowly pooling around my head, I saw with terrified fascination how he seemed to experience a kind of frantic energy from the violence he inflicts, as though the very act of lashing out at me was exhilarating for him. There is never any knowing how far he will go; each beating being just a little worse than the last until I begin to see where it will all end.

On that occasion, he looked at me with a kind of loathing, but behind the fury, there was something else. Need? I *knew* he wanted to hold me, make it better. He was grieving too, not just for his mother, but for his lost childhood, the man he could have been, for us, for the life we should have had. One sign from me, a cry for help, some show of vulnerability, some recognition of his power over me and he would have fallen to his knees begging forgiveness. But I wouldn't give him that.

So he pushed to see how far he had to go to control me. When he was finished, I could not move, my heart pounding so hard I thought it would burst. The pain in my legs was intense and I just lay there trying to breathe and praying to the God of my childhood for it to stop.

He wouldn't take me to hospital, questions would be asked. Fixed me up himself, with bandage and animal liniment. Like one of his cows. I know he hates himself. The cut on my forehead has grown into a red and ugly scar and the bruises on my legs, first black, then purple and yellow, lasted for weeks. I have pain still when I walk.

I communicate with him when I need something; otherwise, I stay out of his way, inhabit a different world; live in my head and in my journal. I include in it all the detail of *his* life: childhood, war years, our marriage. He is part of this too—how life should not be lived. If he ever found it, I'd be dead.

I still write home, but now I tell them the truth, plead with them to write and tell me what to do; tell me how I can contact them. I tell them I could die here, and no one would ever know. I beg them.

Sheila didn't have a funeral, Carl said there was no point; no one would come. There were just a few words from a minister over her grave. I don't know what the purpose of her life was, but she has given me something I couldn't have had without her: hope. Every night as I pray to the God that has deserted me, I thank her for that.

Jake is bemused by the whole idea of wallpaper. He says it's like trying to cover the cracks in a life. I tell him that that is exactly what it is. He is very good though, once he knows what to do. Thorough. I like being in the house with him. There is warmth around him. He asks me about the funny song I sing to myself as I paint: *I don't want to play in your yard, I don't like you anymore*...Says he won't take it personally.

He conveys so much without speaking. He is being paid but I know he would help me for nothing. Carl stays out of our way; he is uncomfortable with Jake. When he does see him, he talks loudly, as though Jake is deaf. Jake says that Carl is a young spirit with much to learn, that he has not learned enough from his childhood. I say, I think he is this way *because* of his childhood.

He nods his head from side to side, his way of disagreeing, says that we all choose the life we have, to learn from, so that we can be better in the next. I smile. He said once that *I* am an old spirit of the warrior type, which made me laugh, under the circumstances. When I ask him to tell me again what kind of spirit I am, he says one that is dripping paint all over the floor. I don't understand some of the things he says, but I like to hear them. I think he is the only person I have ever met who is comfortable with himself.

'I haven't told you about Linda,' he says suddenly, out of nothing. His back is turned, his head tilted to one side. He is painting an architrave very carefully.

'Linda?'

'My wife…Of course, that wasn't her tribal name.' He pauses, my jaw drops. 'She was an interesting woman. You would have liked her.' He bites his lip, wipes a smudge of paint with a rag. 'You would have laughed together.' He looks over to me, smiles, nodding.

Jake has always sidestepped questions about his personal life. I stopped asking a long while ago. He dips his brush back into the paint-pot, resumes his careful work.

'Would have? Where is she now?'

'She died in a fire with our young son over twenty years ago. She was the same age as you are now. Suspected arson, no one was ever charged. I should have been with them, but I was out getting drunk somewhere, it was the time of the Depression, there was no work, no anything… It wasn't my time.'

There are some moments before I can speak.

'You never told me.'

'No…It is all right. Don't be sad.' He continues painting, his brow crumpled in concentration. 'It was a long time ago. I don't drink now.'

I stand in disbelief. He glances at me, the little radio on the floor adding a tinny accompaniment of *The Platter's Great Pretender* that seems to undermine the seriousness of what Jake has just said. I walk over and turn it off.

'You must understand, they chose their lives before they were born. It was hard at first for me. Life was…empty.' He stops for a moment, stone-still, looks down at the floor, remembers, smiles. 'My wife was a feisty woman; she was the boss.'

He chuckles aloud as a shadow of memory crosses him. 'She believed that when someone died, they would come back to their loved ones at significant moments in their lives, sometimes leave a white feather as a mark of their presence. She made me a better person, more honest.'

I wonder what he means exactly by this but say nothing.

'My son was strong, a very old spirit. He had big hands; he would have been good at painting.' He spreads out a hand and looks at it, through it, shrugs with an intake of breath, then wipes the surplus paint from his brush on a rag and continues his work.

I look from side to side. 'I don't understand. Why didn't you tell me? I thought… how can you think it's all right to have lost them?'

'I haven't really spoken of my family since they died…You can't share loss; it is like being born and dying, something you do alone.' He glances sideways at me, believing I will understand. I do. 'I blamed myself. I was not a good person then, they deserved better. When I say it is all right, I mean for them. There was purpose in what happened. This life is temporary.'

He turns and looks at me with raised eyebrows, throwing out a challenge. 'In many ways I shall be glad when mine is over and we meet again. I have changed; I think they will be glad. All our lives are preparation for what is to follow. The body is merely a shell. The space we inhabit, the things we collect around us are just comforters, meaningless. Their spirits are safe. They have moved on.'

There are echoes of my religion, what I left in England. When I tell him so, he nods his head from side to side, says Christians have become tangled; have made everything too complicated when it should be simple, too fixed when all things are fluid.

'They believe that the way to paradise must be hard—sackcloth and ashes. That you must enter it by a narrow gate. But how can we recognise the way to go if we close off our field of vision? Farm horses wear blinkers to prevent them seeing things that may scare or distract them; the farmer needs the horse to obey and plough the furrow straight. He is forcing the horse into *his* idea of how he should be. Do you see? The horse becomes broken, his spirit sapped in his service to a master that needs to control him. A wild horse though is a mighty beast. He will protect his herd and live and die a noble creature. Besides', he says, 'Christians do not value women enough.'

When I ask him what religion he belongs to, he smiles, inhales sharply, tosses back his head.

'Look at the compartments humans create for themselves...Think about the hundreds of religions people connect themselves to. Think of the wars fought in the name of their Gods.' He pauses. 'There is only one, and it is all around you, we're all part of it. Earth is part of it, and she has a wide perspective. *She* is my teacher...I take my inspiration from the universe,' he adds casually as though we are discussing what to have for dinner, 'not from some organisation that has forgotten why it is there, who tells me where I should pray, whom I should love, how I should live. True religion is a thing that blows across the heart, carried on the wind.'

'Have you ever found any white feathers, Jake, at significant moments?'

'Many.'

One day I tell Jake that Carl hits me.

'I know this,' he replies.

'You know?'

'If you want, I can help you.'

'How?'

'If you want to be helped, you can be. It depends on you.'

'What do you mean?'

'Nothing is pre-destined. We are offered routes all the way through our lives: choices. If you stay here, it is because you are choosing to, for whatever reason, or because you are afraid. It's possible that you have something to learn here…I don't know. But if you decide to go, you *do* have the strength inside you, we all do, and I can help you. You know, I think it is perhaps the reason we met.'

'You say that nothing is pre-destined, yet you think we were meant to meet?'

'Destiny is a strange word, don't you think? Paradoxical. Life is not random. By the very people we are, certain decisions will be shaped in advance, but we still have freedom within that. It is likely that I am offered to you as a route, which you may choose not to take, just as you are offered to me for some reason.'

'What reason?'

'I don't know, it isn't clear yet. Redemption?' I am confused.

'You think I could really get away?'

'You need to stop thinking of yourself as trapped. Who knows, it may be better for Carl if you left, whether he knows it or not…Follow Carl's habits. Look for weaknesses, there must be gaps in the day when you can organise yourself. Know that you *can* go if you choose to. It is this knowledge and the absence of fear that will free you. You will also need money. Enough to get you home.'

'I have money.'

'Good. That's good…then you can begin to make plans.'

'You make it sound easy, but it isn't. I tried before.'

'The fact you have tried before means nothing. Look at a wasp trapped in a jar. It will never cease trying to find a way out until it is dead. If the jar holder removes the lid for a moment the wasp is out. There is only one reason why the wasp would stay and that is if there is something in the jar that he wants.

'Of course, the wasp has no concept of time, he cannot know that if he does not leave in that moment when the lid is off, he may not have another chance in the future. All that matters to the wasp is the immediate need, in his case hunger. But you are not a wasp, you can prioritise, choose which is more important, your security, such as it is, or your freedom.

'Fear is a funny thing, sometimes we're not aware of it, but we can hold it inside us until it eats away our strength and then something will always fill the void: self-doubt, or worse self-hatred. This is something I know about.' He closes his eyes for a moment, then looks at me directly. 'Or we blame others for our problems; merely hold on to the comfort of not having to act, not having to be brave. Like anything else, if you nurture fear, it will grow. If you hold up a mirror to yourself, fear is what will come back at you. If you really wanted to leave you would have tried again and again until you succeeded, so either you had no real resolve or you allowed fear to dictate your actions.'

There is something evangelical in his manner, as though he has been where I am.

'You must decide not to be afraid. Be like a child without prejudice; receive the courage that is there for you with an open hand. Learn a new skill: not to be afraid. Think of it. Has fear stopped the hurt or pain? Courage is a weapon you can learn to use. So…' He could almost be reading from a book, preaching from a pulpit. I want more.

'Next time we go to town, we can talk about what ideas we have. Whether you act on it, is up to you. Just remember, there is a way out of every dark mist…'

Gradually, Sheila's room is transformed. Its dark ochre is replaced with a light airiness. I move the furniture so that the bed faces the window and I can look out to the sky, the wheat, ready for harvest. I turn the mattress, shake and beat the rug outside till dust-clouds fill the air. I place photos of my family on the dressing table; Carl would not have them in our bedroom, said they made me homesick. I move in my easel. The light is good, perhaps I shall begin painting again. And a small table where I can write, in secret, when Carl is away.

Afterwards, Jake and I sit on the floor drinking lemonade and admiring our work, talking of nothing, the little radio warbling Fats Domino's *Blueberry Hill* in the background. The smell of fresh wallpaper and new paint lifts me.

'So, you've finished?' Carl has crept in, overheard our conversation, hoping for something he could gnaw at. Jake gets up, spilling his drink.

'Mr McCullough.' He looks up at Carl, like a defiant pet dog caught on the sofa.

'Very cosy, I must say.' Carl has a hard bite in his voice.

'Yes. It's nice, isn't it.' I know the signs. 'Much brighter.'

'You should go into the decorating business.' He is snide; his eyes run over the bed, the photos.

'I think you're done here, Jake. If you wait outside, I'll pay you.'

Jake leaves the room without looking at me, though he doesn't rush. His head is high, back straight. 'Open the windows, Alice, get rid of that Indian smell.'

Two weeks later, Jake and I sit in town drinking endless coffees, until I am shaky with caffeine and the idea of going home to England.

'Keep a mental diary. Don't write anything down. Times. Dates. If he tells you he's going to town for the night, encourage him, tell him he needs a break, tell him to go out and enjoy himself. Try to establish a relationship, at least superficially. The thing is, get him to trust you. Act as though you care…and allow him to be kind. He needs to believe that you are content, or are becoming so, then he will relax his guard. Become his ally.'

'I see what you're saying, but it's not that easy. If I act this way, he'll—' I stop.

'…want…more?' He is nodding.

'Well…yes.'

'Men are simple creatures. You know yourself how a woman can get a man to do what she wants.'

'And you are suggesting I do this?'

'I am not suggesting that you do what you cannot, but you are going into battle. You are a warrior; you must use what weapons you have.'

I am speechless.

'I shall find out details for you. Trains, ships, cost and so on. Once you make the decision, you are on your way. I didn't say it would be easy, but it will be worth it. All of these things have always been there for you, I am merely pointing them out.'

We drive back in silence. I stare out of the window, see the landscape without me in it; more complete somehow, like a tear that has been repaired, a scar healed. I imagine the voyage back, the movement of the sea, the homecoming, see faces trapped in time. I do not think about what will happen in between. I am a soldier at *Agincourt* before the battle, thinking only about the future.

Chapter Twenty-Four

America
1957

I like my new bedroom. Six months on, I derive pleasure, still, out of closing the door at night. I have my own transistor radio and listen to *Moondog* without Carl telling me to *switch off that trash*. I have taken to wearing talc and even scent occasionally, now that being attractive is not the threat that it was. I got my hair cut last time I went to town, had a shampoo and set. Jake laughed when he came to pick me up. It wasn't the reaction I expected; said I looked like Elizabeth Taylor. When I got home, Carl asked me why I was tarting myself up. I told him I wanted to look nice for him. He growled.

'It's wasted on that fucking native anyway.' I bit my lip and said nothing.

I told Carl I need something outdoors to occupy me, did he have any suggestions. Perhaps I could help him with the lighter farm work. I am following Jake's advice, letting Carl think I am putting effort into this shared life. After he stopped laughing, he said he would think about it.

He has given me a corner of the yard to plant vegetables, flowers, whatever. A scrubby piece of ground but protected from the sun. I know he is patronising me, waiting to see me fail. I have never gardened, so on one of my trips to town, I made my first sally to the fusty corner of the hardware store, which passes for a library, and took out a book entitled *Grow Your Own*. It is so old the pages are brown and flaky, but it'll do. As I went towards the counter to pay for it, a large-bellied man in farm clothes fingering a pitchfork stared sideways at me.

'You're a bitty thing for such a big book...' I think he was being friendly. I've forgotten the signs.

I have dug over the plot, fertilised the soil with rotted manure from the barn and planted seeds. I just have to wait now. I can't help but see a parallel between my fumbling efforts in gardening and my labours with Carl. Stony soil.

When Jake speaks to me of train connections and sailing dates, of projecting myself forward, I become impatient. I need Carl to trust me enough to stop watching my every move, to open the lid on the jar just long enough for me to fly out. I could go on one of my trips to town and not come back, but he clock-watches me and knowing there are few ways of leaving, I fear he would find me before I reached the coast. Jake has suggested that when the time comes, I could ask Carl permission to go to the city and stay overnight to enjoy the sights. If I ask him now, he will never believe that I would want to do this, so I must start showing interest in an excursion, let the idea settle.

I have started baking again, another ploy. I stopped after Sheila became ill, there seemed no point. I know Carl is partial to Pecan Pie and so every time I go to town, I buy pecans. Last time, as he ate, he stared unblinking at me through his eyebrows.

'You up to something?'

'What do you mean? Don't you like it?'

'It's fine. What is it you want, Alice? C'mon now, you're acting suspicious.'

'Well…there is something…'

'I knew it. Spit it out, why don't you.'

I seized my opportunity; thought on my feet.

'How long have I been here, Carl? Here in America.'

'I dunno, years.'

'I've been here close on eleven years.'

'Yes…so?' He was scraping his bowl to get the last of the ice cream. The noise jangled my nerves. I felt my breathing shorten.

'I'm thirty-three years old and I've never been to the city except the day we came through it when I first arrived here.'

'City's a long way, what do you expect? I don't go either. Why would you want to?'

'Don't you see, I…I need a change, see the sights, go to see a show maybe.'

'You want me to take you to the city? Is that what you're fishing for? All dressed up and nowhere to go?' There was ice cream on his chin. A sneer played on his upper lip.

'I know you're busy. I could go alone…?'

'Oh no. Do you really think I'm that stupid?' He banged down his spoon, got up, almost threw the bowl into the sink. I was kicking myself; too soon.

'Of course, I'd rather go *with* you, be nice to have company, but I knew you wouldn't consider it.' I back-tracked wildly.

'How do you know what I would or wouldn't consider? I sure as hell wouldn't let you go on your own.' His fingers were white. His eyes had that wild look.

'Would you take me then? It might be like old times.' I gritted my teeth. Stood up, moved close to him, face to face. Tried to look sincere. If he were going to strike, it would be then. I braced myself.

He stood for a moment shaking his head. Scratched the side of his face, looked perplexed.

'What are you saying? You can't bear me near you, but you want me to take you sightseeing, *like old times*,' he mimicked. 'What game are you playing, Alice?'

'I just thought it was about time we did something together. You never know, it might improve things.' I felt sick.

'It's gonna take a lot more than a trip to the city.' He was placated. Shocked but placated. 'I'll think about it.'

I had sown a seed, now all I had to do was water it.

A week later there was a knock on my bedroom door just as I was dozing off. I pretended to be asleep. He knocked again then walked in, sat on the edge of the bed.

'You awake? Alice?' I feigned sleepiness. 'I was thinking…a trip to town isn't such a bad idea. Could do with a change myself. We could make a weekend of it; get old Jake to help Wayne out on the farm. Have a vacation like.' I stared through half open eyes, knowing what was coming. 'Like old times you said…'

'Yes,' I whispered weakly.

'Mmm. Mind if I cuddle in with you? See if we can remember what it was like?'

This was the moment. I told myself if I failed now, I might as well forget the whole thing.

'No. Come in. I've been waiting for you.'

That was all it took. A tiny encouragement and Carl was revving like a tractor engine. He pulled up my nightie till it covered my face. I left it there. It was easier for both of us if we didn't have to look. I tried to fantasise, imagine pleasure. A handsome stranger, a chance encounter. I surprised myself that I almost managed it. When it was over, he did not get up to wash as he always did, nor did he turn his back. He lay on his side staring at me, his arm draped around my middle. I was sweating nausea and guilt.

The next day, as I tended my patch in the yard, I saw scores of tender green shoots pushing up awkwardly, higgledy-piggledy, from the earth. I think I felt joy.

Chapter Twenty-Five

America
1958

We've grown into established patterns, habits. Despite my fawning, thin-lipped smiles, visits to my room in the dead of night, Carl and I keep slipping back to mutual distrust. Point scoring. Always there is a lack of generosity between us, a sense of my waiting for things to get better without actually orchestrating change.

Each time I succeed in snaring his belief in my sincerity, some small act will shake it. The way I look at him over dinner, off-guard, hawk-cold.

'Hell Alice, I can see right through you. You're like a fucking vulture waiting to pick my bones.'

My responses to his *lovemaking*.

'For Chrissake…Where the hell are you?'

Even the way I dress.

'Who do you wear that for? Sure as hell ain't me.' And always a look that is both hopeful and scathing, a child that wants its own way, but more, just wants to be held.

Then I snap.

'Can't I do anything right? What does it take to get you to be normal? I'm trying to make an effort. I don't know why I bother.'

'Is that what you're doing? Bothering? Nice of you, I'm sure. Jeez, I'd hate to see you when you weren't.'

I cannot imagine Carl *working* with anyone. He thinks that *I* am the problem: I am *spoiled, superior, critical …a fucked up English rose: thorny, past its best.*

When I tell Jake, he responds, after an indecent pause, 'we are all of us flawed', which annoys me, makes me question who the hell is *he* to judge? And I feel like packing in the whole idea.

'I don't know what you are, Alice, except that you're human. He isn't your judge, nor am I. And you're a harsh one. You don't deserve punishment, but some deep guilt you carry like a stone on your back has caused you to offer yourself up like a sacrifice. One day there will be nothing left. You will have been consumed, and he will still be hungry. You will have made no difference. You must stop going back to the beginning every time it goes wrong.' And I relent.

But now I have a plan. I have begun to realise that each pliant act, each submission adds up. I am wearing him down. Slowly. Two steps forward, one back. Every weakness I portray gives me a little more control, because I am doing it consciously. Every time I think of his size, his strength, Jake reminds me that the wings of a bird are light, delicate, easily crushed. Put to flight they have immense power, able to cross continents. And, despite my impatience, Carl *is* becoming more relaxed. The rocks beneath his feet are shifting.

He wants it to be true, wants me to love him as he imagines he once loved me and I've discovered that I *can* pretend, am, in a way, beginning to enjoy my emerging power. I can laugh at his jokes, smile in an affectionate way when he tries to be kind, take his hand as though to dance when *Peggy Sue, Kisses Sweeter than Wine* or some such song comes on the radio, which he will shake off as though I am being silly, but smile despite himself. I am the buzzard hanging in the still air, circling, biding my time.

I have taken out my old red dress. I have not worn it yet, but it hangs there for when I am ready.

*

We speak little all the way to the city, which is fine, almost enjoyable. We listen to the radio; at least I do. I remember how it feels, wanting to dance. Carl, hands on the wheel, stares fish-eyed, unblinking at the road, his jaw jutting forward. I look at him in profile; see a likeness with the face on the radio: ...*well I bless my soul, what's wrong with me? I'm itching like a man on a fuzzy tree...I'm in love...I'm all shook up...* I turn up the volume.

When we get there, at a loss how to spend our time, we queue for tickets for whatever has seats for the following evening. There is a melodrama on at the main Victoria Theatre: a woman forced into prostitution by a husband who deserted her for another, left her and her children penniless. *Superb* says the programme. *Brilliant portrayal of a woman's fight back to respectability.* Not exactly Carl's cup of tea.

Muffled with scarves, we trot along the frost-hard streets, and, for some reason, perhaps because I am finally doing what normal people do, I suddenly think of dear Lily from Middleton. Imagine her now living in a leafy suburb out of town going to lots of plays in New York. Shopping in Bloomingdales or Saks, dressing like Jackie Kennedy. She will have changed, dyed her hair back to its natural colour, have opinions, chair women's society meetings, wear low heeled shoes. Go to church. Become American.

Every time I watch *I Love Lucy* on the television set that Carl bought last spring, I see Lily; realise how much I have missed her. Despite all my letters, she never wrote.

Carl is coiled tight as a spring. Nibbles at thick farm fingers, plays with his hair in shop windows assuming his narrow-eyed James Dean expression, shuffling me sideways whenever a man comes too close. Whatever we do, he looks around, runs his hand over his jaw, weighs up what better way he might spend his time and I realise with a peculiar wry sadness that Carl does not know what to do. In the big city, he is nobody and he knows it.

Walking around the city blocks, I scan the billboard hoardings for any opportunity to return at some future date; something advertised, an exhibition that Carl would hate, or a course in something innocuous. It would have to be his idea, something that he would think would make me happy; be more content with him.

I surprise myself that I find him embarrassing whenever we are around people. I thought I would no longer care. His trousers are all too short, I hadn't noticed. His green ones make him look simple, a bumpkin. His tartans, ridiculous. White shoes…Better in his farm clothes. But then I look at myself and compare the way I am dressed alongside women wearing suits with big buttons, stilettos and the bobbed hair that they seem to favour now. We are a pair trapped in time and look so much older than we are.

But it isn't just clothes. Carl's behaviour is awkward and discomforted here is the city. He coughs up and spits on the sidewalk. Grunts when people are polite, glares as though I am stupid when I hold a door open or pass the time of day with a stranger. He seemed so gentlemanly in England all those years ago, or did he? Perhaps I just chose not to see it. I can't remember anyhow.

And he talks too loudly; I feel eyes burning into my spine. I want to shush him, tell him *really*, folks aren't interested in our conversation. I think he believes that somehow his slow farm drawl may impress them.

I watch as he scratches the inside of his ear with a toothpick while we have dinner in a restaurant, his elbow lifted high into the air, his face contorted in concentration, one side of his top lip curled. This small act makes pink spots on my cheeks and neck. Makes me want to tell everyone *I don't love him, I know he's a buffoon, I shall be leaving him soon*…but why do I care? They don't. At the end of the meal, he pulls his chair close to mine, hangs his arm about my neck like a loose rope. Orders more beer. I smile flatly, feel my hairline prickle.

I imagine the nights will be the worst. *City Slicker Motel* lies. It is a long, thin, drab sort of place, outside the city. No bedside lamps to create the lie of homeliness, just a glaring bulb in the centre of the square cardboard-like box, under an unforgiving shade that creates none. The tap water runs river brown and lukewarm. There is a smell of last year's tobacco, spilt beer, stale clothes. We are tired; have been up since before dawn, driven for six hours, and have trailed around the streets being a couple, trying to be breezy. Still, I am surprised when, after showering, Carl gets into the sagging too-small bed, turns his back and falls into a heavy sleep. I relax, grateful, and sleep too.

Tonight, the second night, after the theatre, isn't so good. He watched the play with both our eyes, its ladles of sentiment stirred up with dollops of female retribution. Men were cads. It was melodrama, but Carl drank in the meaning I would take from it, brewed strong and thick.

'What is it with women these days? They only happy if they make a guy look dumb? Plays like that just cause trouble.'

I agree. Part of the game. Still, he has to scrape away at the man thing once back in our room. It's the way he is, once he has an idea in his head, he won't let go, shakes it like an angry dog, taunting, frenzied. It isn't me he's with, but the sassy actress who has it coming, who needs a lesson; one he can give. Heavy, he forces his mouth on me, his charcoal breath suffocating as he tries to ignite what *every woman* has inside her. Giving what that actress clearly wasn't getting: a *good doing*.

When I eventually sink into a bruised sleep, I find Walter. In my dream he lays me down very gently on the grass and carefully removes my clothes—like a surgeon entering a body, never looking at my face, just concentrating. Then the grass becomes hard and elevated; an altar in a church, around it statues of the Virgin Mary, Saint Jude holding a tiny infant. Hanging directly above me like the sword of Damocles, a crucified Christ swings precariously on large heavy chains. There is a priest in white vestments, a tall dark figure watching, and a nun, whose rosary beads rattle against the marble altar as she lights candles around me. Having delivered me up, Walter then turns away, his heels striking the stone floor while the priest begins: *We are gathered here in the sight of God...*

At breakfast Carl gleams, his face soap-shiny, almost happy.
'You okay?' He scoops the yoke from his plate with a pancake.
'The eggs are good.' I smile.
There is a short silence.
'Sorry about...it wasn't...' He shakes his head, gives a look like a question, his face pasted with remorse.
'Don't. Don't say it. It's fine really.' I butter my toast, sip my tea, cough.
Another silence.
He drinks some coffee, gulps and I watch his throat move, hear its awkward swallow, as though he is forcing it. He smiles an old smile and nods slightly. He is glad to be going home.
'Enjoyed the bright lights?'
This is my chance; it is the right mood.
'Oh yes,' I give a young blameless smile, tilt my head to one side. 'I'm happy to go home now.'
'Good,' he says in a rising cadence, staring at my eyes, a trace of a frown pushing at his eyebrows as he tries to decipher duplicity. 'That's good, Alice.'
It is the first time he has used my name in months. It is a sign.
'I'd like to come back, not yet...in a couple of months or so, you know. Wouldn't you?' I look him straight in the eye, with as much fondness as I can muster.
'Dunno. It's not easy leaving the farm. Don't trust anyone else. We'll see. Let me think about it.'
I want to push it, but back off. I am learning. We still have the morning before we set off home. Once at Home Farm, it will be forgotten, replaced by familiar distrust.
'Never mind. Sometime, maybe.' Two steps forward...
Then he says it.
'*You* could...if you like. Can't think what you'd do here alone, but if it makes you happy...?' His voice was soft, yielding, but happy to be in control.
'Oh, I don't know, I'll think about it. It's not important.' I mustn't appear keen, the brakes will slam.

'Yeh, think on it. You could get the Friday Greyhound from The Cross. Take you all the way…if you wanted?'

'Mmm. We'll see.' I wipe my mouth with my napkin, put my knife and fork together, can't stop an accusing glance at his own, spread-eagled across the plate. He doesn't notice.

A smear of disappointment rubs over his face that I haven't somehow been more grateful. I have to act before it becomes anger.

'If there was something constructive I could do while I was here, then perhaps…What do you think?'

'Well now…you're getting green fingers, you could do some sort of course at the college, though what city folk know about growing stuff you could fit on a dime…' I laugh as though he's made a good joke. He laughs too.

'Thanks *love*,' I push out the word, worry it is too much. 'It sounds good. I'll look into it.'

And that is it, easy as pie. Carl even makes a detour around the city for me to pick up information from the college. It is all *his* idea. The prospectus I get gives us something to talk about on the way home.

'How about electrical engineering?' I joke as I leaf through the tome of information.

'You? You'd never figure the goddamned equipment, let alone do anything with it.'

'I'll have you know I did plenty of engineering on the Lancaster bombers during the war.'

'Only because there were no men around to do it.'

'Which proves that we *can* do it if we're given a chance.'

'So, you want to be an electrical engineer?'

'No. What made you think that?'

He laughs, like none of the years have happened. I am almost happy. We finally settle on a course entitled *Horticulture for beginners*.

'Are you sure it isn't too long?' My heart is racing with the prospect of a whole week to get away before he realises I have gone.

'Can't say I like it. You'll have to fix up some meals for me to have while you're gone. Might give you chance to miss me.' He looks over, a half-smile flitting around his mouth, enjoying the newfound power of generosity. His head bobs to the Everly Brothers singing *Bye Bye Love*…on the radio.

'It says here the courses begin next month. The horticulture one is on the…where is it…25 January. Is that too soon? There's bound to be another later—'

'Hell no. Do it if you want. Give you an interest. You could grow us a garden come the summer. Make Home Farm the prettiest around.' He is on a roll.

I feel a grin creep up over my mouth and cheeks. Feeling transparent, I stare out over the undulating acres, the pink spreading up from my neck like oil on water.

Chapter Twenty-Six

America
1959

I pull my coat about me till I am thin with it. Move my arms around my waist like a cross-over belt. See my white face and dark body reflected in a bus window as it glides slowly past coughing grey clouds of exhaust smoke into the sunless white of a winter city morning. My own misty breath freezes in the pale air. I restrain a nervous smile, prevent it spreading out of control like spilt milk. I have creatures in my belly fluttering like moths around a bright light, I am happy-sick with them.

It is bone-cold but I prefer to stand outside the bus station in the open. Standing against the West entrance I am protected from the wind's knife-sharp gusts; sheltered from the tiny flecks of snow that float upward and dither uncertainly, mesmerising.

Jake will be here when he can; there are things he has to sort out. Between ten and eleven, he estimated. I must meet him in the coffee shop across the street, half a block from the depot, where he will hand over all the travel documents he has kindly arranged for me.

I see it clearly: couples and women talking, children in the window nursing steaming mugs in gloved hands watching the world through a flurry of racing and whirling snow eddies. But there's a good view from here, I almost enjoy the comings and goings. I'll go in if he's late. Not yet. The cold produces a kind of dreamy euphoria in me, I enjoy imagining how it will be when I get home, begin remembering how it was: winter in Yorkshire. I slip into daydreams of my homeland, revisiting places I haven't been, even in my head, for years...

I picture the snow settling on the moors behind Slack Bottom, the top of Widdop Road where the Baptist Chapel sits at the fork. The dry-stone walls are peaked with it. Solitary footprints lead up Horsehold, to our door, where a green wreath of holly, plucked from the garden, hangs, thick with berries, weighted by childish decorations made with dough, secured by flower wire; decorations dragged out each year to show me where my life has been. The apple tree branches are ridged in white, bare except for a few crinkled apples that hang stubbornly, edible baubles for robins to feast on…

Snow is different here. There are no hills to halt the horizontal wind, ice-flecked and cruel, straight from Canada. A sea of white crashing over the land; a tidal wave of joint-cracking cold. Here winter is about survival.

This year was the same as all the Christmas's at Home Farm. The only difference in the past couple of years, Sheila had not been not there. Two people instead of three threw words back and forth as though there could be only one winner. Christmas before last had been the most difficult of all. This last Christmas however, being ostensibly *happy* together, result of months of effort, made it surprisingly tolerable. And there was the knowledge that everything was for the last time.

The last time I would cook a goose just how Carl likes it, its soft belly wet with fat, potatoes gorged with it. Or make spread for toast from stock for a Boxing Day breakfast, the way Sheila did, its morning smell thick and rich. The last time I would endure *goodwill to all men*, or sob my pillow wet till feathers showed their curve, their hard point through the cambric pricking my cheeks.

Since we got back from the city, Carl has been affectionate, kind even. He hasn't hit me once.

Being someone else; subjugating my instincts to react, has made me finally realise that Carl *can* be nice. Could even be a good husband were I submissive enough. But there is baggage, miles of road travelled. If I had had no choices, no way out, I could see that if I played my part well, swallowed my true nature, life could improve.

In some ways, I feel bad about what will be left. Sheila was right; Carl might have been a decent man. But he is not my child.

And so, I have left him. There is no going back. I do not feel a black crow on my shoulder; there is no man in a black cassock, or Amish minister about to interfere this time. I think of Sheila suddenly, whisper a quiet 'thank you' and despite every instinct, cross myself for her departed soul: *Eternal rest give unto her O Lord, let perpetual light shine upon her. May she rest in peace. Amen.* And where would I be now without Jake? He would say all he did was unscrew the lid. If there is money left over, I shall tell him to keep it. When he arrives, I shall hug him for the first and the last time in this life, tell him that, in my own way, I love him. He will tell me not to think about it, that I shall see him in the next.

He has the bus and boat tickets. I have my passport, which had to be sent to Jake; we thought it would never arrive. When it did and I compared the photo of me now, with the one in my old pass, I wanted to weep. Even Jake found it hard to believe.

I know that I shall travel by greyhound to New York, board ship on the lower East Side and sail to Liverpool. Then home. I roll the word around my mouth, allow it to melt like chocolate.

But right now, I am rigid with cold, time to go inside, buy coffee and doughnuts and thaw my feet. I smile when I hear the piped music *Gotta travel on* and feel it is being played just for me. I am thirsty and feel like tea but if I order coffee, they will keep refilling my cup. I can order food if I get hungry and buy more time. The coffee shop is half empty; I am not taking space.

I gaze at the headlines of a newspaper that a man sitting opposite is reading: *Judge in Atlanta orders African Americans to be admitted to segregated colleges...* The world, with all its injustices, is going on somewhere else. I stare out of the window towards the bus station to see whether I can see Jake, blow on my hands. I can see the clock from here; six minutes past eleven.

Then I think about the segregation right here. Think about the reservation where Jake lives and know the world has still a long way to go. He took me there after one of our trips to town, the day I gave him a Christmas hamper. He was so happy with his gift even though it was nothing special, just a scrawny rooster I had cooked, some root vegetables, fruit I conserved in late summer and seeds from my summer plants. Carl gave him two bottles of ale, assuming, he said, that 'all Indians liked alcohol'.

Over coffee in the drugstore, where, as always, other shoppers passed disdainful stares at my sharing my coffee and conversation with an *Indian*, I told Jake of the plan for the horticulture course and he smiled till his face was tight with it, told me I would be growing more than plants. I remember he did a strange thing—he took my left hand turned it over, palm upward, traced the palm lines with his finger, smiled and closed up my hand like a bud. 'You have been many places; it is all here. And here,' he tapped my temple, 'but you will go further, now or later.'

When I asked him if he was reading my palm, he said, 'Of course not, it's a lot of baloney, isn't it?' He liked *baloney*, said it was a word I had taught him. Sometimes I think he plays with me like a cat with a bird.

When we'd stocked up with necessities and some Xmas luxuries: gingerbread biscuits with red and white icing, a bottle of Sherry and some silver crackers with bells on, I was surprised when, on the way back, I managed to persuade him to take me to the reservation. It was something he had promised to do, though surprised, bemused even, by my curiosity. I told him if it were not now, then it wouldn't happen, because—and I repressed a squeal of joy—I would *be in England*.

After we left the highway, and my Christmas babble died away, we spent a long time silently criss-crossing miles of ploughed silver brown acres until gradually the tended land fell away behind us and the area became more scrubby, arid, sand-gravelly, with occasional tufts of blue-eyed grass and locoweed. When we finally pulled up from the long straight dirt road, having passed stragglers and people sitting around against the wire fences for some half-mile, I was shocked to see young boys and old men doing some sort of dubious trade by the makeshift entrance. There were heaps of garbage slung either side of two concrete posts.

'What are they selling?' I asked as Jake swung in and to the right of a collection of huts.

'Alcohol mostly. You've heard about *Indians*, haven't you?' There was an edge to his voice I had never heard. I said nothing.

He stopped the car suddenly, I had to grab onto the dashboard to stop myself falling forwards. A swirl of silver frost-dust sprayed around the truck. I looked at him accusingly, but he just got out and shut the door. I stepped out after him and immediately noticed the smell. It was the same that clung to Jake's clothes when I first met him, only stronger. Of leather, animals and earth, of surface drains. In the background lingered a faint waft of excrement. I looked around; felt a mild panic; I was out of my depth.

Shacks cobbled together with bits of wood and clapboard lay sprawled in untidy rows. Attempts at extending the ground-space of some with sheets of corrugated iron and poles made a higgledy-piggledy mess of the whole. Pieces that had fallen off or had not yet been used, lay around in piles. An improvised system of electrical wiring meant cables looped and swung between shacks and made whistling noises when the wind blew.

As we walked around, weaving through the scruffy collection of shanties, ducking beneath washing lines and rugs left out for airing, where animals, dogs, cats and the odd goat and chicken, wandered freely down frozen ridged alleyways—that must have been a mire in the rains, and an airless smelly labyrinth in the sun—I was embarrassed at the two layers of existence only a few miles apart.

Jake was greeted with nods and a furtive curiosity about his guest. A woman was boiling potatoes in a pan over an open fire of twigs and wheat stalks and something that smoked a lot, she half smiled, head tilted, while several pairs of eyes looked out from a tiny dwelling behind her, then she looked at my shoes with a vacant stare.

Two young men leaned indolent and provocative against the porch of one shack, smoking and drinking something dark coloured from an odd, square shaped bottle. Their curiosity was tinged with hostility; if I had been alone, I would have felt threatened. It wasn't what I expected.

There were people everywhere, poorly dressed, lethargic, handsome. I couldn't see where they would all sleep.

When we reached Jake's house, even smaller than most we had passed, the dirt-grey linoleum floor and bare light-bulb, that swung in the shaft of air from the open door lent a soulless aspect to the place. It was cold and I could see no direct form of heating. A bed cobbled out of boxes, a mattress slung over them, and several blankets folded on the top, was pushed up against one wall. A small shelf above it had books, candles, a box of matches and a tiny leather shoe, scuffed and worn. I hesitated, in response to his invitation to sit on a small stool next to a wooden table. I couldn't speak for some moments for fear of shaming him. He was clearly unaccustomed to visitors, awkward at my shock. I shuffled and stuttered my appreciation at his attempts.

'How…how do you keep warm?'

'There's the stove, it's fine…'

I felt asphyxiated by his poverty, ashamed for having complained of my lot to him. Yet surely, my inner self chirped, he didn't need to stay here? He must be able to manage more than this. Then I remembered what Carl paid him, how he was always looking for more work, how Indians seemed to find it hard to get any jobs at all, let alone half-decent ones. And I realised I had no room to talk; I was still here, wasn't I?

The waitress fills my cup for the third time, and I smile my thanks, despite the foul bitterness of stewed coffee. I ask for the menu and a glass of water. My hands are shaking.

At three minutes to one o'clock, I go outside. The coffee shop has filled with people for lunch, and the waitress, her squeaky white shoes and bustling air, has pointedly cleaned my table and with a brisk smile told me to *have a nice day*. I walk back to the depot wondering whether I had correctly understood the arrangements; begin to doubt myself. We couldn't write anything down. Then I remember the one greyhound a week and know it could have been no other day or time. That we calculated I would have nearly twenty-four hours before the course Carl booked for me would commence, a safety net, by which time I would be well on my way.

Having warmed up over lunch I feel the snap and pinch of the wind and this time go inside the depot where I find a seat and wait. I notice a man staring over from the ticket booth and I try to be invisible, sink into my coat, lift its lapels until I am cocooned in my separate space.

After three hours, panic has wedged in my throat, I find it difficult to swallow. My body is stiff with inaction, cold, fatigue and torpor of crushing, insane disappointment. The man at the ticket booth, having seen me stand to leave, and registering the blanket of desolation wrapped about me, comes from behind the booth to address me.

'Excuse me, ma'am, you've been here an awful while, can I help, I mean are you waiting for someone?' For a moment I brighten.

'Yes I am. Has someone left a message?'

'No ma'am, leastways not that I know of. I'll go check for you. Don't go away now.' He clicks his tongue and wags his finger in a gesture that is friendly and concerned that, for whatever reason, I am about to run. He returns almost immediately.

'No ma'am, no messages. Is there some way I can help, get you a hot drink or a cab maybe?'

If I attempt a response, I shall make a fool of myself. With a shake of my head and a quick polite smile, I walk out, hail a cab and ask the driver to take me to the City Slicker Motel, the same that Carl and I stayed in, which he booked for the week in my name. There is still the merest candle flicker that Jake, being held up, will make his way there, though we made no such arrangement.

Nestling uncomfortably beneath this small glow is a very bad feeling. I begin to feel sickly, tremble from some profound knowledge at the core of things. I push it away, take deep even breaths. Remember that Jake once told me his wife had 'made him more honest', that he was 'not a good man before'. I think of the two rolls of money I entrusted to him, more than he or I had ever seen, think of the cold shack in which he lives. Then I remember that Jake was a man like no other; he could not do it. Remember the last thing he said to me before he gave me his dream-catcher so that mine may come true:

Life is the flash of a firefly in the night, the breath of a buffalo in the winter.

It is the little shadow, which runs across the grass and loses itself in the sunset.

Chapter Twenty-Seven

I watch Carl tinkering with the engine of the tractor he bought from a farmer's widow over in Scobey, just west of Plentywood.

'She had no idea of its value, just wanted rid so she could get on with her life…'

I observe him, as though I am watching a film of someone else's life. I can't believe I have got away with it. When Carl picked me up from the cross last week, I noticed his hands shaking and a glower masked by an uneasy grin, but he said nothing. Even seem pleased to see me in his can't-you-see-I'm-making-an-effort sort of way. I left no note when I left, gave him no reason to suspect. Yet, because I see my guilt mirrored in him. I cannot believe he has not worked it out.

I try not to think, tell myself there has been a problem, something of which Jake could not warn me. Impossible. All week as I learned about the content of soil: *sandy, clay, lime, ericaceous*…the feeling grew in me that Jake did not meet me because he could not, that my departure is merely postponed.

Completing the horticulture course has given me a reason to go back to the city, to continue with my studies. I tell myself over and over: I have to be practical; I must look only forward. There is a way out of here, I know it now. Jake taught me that. Part of me wishes I had somehow managed to depend only on myself, yet I know I couldn't have got so far without him.

I worry that he is ill and about the money… I shall know nothing until I speak to him, and I fret and pace because I must wait. I know he cannot come to see me until the day he would normally take me to town, two weeks away; Carl would suspect his motives. Jake knows that. It is all I can think of, that and preventing Carl from finding out.

He sees me watching him from the window, lifts a hand, stares for a moment too long, as though there is a question in his head, then returns to his work, his cloud-breath visible even from here.

In some ways, my week away was not entirely wasted. Not Sunday. Cloaked in self-inflicted misery, the seedy surroundings of the City Slicker Motel feeding my crash with its bleak lights, shoddy furniture, collection of stale smells, and the dubious pleasures of a mini-bar full of tiny bottles of coloured liquid, like a kitchen in a doll's house. I spent half the night draped over the pan wishing I hadn't been born.

The other half dreaming of a slip of a girl with cornflower blue eyes and dark hair, standing on the edge of a sunlit tarn in her petticoat, up high on the Yorkshire moors, the only sounds: those of a pony ripping grass and water lapping at the edge of the fern fringed pond. In the water, a half man, half fish moving with consummate ease before stopping and beckoning. Then the feel of cold as she jumps into the deep water beside him and begins to sink, all the way to the black mud at the bottom until it swallows her whole.

Then, an alarm clock, a punitive voice in my head, and a black crow on my shoulder, meant I managed to get out of bed and turn up at the college for the course I hadn't had any intention of attending.

Every hour of each day in the week that followed, I imagined where I should have been, had our plan been successful. Either way I told myself, suppressing panic as I had suppressed so much over the years, in the long run, when I eventually met with Jake to find out what the problem was, I would realise I had lost nothing. Gained nothing either.

There were some nice people who wanted to grow things and Jo the teacher was kind in her industrious way. Feeling my hands in the soil kept me earthed, though I got the reputation of being a dreamer. *The next thing to notice about these plants...Alice...is that they all have a well-defined texture...*

I told myself knowledge was good, that I could apply what I was learning as easily in England. *So much emphasis is placed on the appearance of flower and fruit that the importance of foliage is forgotten...* I felt I had done the hard part. I had left the Farm, got within striking distance of the voyage home. If it could be done once, it could be repeated; the only difference being, that I will not wait years next time. *One of the most vital elements in a garden composition is the general effect when seen from a distance...*

As the week progressed, fear wormed its way through me, that somehow Carl would guess what I had done. I tormented myself, imagining clues I may inadvertently have left. *The larger and shinier the leaf, the coarser is the apparent texture of the plant...* The only thing that was taking me back was money. I had none. *Are you okay, Alice? Alice...are you with us?*

I thought about not going back, finding someone who could help me. Perhaps there was an organisation that dealt with people in my situation. But what was my situation? On the face of it I was fortunate. Compared to some I had a good standard of living. Carl had not physically abused me in over a year; there were no bruises, no evidence of my life with him. I was just another neurotic woman, unhappy with her lot; an ungrateful Overcomer who didn't know how lucky she was, who didn't appreciate the sacrifices that her adopted country had made for her. And so on.

I could hear the drawling conclusion before being sent back to a long-suffering husband. I had done that with the Amish family back in fifty-one, couldn't do it again. I thought about trying to phone home from the telephone exchange but, like us, my parents didn't have a phone, at least not one that I knew of. In desperation I organised for a cable to be sent. It seemed pretty pointless—they had not responded to my letters—but still, in the face of no other option, I clutched at sticks.

Trying to get home. Please write soonest. All love. Ali.

Trying to explain what had happened to my plans was too complicated in a cable, besides, I didn't know myself yet how things would turn out. But when it was done, it seemed piteously inadequate.

Without the buffer of the week, I would never have been able to face Carl. Now all I must do is wait to see Jake. I have waited for years already; I can bear two more weeks.

At first Carl skirted around me, watched as though I were the one to be feared. It confused me; made me doubly cautious. If he didn't know, then why was he like this? If he did, why no confrontation? He left me alone at night, tried to do small things to cheer me up as though he suspected I had *gone off* him. If I wasn't so defensive, I might feel he was frightened of me, in the sense that he wanted me to want him, and didn't know exactly how to be with me. Surprisingly, he asked me little about the week.

When I asked what he had done he looked affronted, as though if he didn't ask me, I shouldn't ask him, as though I doubted him in some way, defensive. 'I was farming, you know, like always...picked up the tractor... Why, what did you think I was doing?'

I surprise myself how easily I have fallen into the old habits and only two weeks since I thought I would never see him or Home Farm again. I cook his grits, make his coffee after barn work, stare from the old nursery window over the blue beauty of the flat, snow-covered land, animal tracks a clue to the hidden wilderness. I nurse my despair like a strict keeper giving it no space, in the sure knowledge that there is a cure, one way or another. I have had a small taste of freedom; it is addictive. I shall not give it up.

The day before Jake's day, I put on boots and go for a walk in the snow. Carl thinks I have a strange idea of pleasure but pays no heed as I head out in no particular direction. I feel some buzz of energy in me, some frisson at this small free act and I walk for a couple of miles then return because I am choosing to, because yet again I am biding my time. I am the wasp back in the jar, but next time the lid opens I'll be out.

Unable to sleep I have risen early. Jake is not due till nine so I occupy myself with chores that have built up over the last few weeks, try not to think of what I shall say to him, how I shall control myself.

When he is late, I try not to notice, the memory of that terrible wait too fresh. There is washing, ironing and I decide to prepare a casserole for the evening so I do not have to cook when I return. I have little space to clock-watch.

I concentrate, bite my lip as I peel potatoes in long curling helices, drop lumps of meat into maize flour and brown until the kitchen is thick with it, the range speckled with fat. *Hope is important…don't let it go…* I make every small task count for something, a necessary step to climb, in negation of what I am beginning to know. As I lift the heavy pot into the bottom oven and sigh with the effort of it, I know he is not coming. It is almost mid-day. Carl, out in the barn has not mentioned his absence. I must. When I go over to ask him if he has heard from Jake while I was away, he shrugs.

'You think I've seen him? Why would he come here? I didn't book him; there's no work for him.'

'But it's my town day today, remember?'

'Oh yeah…I guess he's just not coming; you know what they're like.'

He does not meet my gaze but continues thrusting the pitchfork into the straw, shaking free the steaming manure and stacking it on the 'clean' pile ready to put down again later. The shiny prongs push deep over and over, rasping as they strike the bare ground beneath the bedding. The air is syrupy with dust and breath, with mewling and crunching from the animal's jaws. I stand watching, waiting. The pitchfork shoves in again and again until I feel faint with the violent stench of ammonia, of animals kept in over the winter. I leave the barn before I retch.

Then I know. The thing I have pushed away as unworthy. The unthinkable. Jake has taken the money and gone. In that moment I know for certain that I shall never see him again. I know he will not return to the reservation. A man like that could work all his life and not see money like that. I want to hate him, but I cannot; I put temptation in his way and now I am being punished.

Of course, I had no option, I tell myself; I did not have the freedom to run hither and thither finding the different options for travelling back to New York and then England. It seems pathetic to me now and pretty stupid but with Carl watching my every move, it seemed the obvious thing to do. I would trust Jake with my life, and if my life, then why not my money?

My hands shake. I feel suddenly old, my joints heavy and thick, barely able to carry me. I am overwhelmed by the loss of the money and what it means, but that is nothing beside the loss of Jake. I feel I have been duped and yet…strangely, I do not feel anger, just an overwhelming sense of bereavement. I struggle to cross the yard as the realisation comes over me like the beating of hail on my skin.

Somewhere in my subconscious, my brain scrambling for clarity, I recall a friend of my mother whose husband died at the age of forty. I remember her grief, remember my mother telling me of her anger when she was told that the husband for whom she grieved, had been having an affair with a young woman in the village, and she hadn't been the first. The widow felt cheated, she said, cheated of her suffering, the grieving a small catharsis left for her after he had gone. How could she grieve for a man like that? The anger she felt was not so much directed at her husband as at the person that told her.

And now I feel the same. Somehow Carl's answer fuels me '…guess he's not coming'. How can I grieve for the loss of a man who cheated me? For the first time in my life, I feel hatred. Not for Jake, wherever he is, but for the messenger. How many ways are there to be trapped?

Hatred makes me vigilant. I watch and I wait, still there is some thread I hold onto in the hope that I have been wrong. Carl seems preoccupied, has taken to going into town again; it takes the pressure off. He returns in the early hours, a creeping teenager that doesn't want to be caught in the glare of dawn. This is what I have become: a miserable shadow that drifts ghost-like; an apparition at an upstairs room, staring at the sky watching the geese go over, dreaming dreams that no sane or respectable person would admit to. How life's disappointments age us.

On the face of it nothing has changed except that Carl and I are skirting around each other once again. It is as if the months of effort counted for nothing; I don't know whether Carl can sense my desperation or whether he has a separate agenda. Why is he so different? Why does he avoid eye contact, shuffle in his round-shouldered way when he is close to me as though he expects a physical attack? I decide he must suspect. There has been no mention of Jake, which surprises me. I know he never cared for him, but he was a good worker, why is he not curious?

When I ask about going to town, he shrugs. 'Why? You've got everything you need right here…You can come with me next time I need to go…' he turns his back, carries on oiling the tractor part that he has dismantled on the kitchen floor.

Waiting and watching has become a habit. I am like Sheila, acquiring habits she had. My fingers fiddle with the table covering or with the edge of my cardigan. I put my arms around myself as if I am cold all the time, tired, as though my blood is sticky and won't circulate, feel as though I have almost stopped.

But still, like a tiny nightlight in the dark, something flickers. Still, I watch the horizon hoping to see Jake's familiar figure. The snows begin to melt, each mound keeping its shape, dripping from inside, until it collapses in muddy pools; underneath, a brown earth, soft with a warming sun sitting in a sky that has lost its whiteness.

While I am waiting, and in the absence of choice—I have no money—I decide to grow things. I gather the pots and seed trays, dirty and cobwebbed from hibernation and set about cleaning them, remembering the first lesson of the horticulturist: plant hygiene and preparation. I collect my seed heads and pods and compost. I make a small space in the barn where I can plant seedlings until the weather is warmer and I can put them out.

I line the floor with old newspapers to insulate the trays and I realise I really can't remember the last time I had the luxury of reading a newspaper, the local ones being full of drivel: cats stuck in trees, the price of milk, inane health tips and so on. And *local* is hardly local when you live out here. The only news I hear is from the radio, which tends to be parochial in the extreme or focused on *Ike,* his sidekick *Nixon* and the recession.

But the headlines and by-lines catch my eye as I spread the papers out on the floor: *Man saves drowning dog in the freezing Mississippi. Despair at closure of day centre. PD patrols seize suspects over town robberies.* I drift through some of the stories, get engaged in a half-hearted way, wonder whether I should write something and send it to them; I could do better than this. I imagine my headline "Life as it really is down on the farm" or "Overcomer tells it from her perspective…"—that would really get things stirred up. Then my glance slips back to the inside pages of The Echo. *Meredith overcomes a painful disability to make a bid to be the next prom queen.* Ho hum. *Indian found dead ten miles from reservation. Yes, to new town homes.* I go back, pick up the paper and read:

A 53-year-old man was found dead last night covered in snow lying in a ditch in waste ground behind the city's main bus depot. At first it was believed he was drunk and had fallen, striking his head on the stone culvert, though his neighbors on the reservation insisted he never took alcohol. His death is being treated as suspicious.

The discovery has created a wave of panic in the town. Councillor Bob Graham said yesterday, 'These people on the reservations are a law unto themselves. Likely this is some tribal problem, we've seen it all before, local people shouldn't be worried.'

His comments caused consternation amongst the local Indian population. Asked for his comments, Mr Blue Davis of no fixed abode said, '…we're just second-class citizens in this town. What is it going to take to make people take notice of us?' The dead man is confirmed as Mr Jacob Miller.

Over and over in disbelief I read it, look at the date on the newspaper. Jake is dead. He is really dead. All the time I was waiting for him in the city, he was lying dead in that cold ditch. And this is what is left, a shoddy article in some hick newspaper. I can't breathe. I feel the cold come up through my knees. I am shaking.

'Alice. You in here?' Carl shouts suddenly from the barn door. 'Hell, what's wrong with you,' he says as he walks over and finds me folded up on the floor. I can't speak, I hand him the newspaper without looking.

'Meredith overcomes painful disability…' he reads in a childlike stilted manner.

'Not that, the other,' I spit.

'Okay, okay, steady on. *Indian found dead...*' He goes quiet, reads the article. 'So, he's dead... That's a shame, nice guy for an Indian, but hey, he's nothin' to us, no need to get all upset. Probably a fight, you know what they're like. C'mon now, don't make a fuss?'

'*Fuss*!' I screech. 'He was my friend.'

'He was a farmhand, that's all. I'm sorry he's dead. I'm sorry you're sad, but don't go making such a big deal of it.'

'*Big deal*?' I shout. 'Isn't murder a big deal to you? Especially of someone we have known, who was a friend.'

'He was no friend of mine...and frankly...you were just a little too chummy, if y'ask me,' Carl says under his breath, and walks out of the barn into the milky sunshine. I hear him cough, clear his throat.

My friend is dead.

My friend is *dead*.

I have been here before.

Jake did not betray me. I betrayed him. If he hadn't had the money, he wouldn't have been robbed. Black crows gather on my shoulder, I am bloated with self-hatred, ugly with it.

The next few days I stay mostly in my room. I have eaten little since I found out and have cooked nothing for Carl. Strangely, he has left me alone, but even if he hadn't, I wouldn't have cared. I feel as though my heart is breaking. After about a week, it becomes clear that Carl has taken my response to Jake's death personally, as though what I give to Jake is taken from him. The air around him is thick, like exhaust fumes from a dirty engine, his face tight with something he wants to say, his fists grip whatever he is holding back, veins ridged under his skin like rope.

'For Chrissake, what is it with you? I've had it, you are some moody bitch,' when he catches me sullen, staring from the old nursery window.

'Leave me alone,' I say quietly. He is warming up, revving the engine, but this time I simply don't care; he can do what he likes.

'Why should I leave you alone. I haven't had a decent meal in days. Pull yourself together or I'll do it for you.'

I turn and yell, 'I'm sad. Is that okay?' I'm like someone suddenly let out of a box, all sense of proportion gone. 'And I feel guilty, I ache with guilt. I ache...but you wouldn't know about guilt, would you?' I am shouting, spitting, hissing, choking.

He stares, confused, shocked, takes a backward step. I gain momentum, move towards him. 'For Jake. For Jake. Who the hell else?'

'Guilt? Why guilt? Is this some Catholic thing? Every time someone dies, you carry the fucking crucifix? First your soldier-boy, then my mother, now some two-bit Indian farmhand. You've been guilty so long you're pinned to the fucking ground by it. Why should *you* feel guilt?'

'Because…' I begin to weep, 'because I killed him. Indirectly, I killed him,' I whisper.

'What? What's that? What're you saying? How could *you* have killed him?'

It doesn't matter what Carl knows or doesn't know. It's over.

'I killed him because he was trying to help me, trying to help me get away from *you*.' He stares, his eyes darting from side to side, trying to collect his thoughts, work it all out, shaking his head slowly. 'Yes, from you,' I scream, hysterical. 'You…who stole my life. You think I could come back from the dead and love you after all the beatings, the rapes, after being a prisoner for all these years? You disgust me. You disgust me.'

I shout so loud my voice almost gives out. 'You…pathetic…thing. If…if Walter had lived, I never would have married you. You and your warped family…You…yes, go on beat me. Finish me off, I want you to, do it, go on…do it,' I scream, hitting him as hard as I can.

I feel no pain. Carl has hit me once, hard, with the back of his hand, blood drips down my face, I sink onto my knees, but I feel only numbness. I want him to kill me now. I want to feel nothing.

'I'm not so pathetic,' he growls as he grips onto the door-frame. 'I knew you were up to something; I knew. All that work you put in…you fooled me for a while, sure. But I knew, you scheming little bitch. I'm going to make sure you live long enough to regret it; I'm not going to dirty my hands on you. You think you've been a prisoner, you've no idea…'

I wait for him to kick me, to lift me up to knock me down again but he doesn't. He just walks quietly away, leaving the door open behind him. I hear him scratch some things together, hear the rattle of his keys, the truck engine start up and the scrape of the tyres as they spit and crunch their way out of the yard.

When he has gone, despite my face swelling and the thick dribble of blood from my lip, I have to get out of the house; breathe. I start to walk again, think of Jake telling me I walk in circles and that is what I do, a huge circle around

Home Farm, until a kind of peace settles on me; a relief I can't quite understand. I am calm. A rare mist has settled over the land and, as I return, the house seems to glow red, floating in the white evening air.

I imagine, as I walk up the front porch, painless ways to end it. All of it: the loneliness, the beatings, the rapes, the unrelenting boredom. End myself…whoever that is. And then I realise, I don't know who I am anymore; I have been stolen. My very self has been robbed from me. And I ponder how abuse could do that; blow out the flame that makes us who we are; change a person so utterly, that a woman, full of the joy and wonder of things, that lived through the war, that saw loved ones die, could surrender herself to this life, and then could willingly, happily even, consider suicide?

Suicide… a mortal sin. Suicide that only leads to more of the same: eternal punishment. Yet…it seems that it is there for me when I am ready, because anything is better than this. And this is the reason for my feeling of tranquillity, because suddenly, out of nowhere, I have a choice.

As I open the door, something makes me stop and look over at the room with the drawn drapes, Carl's room. I never go in it, or at least not for years. I used to clean it when I first arrived at Home Farm, but then Carl said to leave it, said I rearranged his desk too much; messed things up. I was happy to have one less chore and after that I neither wanted to go in there, nor was I ever invited.

However, in this moment in time, some extra sense makes me curious; I find myself moving inexorably towards it. I walk into the house, down the hall where I see the key hanging on a nail outside. Just the thought of what Carl would do if he found me here, paradoxically gives me courage. I take the key; feel the weight of the black metal in my hand. The lock is stiff, I need two hands to turn the key and with only a moment's pause, I walk into the dark space.

The first thing I notice is the smell. Stale bourbon, socks. I resist the impulse to open the drapes and the window to let out this bad air. Instead, I close the door and put on the yellow light. I creep slowly around the room, touching nothing, just looking at the heart of the man I am married to. It is a room trapped in time, a boy's room. It has a superficial tidiness, but there are layers of dust beneath which, I suspect, are layers of grime. There is a baseball glove and ball on the floor.

I am surprised to see a wedding photo, unframed and curled, propped on a shelf beside a tiny American flag on a stick, together with photos of Carl in his army uniform and another of him and four soldiers posing, arms folded and laughing, leaning against a Nissen hut doorframe, with a sign that reads *Mary Ann Mess Hall*, the *Hall* chalked through.

A cloak of nostalgia swirls about me as I gaze at the photos and remember my brother Vincent and Lily at the dance at Burtonwood, the first time I met Carl. I can hear the band playing: *Boogie Woogie Bugle Boy*...then, like an apparition, it disappears. There is something fitting about the group of photos, bunched together, part of the past locked up in this dark miserable little room.

There is a desk, large and gnarled at the edges, piles of papers and a list of household expenses sitting squarely in the corner. There is a comfortable chair beside it with threadbare arms that don't fit under the desk, and I imagine Carl sitting in it, a bourbon in one hand, his feet on the desk, while he reads the local paper from cover to cover as he always does.

Suddenly, the peaceful mood has shifted; I am wired up and casting. Carl *does* read the paper from cover to cover. His mind is always full of the trivia he has gleaned during his *time out* in his room. Why then did he not know about Jake? Having hooked it, I sit, reeling in this knowledge. He must have known. The more I allow the idea to settle, the clearer I can see. I remember how he reacted when I told him of Jake's death; he was not surprised. He was *not* surprised. Why then did he not tell me? Why?

Wild thoughts crash around my head like storm waves at a breakwater. I am soaked with fear. I look around the room searching for inspiration. I close my eyes wait for the crashing to subside, try to concentrate, remember everything since I came back. I become still, focused. I open my eyes and as if directed by some unseen force my gaze is led beyond and behind the desk to a wall where there are shelves and a single drawer above a white painted cupboard. I walk around the desk, careful to touch nothing and I pull the drawer handle. Locked. I look around for a key.

I feel a heat emanating from the cupboard as though there is something burning, urging me to find it. I think I am going crazy, but I look around, my heart pounding; becoming quietly frantic. Is this what it is like to lose your mind? I begin to open desk drawers carelessly, with no thought other than getting open the white one. I rummage around through bits and skits looking for a key. Nothing. I scan the room, hunting. Then I see a small china bowl on one of the shelves with painted dragons and a lid like a ginger jar. I lift it and there are four keys.

I take them all and try them one by one. The third sweetly turns the lock. I pull open the drawer and see…nothing. Odds and ends, a tape measure, a football medal, an old camera case, a few manuals on tractors and farm equipment. I close the drawer; try to pull myself together, slow my heartbeat, tell myself not to get carried away. I am about to leave when I spontaneously pull out the drawer again, randomly open the camera case. In it are two large rolls of money secured with red elastic bands.

I take a deep breath, replace the money inside the camera case, close the drawer, lock it, return the keys to the jar, leave all as I found it, lock the door, hang the key on the nail, walk out of the house, down the steps and out far into the field.

The light is going, soon it will be dark. I stare at the huge sky scored with rose and indigo cirrus, a horizon of dying golden light above a darkening lid folding over me. It is a shock when I hear screaming, somehow have an objective sense of my primeval self, shifting, moving, squeezing itself out. All the time I am screaming, I feel it compressing, condensing, until it explodes through my head. I feel it. Feel it burst into the atmosphere blasting into a billion atoms.

Suddenly, I am collecting above me like a swarm of bees, spinning, swarming, looking down on myself screaming in a wheat field in winter in Northeast Montana, the land fanning out in all directions, the sea, continents, the strange question mark of Britain on the periphery. Below, is me. What is left. Just the essence of something; a smudge on the landscape from a hiccup in time; a skinny scrap of a woman lying in the dirt.

Book Four

Chapter Twenty-Eight

England

June 1967

I pull on my bell-bottomed jeans and tie-dye t-shirt; being a student is turning me into a hippie. I take a last look in the mirror, check my make-up, push my long curling hair back from my face and decide I look ten years younger than I did ten years ago. I tip my head back as if to say *so?* and smile in the way of someone I once knew. Then I gather my books and writing materials, put them into my briefcase and push down the lock, holding my hand there for a moment as though I have come to a decision about something. I go to the kitchen, wash my breakfast dishes, tidy a little, pick up my keys and let myself out.

After locking the door, I walk a few paces and look back at the little house that I love. My father had a savings account in my name and there was enough to pay the two thousand pounds purchase price, decorate it and leave me enough to live on, along with my grant, until the money from Carl comes through. I wish for nothing more. Not a day passes that I do not thank him for this. The grey-green window-frames, pretty clay pots full of Busy Lizzies, and the door with its brass knocker, shaped like a hand, give me immense pleasure. I have realised I am relatively easy to please; something that surprises me, having been told for so long how difficult I am.

I am taking driving lessons but walk to the stop where my bus will take me into town. It is a beautiful cloudless morning, warm and still and the trees are dressed in a coat of sunlight and fresh summer green.

On the bus I sit by a window and as we pull away a friendly guard comes to my seat with his big leather bag full of change.

'Where to, love?'

'Albert Square please.'

'That's one and six to a pretty lass like you.'

I pay my fare, sharing my smile with a woman about my age, sitting across from me who gives me an exasperated look as two children squirm and wriggle in their seats beside her. I take out my poetry books and try to concentrate. I mull over the mnemonics I created to remind me of relevant quotations and facts about the authors' lives and works. They call to mind the 'courtly love' medieval poets, Yeats's muse: Maud Gonne, Hardy's love poems written after Emma's death, T.S. Eliot's Four Quartets: *in my end is my beginning*...and I think, not for the first time, how love, above all other things, has been the mainspring of inspiration since the beginning of time.

I know what it is like to live without it and thinking of these poems makes me feel part of some universal understanding. I smile again at the woman who is hugging her youngest, whilst he in complete submission, drapes himself all over her.

I alight in the city centre, squinting in the sudden glare from a gaudy and reckless sun and feel a small shifting breeze on my face that carries with it the unlikely scent of apple blossom. I push up my sleeves to reveal brown arms from gardening, don my Marianne Faithful-style sun-glasses, and sense a small frisson of pleasure that comes from feeling just a little glamorous. A man hurrying past looks at me twice and I smile at my vanity. I walk across the wide-open space of the square, the statue of Prince Albert staring down at me, so beloved by Queen Victoria that when he died she wore black for the rest of her long life, and I think again, without love, in whatever form: romantic, filial, maternal, fraternal...there is only black.

The door is open, and a pleasant waft of books assails me as I walk into the examination area, housed in the same building as the library. I am early, so I position myself outside the hall, grateful to have the time to go through my last-minute revision, hoping, given the work I have done, that Woolf, Austen, Eliot and the Brontë's come up. Other students are there already, and they continue to arrive and stand beside us, silently revising. There is the odd nervous smile—we know each other well—understand the tension; nodding in acknowledgement of it.

I ponder why I have so closely focused on female writers, and if not female writers, then works that are sympathetic to women. Perhaps I search in them a voice I need to hear, need to believe that history has not swallowed us whole, or at least if it has, then some acknowledgement of the fact. I try to recall the line in *A Room of One's Own* that says it more succinctly than my crowded brain can muster: *If women had no existence save in the fiction written by men, one would imagine her a person of utmost importance; as great as a man...But this is a woman in fiction. In fact, she was locked up, beaten and flung about the room…* It may be useful if I get the kind of questions I hope for.

While I think, other things pervade my mind—alert, active and finely tuned as it is, from years of study. I shuffle my feet, impatient, nervous, trying to avoid the distraction of unwelcome memories that these quotations stir in me, yet they push through my anxiety like characters impatient to be heard and force me to go back to that time, some seven or eight years ago, when it would have been inconceivable to me, that standing here at all could have been possible.

But stand I do, looking up at the panelled ceiling of this lovely old building; a space with a sense of serenity and civility about it, and wonder why I stayed so long in a place that is just about its opposite. There must have been some way to end it, some way to just…walk away?

This question haunts me, but I know the answer and that haunts me too. No one forced me after the war to give up everything for a life of uncertainty with a man that I knew, subconsciously, I could never love, but this I did. And I did it because that's what women do when they lose themselves; when the person they are, drops slowly into the shallows, like a pebble thrown into a pond, hidden from view, but existing all the while, staring up from the depths darkly.

How much more quickly do we sink when there is no one to catch us, no reciprocation to affection, no one to tell us that we are loved. And then, when we imprison ourselves in whatever way we choose, because, perhaps, we believe we deserve no better, we are only as good as the image thrown back at us by the people we accept as our captors.

People have asked me what happened to feisty Ali and what do I answer? That she simply submerged one day when it all got too much, and when I feel the inadequacy of my answer, I remind myself that they, those that ask, live normal lives; they measure by parameters that don't apply in an abnormal world. They don't understand, can never understand, and I thank God for it. I want no woman, man or child to know it.

I try to focus my mind on the here and now, look at the clock, twelve minutes to go but, despite myself, think suddenly of Jake, of the one person in all those loveless years who saw something in me worth saving; think how he would smile his round smile just to see me standing here, knowing the wasp has finally got out of the jar. My eyes fill but I look around the crowded waiting area and I hold on, hold the emotion in, as I have done for so long. Instead, I try to concentrate on my exam; prepare to answer the questions I have been set, with objectivity, understanding and academic discipline.

And now, in the last minute or two, I write on my spare scrap paper, meant for notes: I am Alice Conroy. Then I go over it again with a heavy hand and I underline it. **I am Alice Conroy**. Whatever else I am, I deserve to be here.

I hope I can answer on Jane Eyre—my personal heroine. Jane, for whom poverty was her gaoler. I ask myself: was the war mine? But the world will continue to fight, to go to war, and I wonder what will become of the women, of their children, their unborn children.

But, like Jane, who is redeemed when she discovers that she is loved, I too am redeemed. I won't be here for long; life is the *flash of the firefly in the night*...but while I am here, I count for something; my life has purpose. And I know that when the time is right, good things happen.

Then, I am jolted from my reverie as the invigilator beckons us into the examination hall. I banish the diversion of my thoughts of the past and concentrate on the task in hand, knowing that the best of my life is yet to come, is full of promise, but that in this moment, I must deal with the present.

Chapter Twenty-Nine

America
1963

The sink runs red with blood, pink polka dots decorate the edges as Carl washes his hands in that frenzied way he has. I watch, my mouth dry, iron-tasting. The smell from the barn has carried into the kitchen on his boots, his hands. I say nothing. I should be used to the slaughtering, but there's something about the way he does it. I mentioned, couldn't he stop the other animals from seeing, from hearing. I said it only once.

'If you're going to eat meat, you should *shut up being such a fucking hypocrite.*'

So I did. Still, I have to cover my ears when I hear the chickens screeching as he hooks them upside down. Sometimes they're hanging for a good while flapping their wings, getting weaker, less frantic, as though they resign themselves. I've stopped petting the calves. Seems they're only just born, learning to live and he kills them. Bleeds them first, less mess. Unless they're cows then he keeps one for milk, sells the other on.

I tried to give up meat last fall. I watched a British cookery programme that said it may be healthier. Carl said I could put myself out to grass if I wanted, but he wanted meat and that meant I had to cook it. So I do. I also eat it; it's just easier.

I brush out the straw he's walked in, scour the sink with disinfectant and start to clean the glob of meat, still warm, he has slabbed onto the table. I chop it into pieces for dinner. Carl likes it fresh, likes to taste the blood, says it's better a little undercooked.

My hands under the running tap are chapped and red. The first liver spots at forty; I am old before my time. I see four hands under that splashing water. Mam is peeling spuds, humming, gazing out over the moor toward Heptonstall; her hands, bigger than mine, longer fingers, pale, thin-skinned, blue veins like worms crawling through shallow pink earth; liver spots like freckles. *Ali set the table love*...She wasn't that much older than I am now when I left. Funny that. I must be grown up.

Long nails. She always wore varnish: fuchsia. Would wedge cotton wool between her fingers to prevent smudging, lips tucked in concentration, head tilted as she made slow dainty brushstrokes like an artist painting miniatures. Then her hands splayed on her lap, emphatic, statement making, while they dried.

I have workman's nails. Half-moons of skin above each shorn nail like fat pink slugs. My father's hands.

There is slippage in my reflection in the small mirror on the windowsill above the sink. I tilt my head so the stark light from the window shows the creases in my brow, my thinning lips, the beginnings of wrinkles that are not laughter lines. My face is becoming a different shape.

I am speckled with the mirror's dried water-splash; there are dark rings under bored, spark-less eyes that seem to have lost their blue. The first grey hair wires its way into a tight curl on my forehead.

I let Carl sleep with me now, only for sex, about once a month, usually when he's drunk, it's easier; he will anyhow. I am not a lover, even a wife, just convenient. I think he's slowly becoming impotent; I hope so. He says it's only with me. He still goes to town, but wears protection, says he's looking after me. It makes no difference. I don't care.

I pull at the fat on the meat that puckers and shines pearl through the flesh like snail-trails, stretch-marks. Mam used to hate hers. Got nothing to show for mine. Carl likes the fat left in, more flavour, but Fanny Craddock says too much is unhealthy, causes heart attacks. I leave some of it in.

I'm preparing a pot roast with carrots and onions and potato. The radio has been relaying a speech made by a pastor in Washington. I have no idea who he is, his name is Martin something...King I think, but I listened anyway because there was a big demonstration and it seemed to be important. It was a wonderful speech, I became transfixed, wept as it finished. With its catalogue of injustice, it made me think of Jake...*With this faith we will be able to hew out of the mountain of despair a stone of hope*...

It's a good job Carl is out of the house, he would make some comment about coloureds that would have ended in a row, so before he came back in and heard snippets of it, repeated over and over on the news broadcasts, I switched it off and put on the small television in the kitchen.

I have taken to watching *As the World Turns* and *The Edge of Night*, while I cook, wonder about Charlene and whether she'll tell her best friend about her lying husband, but I'll have to wait till tomorrow to find out. The new series, *General Hospital*, is on soon.

Yesterday, there was *Dixon of Dock Green*. I like British programmes even when they are old. Good old Bobbies. I wonder if they still wear those big hats. Couldn't help thinking about the only time I have been to a police station over here. It wasn't like *Dixon of Dock Green*.

It was some time ago; Carl took me to town for provisions. I don't go very often now, he prefers I stay home, which means I have no choice. I managed to persuade him that time, to go and have a beer whilst I went, ostensibly, to the new shopping precinct they call The Mall. Instead, I went to the county sheriff's office to tell them it was possible that six months previously Carl had murdered Jake to stop me leaving him. Just like that. It just kind of tumbled out piecemeal. The officer looked at his colleague, a frost of annoyance tinged with a long-suffering smirk formed on his face. He wiped the sweat from his neck with a handkerchief, adjusted the fan on his desk.

'So, let me get this right. Six months ago, your husband murdered Jacob Miller? Because you were leaving him? Look him up in the files, Willy,' he said over his shoulder.

'Well, for helping me, you see I gave Jake some money to go and buy—'
'How much money?'
'I don't know exactly…I never counted it. A lot and…'
'You gave an Indian a whole lot of money and expected him to help you?'
'Yes. He was a friend. I trusted him.'
'I see… You're not American, are you, ma'am?'
'What's that got—'
'Why did you want to leave your husband?'
'Lots of reasons. I…I was unhappy…We should never have married. I wanted to go home…why do you need to know that?'

He looked at his colleague who was nosing through a filing cabinet, lifted an eyebrow and inhaled loudly.

'You wanted to go home. You don't like America?'
'Yes… No…yes.'
'You know, we got someone for the Indian's murder, pretty damn quick actually. Cut and dried. It wasn't the only one, we've been after him for some

time. Doing time way down in Texas where we caught up with him,' *Willy* said throwing down the file on the desk.

'That's not possible—'

'He's on death row lady, better be.'

'I don't understand…'

'Well, that makes three of us,' the officer at the desk nodded, casting an ironic look at his colleague as he swung from side to side in his swivel chair. He glanced at his watch. 'Of course, now you've made this allegation, it has to be investigated…'

'Did he confess?'

'Who?'

'The man in prison.'

'He's an Indian, they never do, they like to see themselves as hard done by.' 'Course, now I know you gave Miller money, well…there was a motive. I suppose the widow will enjoy it when he's dead if he hasn't spent it already.'

'I think you'd better leave it. I mean, I withdraw my allegation.'

'No can do, not when a man's on death row. New evidence. It's a whole lot of work for us lady…Right,' he sighed heavily, giving a look that said *we've got a crazy one here*…his breath acrid, smoky, 'we'll just take some details then…'

I told them Carl would probably kill me too, if he knew I'd been to see them. The man standing shifted, stifled a snigger. They asked what evidence I had, I told them about finding the money in Carl's drawer. They said that wasn't evidence, it was my word against his, so I told them everything. They started to question me until I felt like the guilty one.

Of course, a few days later at home, when a rookie 'interviewed' him, Carl was all sweetness, butter wouldn't melt, made signs behind my back, tapped his finger on his temple, raised his eyes. I heard the rookie titter. Carl said his mother had left him the money when she died. I hadn't thought of that, maybe she'd divided it up, but she said… What did she say? He tangled me up in doubt, made me look stupid. I realised that I hadn't thought this through.

When the officer had gone, Carl gave me that stare through his brows, teeth clenched.

'What the hell…?'

'I thought that with the money…'

'The money? The money my ma left me? Why would my mother disinherit her only son? Now tell me that?'

'She gave me money too.'

'Well, I'll be damned… and now you think… Fuck…you really think…'

'You weren't surprised when I told you he was dead, you—'

'Of course, I wasn't surprised, I read it in the goddamn newspaper, I just chose not to tell you, I knew you'd make a fucking drama out of it. You're a lot of things, Alice McCullough, but I never had you down as stupid. You run off to the police with this cock and bull shit and make me look like a fuckin' criminal? Holy cow, woman. I saw enough in that godforsaken war to know that killing ain't something you do because it's convenient. You thought I was a murderer. You…you…my fuckin' wife…?'

Carl hit me so hard that I fell right across the room and hit the doorjamb on the other side. I curled into a ball knowing what was coming, but he grabbed my arm and threw me down the steps into the yard. He paused for a minute to be sure the rookie wasn't coming back, then he dragged me over to the barn, shoved me into the shippen and kicked me into the corner. He then walked out drawing the bolt across the door. He left me there until the next day.

I wept all night, for myself, for Jake, for my family who had deserted me. When he let me out, he told me to clean off the cow stink, get in the kitchen and make his dinner. And I knew then that one day soon I would leave, one day when it felt right, when the small flame of defiance his last beating had ignited, smouldered in me until it became a fire. That day I would go, even if I just walked out the door with no money and kept walking…that thought allowed me to stay trapped, for now.

Dixon of Dock Green. I don't like the adverts, they break up the flow, make me feel I'm missing something.

Sometimes I think of Jake, imagine his body in the earth. It'll be a skeleton now. Eaten clean. *More life under the ground than on it* …I feel my face with my fingers, the cheekbones, chin, the indent of my temples, imagine myself as a skeleton. Think of my teeth like a toothpaste advert, *a ring of confidence,* my nails and hair still growing.

The Indian has probably been executed by now, never admitted his crime. Carl made a big deal of reading the article in The Echo out loud: *Local man falls foul of Texas state Death Penalty…*

I don't know who killed Jake, Carl couldn't have done it, too much of a coward anyway. It must have been the Indian. It's easier that way. Either way, it makes no difference to Jake now. Or to me.

I wipe down the blood from the table, disinfect while the fat sparkles on the range browning the meat. Enough for three meals. Tomorrow, I'll slice some of what's left, make a mushroom sauce and some fries. On Thursday, I'll use up the rest in a casserole. Never could have done it without the Frigidaire. There's a little compartment at the top where I can freeze the fresh meat, means we can have meat all year long. I want a Bendix now, one that does the washing for me, this one's worn out.

'Coffee?' Carl stamps his feet, more bits of the barn. I say nothing. His sharp voice and narrowed eyes beneath knitted brows suggest he thinks I've forgotten. He sits down, clearing his throat like an old man. Only thing he doesn't do is spit, he would if he were outside. He drapes his forearms, fat with old muscle, over the table, sniffs. He has put on weight; the chair creaks as he shuffles. There is an old clothes smell around him like something beginning to decay.

When I sit opposite, look at his face, see the way he is with me, I feel like his mother. I do his washing, cook his food, clean up after him. I just accept it. For now. I have become Sheila.

'I'm having a bonfire in a day or two… I've got some crates need burning, and that partition in the barn that's split, the one I keep fixing, is coming out. I don't know why I've kept it…I'll just get rid. So, anything you want clearing, rubbish, anything that'll burn, make a pile and I'll add it to mine.' He grimaces as he tries to sip the hot coffee, then blows to cool it.

'Thanks, I'm sure there's stuff I can give you…'

'You're not doing me any favours here.' He chuckles, shakes his head as though at a stupid child.

'I only meant—'

'Must you have that thing on all day?' He stands up, switches off the set and turns the radio back on, where the new band from England are singing their hit song: *Please Please Me*, which seems ironic in the circumstances. I notice the bagginess of his blue jeans, the crack of his backside, the dimpled flare of fat that begins to bulge around his hips, the smell of stale sweat from his armpits, like pig fat. I inhale, hold my breath, see that he would have grown this way. As I get thinner, he gets bigger. One day, I'll fade away and he will fill the space.

'It's company, I like having it on.'

'Why don't you do something. You used to paint, whatever happened to that?' I hate the fact that he is right.

'I used to do a lot of things.' I am sorry as soon as I have spoken.

'Meaning?'

'Nothing. You're right. I mean, you are…right.' He half smiles, I can't decide if it is smugness or pleasure. 'I should do something. I should grow things again and clearing out that's good. Be like a late spring-clean.'

When he has gone back to the barn, I put the pot roast in the oven, wipe down the slicks and spots of fat that have splashed on the range and go upstairs to see what I can find to burn.

In my bedroom I become distracted by a skittering in the yard. I stare out towards the barn, must have been a cat. I stare past the yard, the barn, into the distance, not seeing, but thinking. Carl *is* right. I do nothing. I am nothing. I have stopped, like a clock that has no one to wind it. Even my journal goes months with nothing added, and when I do write, it's all stuff from the past: my family, the war, Walter's death, Carl before I met him, way back during the Great Depression; his screwed-up family.

Whatever *was* me, the girl I grew up with, the witty, pretty girl that read books, sang in the choir, loved high places, that had a family… has gone. I am boring, dull-eyed. I look at my feet; old slippers, pressed down at the heel, a colourless shift clings to my body and makes a shapeless bag of me. I don't deserve anything better than Carl—he is what I have earned for myself: my reward.

Suddenly, I see myself from the other side of the glass, a ghost. A hint of window glint obscures my form. Just like Sheila: standing there, listless, looking out, grey washed, life stripped. I watch myself put my red chapped hands on the window, feel the glass. See me press my face against it till I am squashed on the pane, then I draw back, make a picture with my breath. I hear Jake's voice clear as if he's in the room with me: *a wasp in a jar.*

Chapter Thirty

The pile is so big I have to carry it downstairs in armfuls. Mostly old clothes. I don't think we've had a clear-out like this since I've been here, and I am ruthless. Even stuff I'm not sure about goes on the pile. I realise I'm enjoying myself; cauterising.

There are some small bits of furniture: a shabby bedside table of Sheila's that smells old-fashioned. I shuffle down with it, one stair at a time. A towel rail, old, stained wood, water splashed, tatty with one *wing* missing. I'll get a new one that fastens to the wall. I'd like to burn the old wooden kitchen table with its stuck-on plastic lace tablecloth, get a new Formica one. I'll broach that later. Once I've started, I can't stop.

Apart from Carl's room and the loft, I have scoured every space in the house, and I am hungry for more. I look up at the square in the ceiling, access to the loft. I know there will be stuff up there that can go, old things of Sheila's. I think of the circular window high in the gable that I see from the yard but have never looked through. Suddenly I want to, but there is no loft ladder.

When I want things shoving up there, Carl slides back the cover, stands on a chair and pulls himself up into the recess, easy for him being so tall, and I pass it to him. I pull a chair from my bedroom as Carl does and stand on it. Not high enough. I look around trying to find something else. When I can't, I trudge over to the barn, mildly irritated to have to stem my flow of activity.

'Carl, there's a whole pile of stuff for burning in the hallway. Where do you want me to put it?'

'Leave it there for now, I'll sort it later.' He doesn't look up as he pours feed into a narrow trough for the chickens.

'How can I get into the loft?' He stops, looks up, the sack he is holding continues to pour small grains into a growing pyramid on the floor.

'Carl!'

'Shit!' he says, putting down the sack. 'Why do you want to go in the loft?' His voice is raspy, agitated. He wipes his hands on his jeans.

'I thought while I was at it, I could clear some stuff from up there, hasn't been cleared the whole time I've been here, must be heaps of things to go.'

'I'll do it.'

'I just thought—'

'Well, don't. I'll do it. Hear?'

'Why?'

'Why?' He mimics me 'Because I said so, because you're too short, because…because.'

I shrug my shoulders, irritated.

'So leave it, okay?'

I walk away, mumbling. He stops what he is doing, walks after me.

'Did you hear me?' He spits the words. Pinball eyes glare through veined white.

'Yes. I hear you.'

'You want stuff clearing from the loft, I do it. Are we clear?'

'Yes. You've already said.'

'Just don't want you breaking your neck,' he says after a minute or so, his voice softer. I smile as I cross the yard. How considerate.

When my frenzy is over, I kick the clothes into a pile against the wall, the bits of furniture already out on the steps. I notice something bright in amongst all the drab stuff. I pull on it. A red dress snakes out. I smell it, a whisper of *Evening in Paris*. It is crushed and creased. I shake it, hold it against myself in the hall mirror, wonder whether it would still fit, throw it back on the pile.

After dinner, I switch on the TV for the evening movie. Make myself some tea, try to settle. An old Bing Crosby film is on: *The Road to Bali*. I think about Carl. Dorothy Lamour sashays barefoot over a beach. He was upset; didn't want me rooting. Why? The idea needles me. Makes me want to go up there. A voice like syrup and a beach in Hawaii. *Welcome to paradise*…I curl my toes. Think about the loft.

On my way to bed I see the red dress in the hall lying on the heap of clothes to be burned. I pick it up, smell it again, tuck it under my arm and take it upstairs. Once in bed I push the dress under my pillow, the scent of old perfume comforting, my hand stroking the silky label inside the dress until I fall asleep.

*

I wake early, hear Carl rattling around in the barn, smell coffee, he must be going to town. I yawn, stretch, shudder, slide my feet onto the rug, feel the joints in my ankles, stiff from inaction. I stretch again, curve my back to loosen it up; try to feel my youth.

When I hear the last snap of the screen door, his car pull away, I go downstairs. I know when he goes to town because he never tells me. Then I won't know, and he won't have to acknowledge his *activities*. As if I'd care. He is not organised enough to have everything done in early morning otherwise; has to have that thirst in his belly. He is always nicer when he comes back. Subdued, obsessive; washing himself, but easier to live with, less volatile.

I make myself have breakfast: cereal, toast and tea. Dress. Then I do it, the thing that has festered like a sore since the bonfire last week. I open the loft. There had never been any reason to do so before, and the only stuff Carl has put up there, to my knowledge, has been junk that I wanted to discard but that he had insisted on keeping. But now I want to see what he is hiding.

I lug the ladder from the barn over the yard where it traces train tracks over the clay. It is lighter than I thought, but still, I must stop several times as the wood cuts into my fingers, causing splinters. I have to slide it up the stairs, pulling from the middle, using the rungs to heave it up. It is filthy, my palms have lines of black and there are slivers of wood and barn-dirt all over the stairs. Evidence I shall have to remove.

Fortunately, the loft hatch is at the end of the landing, no corners so I am able to wedge the bottom rung against the landing newel post, once I have lifted the top into the open square that is the loft hatch.

I am surprised how bright it is up here. The small round window throws a shaft of cob-webbed light across the entire space where broken bits of old lives reveal themselves in worn and stained pieces of furniture that have the patina of humanity upon them, and as my gaze moves over the years, the lives stare back at me, dating back I should think, from when the house was built at the turn of the century.

It is cleaner than I expected, clearly Carl has been up here more than I realised, the boards on the floor have a kind of pathway around the junk, polished by years of feet. I wander over, head ducked around the sloping eaves, towards the round window. I want to clean it but dare not. I look out, love the perspective the height lends over the land, and the impression, from this angle, of the yellow wheat waving in ribbons, shimmering in the fat summer breeze. Moving back into the loft, allowing my eyes to adjust to the comparative dark, I almost trip over a small black chest. Like a sea chest, though that seems unlikely.

Initials are scrolled on the side and there is an open lock in the middle. I lift the latch just because it is there. Then I see it: my name on an opened envelope of a handwritten letter. Hand-writing I recognise. I feel a chill that runs from my scalp down to the base of my spine. I push the letter tentatively to one side. Underneath it is another and another. I pull them out gently as though they would break, and they spill and fan over the floor.

There must be a hundred letters, addressed to me, all of them open. And as many again in my own handwriting addressed to my family, letters I thought Carl had posted to England. I feel my heartbeat racing in my neck, my head flooding. I am trembling as I pick one at random.

Hebden B.
April '47

Dearest Ali,

This is probably a waste of time, but I write in the hope that one of these letters will reach you (or that you will decide to reply). Your Mam and Dad said you won't, but if you decide not to respond to this, please, please Ali, let them know you are all right.

I have been home eighteen months now. I didn't tell you in my other letters, but I came to try to find you in Salisbury after you left Manchester (Ned told me where you were). I chased you to Southampton Docks, but I was too late. I stood on the quay scanning the faces waving goodbye, but I couldn't see you.

What can I say? I don't blame you love. I told you to live your life and I know you thought I was dead (such a strange thing that...) I'm glad you're happy Ali. I didn't go to stop you leaving...well I'm not sure now what my motives were. I think I just wanted to say goodbye, you know, have some sort of closure. I'm glad you found a good bloke after everything you went through; I know it can't have been easy. I hope he deserves you. I know I had my chances...Mam always said I go forwards and meet myself coming back!

I'm sure you have been wondering how I come to be alive. I wanted to tell you in my other letters, but I suppose I didn't want you to think ill of me. Now though, as we'll maybe not see each other again, or at least not for a while, I decided I wanted you to know. I suppose the technical term is AWOL. I deserted

Ali—not something I'm either proud or ashamed of—I didn't plan it, it just happened. I went for a swim, apparently 'drowned' and woke up in the house of a local woman who found me on the beach of Lake Trasimeno in Italy...

I look up from the letter as I absorb the fact of Walter's life. I do not blink, tears creep warm down my cheeks. A cobweb, over the round window, sways in what feels like still air. A small fly struggles, caught in its stickiness.

I am in Italy, imagine the scenario. Walter washed up on a beach. Flotsam...

A woman in black walking along the road some twelve miles from where Walter had entered the lake the previous evening, noticed a large fish beached on the lake shore. She knew the legends of huge prehistoric-type fish that had entertained the local population for generations. Curiosity and the urge to have a story to tell, led her over onto the sand. When she got closer, she saw that the fins were hands, snaked and entwined with weed, the tail: legs, twisted as one, black with lake mud. She ran over, half in dread. What she found was a naked man half in and half out of the water, face down in the sand.

She rolled the body onto her knees, cradled his head and neck, guessed by his whiteness, his sandy hair, that he was not Italian. German?

'Sei vivo? Che ti succeed? Dai, rispondimi! Apri gli occhi—per favore, dai...'

'Alzati. Riesci ad alzarti? Bravo. Vieni con me. Ti porto in un posto sicuro. Metti il braccio intorno al collo e prova a camminare. Cost, dai.'[1]

After she had washed him with water heated on the stove, she gave him night-clothes, fed him salami, pancetta, water and a little wine. She folded him into a clean bed and closed the shutters. The man had not spoken.

When he woke it was almost dark. He lay for an hour or more staring, a leaden feeling in his body, joints stiff and sore, had no idea where he was or what he was doing there. When he put on the bedside light, he saw a simple room, dark floorboards, a rug beside the bed in all shades of red.

---

[1] *Are you alive? What's wrong with you? Come on answer me—open your eyes. Please, come on.*
Get up. Are you able to get up? Well done. Come with me. I'll take you to a safe place. Put your arm around my neck and try to walk. Like this. Come on.
Translation: Paolo Giagodi

There was a dressing table with peculiar turned legs, animals and birds carved into the wood. A severe wardrobe leaned toward him from the foot of the bed. The door, not quite closed, had caught the hem of a summer dress, its colours reflected in the glossy dark wood. On the dressing table was a photograph of an Italian serviceman. His head was high, stiff, like something from the past. Over the mirror: dog-tags.

There was a jug of water, a glass by the bed and a clock that ticked loudly. He drank from the jug until it was almost empty, then rolled back into sleep, dreamt of running breathless, a fire at his back, until the sun came up and the smell of fresh bread and coffee drew him to the knowledge that he needed food.

'E tutti bene?' she said softly when he appeared at the door of the kitchen. He stared at Signora Luciana without inhibition, dazed by sleep. He looked around the room, part of a large old house: simple, no clutter. She, about thirty, dressed in a loose black shift, smiled, beckoned him to sit. He could see grief in her face, had seen the same look in his mother's when he was just a boy. Had seen it in soldiers' faces, even in the expression of caged animals. She was once beautiful this Italian rescuer: she moved with grace, had a face to laugh in, which was now plain and a little baggy. Eyebrows rested heavily over hooded eyes.

She didn't try to communicate verbally much. He established his nationality and used sign and body language for the rest.

The mere act of sitting in a kitchen in a house gave him immense pleasure. He noticed domestic appliances, furniture, the shape of a chair leg, the wrapping around the cheese, butter on a slab, keys on a hook. Things he hadn't experienced for nearly three years. He noticed the roundness of her shoulder, the point of her elbow with its dimple, the downturn of her mouth despite her smiles.

She seemed puzzled by him. He knew she would like to know how he came to be in the water, but she didn't try to ask. He sensed her pleasure at being able to help. She kept remembering little things that he might like, a razor, a toothbrush, day clothes, more coffee, tutting each time to herself that she hadn't thought of it sooner. The loose-fitting cotton dress covered her full figure. Sandals on brown pretty feet. She had shapely legs.

He would not be listed as missing yet. He could take a little longer. Besides, he was exhausted. Moving made him breathless and he was hungry all the time. She seemed happy for him to be there. She made no effort to contact the authorities.

After three days Walter became used to Maria's quiet movements around the house, her unquestioning acceptance of his need to be there; her need. He knew he must leave in the morning. He had stayed too long. If he didn't, he might not go at all. There was something about being there that evoked memories, feelings, that a life with men had suppressed.

That night as he was drifting into the first relaxed sleep for a long time, he opened his eyes to the lazy creak of the bedroom door being opened very slowly behind him. A shaft of light fanned over his bed, over the floor, then fanned back into darkness. Nothing. He held his breath, closed his eyes, heard the faint press on the wooden floor of bare feet. Then he knew.

The warm body of Signora Luciana slid into bed behind him. He felt the coarse cotton of her nightgown against his bare skin, felt her arm slide up his back over his shoulder to his neck, down his arm, her breath on his skin made him shiver. Her voice *andante* powdered the silence: 'Va tutto bene. Non ti preoccupare di niente…' Then she was still. A tension filled the air. He turned, looked at her in the semi darkness: wide-eyed, expectant, nervous. He kissed her on the mouth, then slid his arms around her shoulders and pulled her to him so tight he almost couldn't breathe.

In the morning, there was affection and the unspoken knowledge that he would go. As she prepared food, she snatched looks at him, darts of tenderness, a small sad smile signalling their imminent parting. He left early, before the breakfast she had laid out for him, before it became unbearable. Maria's husband's clothes were a little big for him. She gave him a bicycle and a sealed letter, which she wouldn't let him open, 'Domane, prego', she begged him. She gave him a small basket of food tied to the handlebars, kissed both of his hands and quickly closed the door…

Yes, that's how it would have been…

She was kind, Ali, and I must tell you, I left something of myself there. Sitting in that house, I saw that somewhere life went on, that the one we'd all been living wasn't all there was, that the death of so many pals was…well, pointless. I hadn't meant to desert, never consciously intended it, but once done, it felt like the most natural thing in the world.

I travelled by bicycle across and up the eastern side of Italy (it was so beautiful, Ali, you would love it there) and somehow found myself working on a farm for a widow that had lost her husband and two teenage sons in Greece.

I stayed there for several months after the war finished. I wasn't sure whether I'd be treated as a criminal on my return. I couldn't let anyone know—do you see? Eventually I wrote to Mam. I know I was selfish, but I think had I stayed with my unit I would either be dead or have lost my mind. War suits some blokes; best years of their lives to hear them talk. Not me.

I know you'll be angry when you read this, I don't blame you. I know the pain I must have caused. Maybe you already know all this and that's why you haven't replied. Somehow it just felt right to be where I was, growing things instead of killing them. It's all in the past now. Strangely enough, I have no regrets, though there are those that would call me a coward. Perhaps I am—I don't know.

I hope your husband won't mind me writing to you from time to time. We go back a long way, don't we, Ali? I'd love to hear from you, we all would. Sometimes I feel like getting on a boat and coming out to see you, but Shirley, my new lady-friend (more of that in another letter), said she wouldn't be best pleased and I'm not sure how your husband would react. (I hear he's a big bloke!)

Tell me what life is like in America, Ali, tell us all. (Your parents still miss you so...I know about you and your dad, but take it from me, he hates himself for letting you go without seeing you.)

Whenever I walk up by Stoodley Pike, I think of you, perched on a rock, a feather in your fingers!

Be happy, Ali love, write and tell us how you are.

Love always,

Walter

I am blasted, bare. A bird blown into unknown territory. Walter is alive; a deserter, just like me...I look into the trunk where there are more letters. I pick up another...

Horsehold cottages,
Hebden
Dec 1951

Darling Alice,
Just a quick note this time, as I'm going to the Post Office, to tell you about Vincent's wedding. You'll remember he wanted a Christmas wedding (foolish man!); well, he got it. It was a white wedding in every sense of the word, the snow was a foot deep!

We had a lovely day, Ali—we all raised our glasses to you, Vincent included you in his speech, said the only thing missing from the day was 'our Ali'.

She's a lovely girl, Margaret, I know I've told you all about her, but she really is sweet. I think she misses her home in Hampshire, but she doesn't go on about it. I really think they may move there one day. I hope not, of course, but I don't say anything. Ned's children are coming along. David is three now and very full of himself. Alice is six months and already rules the roost! Anyway, I'll stop here, or I'll miss the post.

I'll keep on writing, Ali, as long as I live, in the hope that you are reading all about us and that one day we'll see you...

Love as ever,

Mam and Dad XXXX

Gradually, the brightness begins to fade from the small window as the sun moves over the sky. The evening light gives the room an unearthly pink glow. The cobweb floats, now gold like silk, the small fly has ceased struggling in the maze of it, and I have the strangest sensation that I am not alone. My whole family are here with me including those I have never met. A small boy called David stares at me with cow eyes, an uneasy smile waiting for encouragement. A baby called Alice is me. She holds a hand out to me, impatient for a response...I have been replaced.

I realise I have been up here for hours reading letter after letter from my family, even two so far from Lily. My legs are locked, my feet numb and still I have not read all the letters. But I have read enough. I tuck four of them into my pocket and go back down the ladder. I am calm. I am thinking more clearly than I have for a very long time.

Downstairs, the radio is playing Ray Charles: *Take these chains from my heart and set me free*...just the sound of the waste in his voice makes the tears come thick and fast and I can hardly see for the blur that falls down my cheeks. I let myself into Carl's room for the second time in years and walk straight to the drawer where he keeps his cash. The rolls of money in the red elastic bands are still there. Why? Guilt? There is also a wedge of twenty-dollar bills two inches thick in a brown envelope.

I leave the envelope and its contents and take the two rolls of money. I leave the room and go to the kitchen, make myself four sandwiches, take some fruit, a bottle of water and pack it in a bag along with the money. I go to my room, dress for a journey, take my passport, hidden since Jake's death in the leaves of my gardening book, my journals from under the range, a creased red dress, Jake's dream-catcher and the four letters, then return to the kitchen where I pick up the bag of food.

Suddenly, I remember something. I fetch a cardboard box from the pantry, find Swallow, our new kitten, who purrs then meows as I put her into the box. I take her and the small bag of belongings and food and calmly go out of the door, down the steps into the balmy evening and walk. I do not look back.

Chapter Thirty-One

September 1963

If I walk through the night, I shall be less afraid. Less likely to see anyone who may be tempted to enquire about a woman alone. I stay away from the road but keep it in view, a rule running straight into seeming infinity. It is not difficult, a fat sickle moon lights my way, cutting a milky swathe through the recently cut wheat, in what is a late harvest. The ground underfoot is furrowed and slow to traverse and at around midnight I cut over to the road, there has been no car for a considerable time, and the relief of walking over flat ground is immense, my ankles grazed and sore from the sharp stubble.

Notwithstanding the discomfort, I feel light, glad to be using my body. My energy surprises me, an ecstatic tremble enlivens my progress such as I imagine a captive bird may feel when it is released. Swallow has stopped following me finally and I am sure she will make her way to the Amish house that we passed a short while back.

It is three in the morning. I have been walking for seven hours. The soles of my feet ache and I could wish for a better pair of shoes. I look around for anything that could provide shelter for me to rest, but there is only the wheat or stubble stretching out: a flat, featureless desert. I leave the road again and head into the land. In the middle of a borderless field, I make my bed where the wheat remains uncut and so will provide a better screening from the road. I flatten a small circle, spread my cardigan on the ground and lie down exhausted, using my bag of food as a pillow.

Despite the physical discomfort, my fatigue and the bizarre nature of my situation, I feel, for the first time in years, mentally alive. My mind scurries hither and thither trying to make sense of my past; the years spent in isolation at Home Farm, unaware that my whole family were there too, hiding in the loft—one of the letters I read, rejoicing at the receipt of my telegram, the first contact they had received for years, and the long wait for me to arrive. Then the decision, in another, made recently, to come out to try to find me.

But I shall get there first. This time, I shall get there…

These random thoughts assuage for a while or perhaps just distract me, from the rustle of harvest bugs that make me jump and scratch. I try to imagine that I am protected by a benign universe fanning around me—I think of Jake suddenly—a giant cloak protecting, guarding, ensuring that nothing can hurt me, because this, lying here in the earth under the stars, on my way to wherever I am going, is what I am meant to do. Finally, in half sleep, I experience an overwhelming, almost euphoric sense of well-being; I think it is joy. In my head the refrain from the music on the radio yesterday repeats over and over, as Helen Shapiro's *Walking back to happiness*…rocks me into sleep.

A rumble in the earth and I am in a car with Jake driving far away, his leathern smell comforting. He is smiling a circle saying *I told you so, I told you*…The dream-catcher, that hangs from the car mirror, swings to and fro. The engine noise gets louder and louder until I can't hear him speak, until I want to cover my ears.

I wake suddenly, open my eyes and find myself in a field, an early sun, sharp and white, blinding me, a combine harvester droning uncomfortably close. There is a rustle and frantic scurrying all around me. I sit up, rigid and cold, hardly able to move my limbs, and see the red predator moving up the field, having come within ten feet of where I am lying. I force myself up and flutter stiffly towards the road before I am caught in its sights.

I know I cannot stay on the road. Carl will come along on his way home. I head up the first dirt track I come to, hoping it has a destination, rather than just the middle of another field. I cannot stop scratching the insect bites that cover my ankles and wrists and I ache all over from lying on hard ground, but still, I experience a frisson of pleasure, smugness at my bravery for having survived my only night ever truly alone. And I am certain that in the distance, I see the pall of the town.

The rattle and swerve of the Greyhound is soporific and rocks me in and out of sleep. Waiting for the bus, at the edge of town, having walked almost all night and all day to get there, gave me a sense of achievement, but I am worn down by it. Each time I surface from somnolence I remember I am an escapee; that I could still be netted. I have been here before, cannot afford complacency. In one of these anxious moments a grey truck noses past us on the freeway and a burly male driver glances up at my supine figure resting against the pane. I start, thinking it is Carl. He drives on, eyes forward, having seen nothing of interest.

Within six hours, I am in Canada, having been advised at the depot in Glasgow, my first greyhound stop, that I would save time going North, making my way from there, rather than waiting around for the infrequent buses going South-East. New York is over two thousand miles away. Wherever I want to go, the distance is immense. I don't think I realised quite how isolated I have been.

Putting miles between Carl and myself is my priority and Canada would be the last place Carl would look, should he follow me. There also just happened to be a bus leaving for Calgary, some five hundred miles west, which feels like the wrong direction and yet bizarrely, seemed like a sensible solution. I am not sure I am thinking clearly.

We crossed the Canadian border at Coutts and within an hour caught up with Milk River, which we had followed on and off all the way from Glasgow. Then we lost it for a while at a place called Havre. Milk River. *The colour of tea with milk.*

As the bus moves along fast on empty roads, I have a clear view to my left of the Rockies, spectacular in the incipient dawn, the sun sitting on the horizon on our right, highlighting all the ridged detail of the mountains: grey downfall, waterfalls of rock, the peaks beginning to pink as I think and watch. *When the sun comes up its like honey spills over them...* The passengers are all asleep.

The driver, just in front of me, spying my awe through his mirror, says softly: 'Quite something, ain't they?'

I am unkempt, grubby, aware of a mild body odour that for some reason reminds me of my infanthood. I am also hungry and haunt the backstreets of the city for somewhere to eat. I settle for a smoky diner where I shrink into a leatherette booth by the window, listen to *Peter, Paul and Mary* singing *Blowin' in the Wind* playing on the juke-box, and watch people with lives, rushing by to do important things. I am trying not to be noticed; I have spent so long being invisible it is not difficult.

The waitress though, casts a look at my dirty shoes and wispy hair, the bites on my wrists, perhaps imagining I am a vagrant come to nurse a two-hour coffee. I order eggs and ham and that seems to appease her sense of begrudging superiority. On the table is a local paper left by the previous occupant and I pretend to be interested by the news: *Ku Klux Klan group responsible for dynamite that kills four girls in church in Alabama... US Army soldiers land in*

*South Vietnam pursuing communist Viet Cong guilty of attack on Vietnamese outpost...Minimum wage in US increased to $1.25 an hour...*I shudder at my ignorance of the world and am sad to know that for some, their lot is far worse than mine. Then my attention is caught by an article about a British airline, which has begun flights between several Canadian airports and London.

Flying home?

Since plotting my escape from Home Farm, the possibility of flying had never occurred to either Jake or me. When I had mentioned to Carl over recent years of taking an aeroplane home for a visit, his response was laughter, as though I were a child. *Flying is for the rich and famous, politicians, film stars and the like. Fancy yourself as a film star, do you? You need to get real...*

But it seems things have changed. The fare outlined in the article, though apparently more than twice the shipping fare, is within my budget. Suddenly, I have energy. Perhaps I don't have to travel on to the coast, perhaps I can head to an airport, get home that way. Everything seems to be falling into place. I finish my meal and head back to the coach depot and ask how I can get to the nearest international airport.

As I sit waiting for my flight, I am amazed how easy everything seems to have been. Although there are only two flights a week, there is one this evening and there is space on the flight. Jake always told me that when things are meant to be, they happen easily. Everything fits, he said, like a puzzle that waited for someone to come along and work out the solution. The only small problem being that the airfare has taken all my money, save fifteen dollars and thirty cents; I don't know what I shall do when I get there. Even that though, seems miraculous, as though the amount had been calculated in advance.

I go to the comfort station to try to freshen up. Despite my tiredness, there is a youthful vigour in me. I feel it in my muscles, my demeanour. I smile at my reflection in the mirror as I wash my hands and jig to the piped music: *He's so fine...* feeling suddenly young, though am surprised to see smiling back at me a middle-aged woman with wispy grey-flecked hair, thread veins around her cheeks and a grey pallor. I splash the water onto my face, erasing the image. I shall shed this skin and begin again. I am not old; I am not yet forty. I can have a life. I shall be with my family; that will be enough.

I smile again at the idea that in a few hours, I shall be out of this continent for good. I push back my shoulders, stand straight, feel a rising excitement in my gut. I brush down my clothes, attempt to clear the worst of the dirt from my shoes, check my ticket and passport. Then check it again. Satisfied, I push open the swing door onto the main console and hear the tannoy announcing my flight. Suddenly, like a nightmare barging in on the daylight, I catch, in my peripheral vision, the sight of a man rushing through the terminal, as though he is looking for someone. He is very tall, wearing tartan trousers that are too short.

I step back into the comfort station, my heart pounding, hide myself in a toilet cubicle and sit wringing my hands, a quiet wail escaping my lips. I have no perception of time, only of the need to suppress my panic. I cannot go back to Home Farm now, shall not go back. He can kill me here, in front of all these people; I shall not go back a third time. I shall scream and scream and scream. I shall not go back. Then I hear the call for the last remaining passengers for the BOAC flight to London to go to gate 3. It is now or never.

I pick up my small bag; keep my gaze lowered, not daring to look around me until I reach the gate, where a few stragglers are queuing to walk out across the tarmac to the waiting aeroplane. As I look up and join the queue, directly in front of me is the tall man I saw rushing. I take a step back convinced it is over, he turns, sees me.

'You late too? Thought I wouldn't make it.' His Canadian accent, his shape, the cut of his clothes—how could I have mistaken him for Carl? I smile, nod, remember suddenly how, when I was told all those years ago—fresh as yesterday—that Walter was dead, I seemed to see him in every shadow, every man with a vague resemblance to him would for the briefest of moments become him. The same is true conversely, when you want more than anything else in the world *not* to see someone.

My trembling hand gives my boarding pass to the pretty young stewardess, and then I walk out across the early fall evening to the drone of aircraft engines, thinking how remarkable it is that only forty-eight hours ago I was trapped in a life. It has taken me seventeen years to remove the lid. The wasp is free. I do not look back as I walk up the steps onto British territory.

'Welcome aboard, Madam.' The crisp English voice is sharp and salty like potato chips. I smile.

Chapter Thirty-Two

England

As I sit in Terminal One at Heathrow Airport, I wonder how I am to get home. I stare at the few pounds the bank has given me in exchange for the dollars I had left. I think perhaps I could take a coach, but I just keep sitting. My eyes water. I dab my mouth; I am dribbling. No one had telephones when I left, it occurs to me that they may have one now, but, if so, I do not know the number.

People are scurrying like rats; skittering, swooshing past; everyone in a hurry. I watch the girls with their pretty painted faces, skirts so short I look around to see whether anyone else is shocked. They are not. Life has moved on without me; nothing is familiar. I wonder how many of the women have the *knowledge*. Of living in fear. Of a marriage that winds around them like bindweed until they are unable to move; where freewill is a drooping flower, choked, that bears no seed.

One in fifty? One in ten? One in five?

I am a statistic, a survivor. One of the lucky ones. The bird that flew away. I want to thank God, but I can't. He has not helped me, only pushed me deeper into the fire. Jake was right. No following of *rules* can protect you from the devil; the only altar passive acceptance can lead you to, is the sacrificial one.

I am smaller now than I was, I could squeeze into any corner unnoticed. I try it; hunch my shoulders, bring up my knees. I am invisible. Why did I let another human treat me that way? Who or what threw that ancient line that knotted Sheila, then him, then me? Without Jake would I ever have severed it? I wonder these things as I sit and rock.

I have not eaten. I feel light-headed and seem to have lost the ability to act, so I sit and wait and be invisible. I am very tired.

I think about the sensation of lifting into the air on the flight, the noisy turbulent grace of it. I watched as the land receded, as we ploughed through what looked like walls of volcanic cloud. The words Cu Nims came into my head. Some distant bell chimed:

'Cu Nims, Cu Nims…' I say aloud now like some ancient mantra. I am taken back to a sunlit day on the moors when I was just a girl and Walter explained to me all about storm clouds called Cumulus Nimbus.

After take-off we bounced around a little until we came out above the cloud, stretching like a pink desert into infinity. A late sun streaming through the windows warmed my face, until it gradually dipped behind a darkening horizon and a fattening curved moon nudged itself above the earth on the opposite side. I did not sleep on the flight, even through the night I kept open the blind and stared into the darkness, the moonlit cloud strewn carelessly across the floor of the sky as I floated in the space between my past and my future. The voyage back.

What a wonderful thing this flying is. I thought of Vincent's letters from the war full of the exquisite joy of flight. I hoped one day I could tell him: *I understand, I know why you love it, because it is remarkable.*

And, I was travelling in a straight line, not walking in circles.

'Cu…Nims…'

And though steady tears fell down my face, tears that had built up over the years, tears of anger, of waste, of apprehension and sheer fatigue; tears that no amount of relief could assuage, still…I felt truly happy.

And now I imagine walking over the fells, listening to the crunch of Tara's bit in her mouth, feeling the soft indent of my steps on the springy turf, youth in my stride, sun on my face. Walter is beside me talking of war, of a future and I can see the future and I want to scream. And I wonder now, what happened? How did we all go so wrong? What misery did I inflict on my family? I can hardly remember. And Carl. Would he have been happier marrying one of his own instead of me: an Overcomer, who, from her very first step onto American soil yearned for what she had left behind.

'Cu Nims,' I say softly to myself.

'She keeps saying that. It's a memory from a long time ago, when she was a girl, she told me. I went over to ask if she was all right…I could see she was in a bit of a state. I've been with her two hours now. She's been telling me all sorts of things about herself, when she lived here, before she went America…all a bit muddled. She showed me some letters, and a journal. Do you think you could help her? She's had a rough time, I think. She's very confused. Look at her shoes, her feet. She said she flew in from Canada this morning, but I don't know…She keeps saying she just wants to go home. I don't think she has money, she's not quite, you know…' She lowered her voice.

The stewardess with the nice face is trying to help me, though I'm not sure she has really been listening, I read part of my journal to her by way of explanation, but she just looked confused. The young man she brings over from Immigration seems to know what to do. They are talking as though I can't hear them. They think I'm barmy, that I'm a doddering old woman; that I'm *one chair short of a dining set*, as my mother would say. I want to say: *I'm just tired—I have been awake for more than two days. I am not old, simply exhausted. If I were going to lose my mind, I assure you, it would have happened a long time ago.* But I say nothing, just nurse my aching legs. Telling her about my life has worn me down; feel I have relived it. As they prattle about my 'predicament', I listen to their British accents, smile a sleepy smile. I am a migrating bird, want only to nest.

'Come with me, my love. What *'ave* you been doing? You look as though you bin sleeping in a field!' His cockney accent reminds me of the war years, my trip to London. 'I think you need some food, this lady 'ere's been watching you, says you 'aven't moved. Would you like a cup a tea, love? We'll get you 'ome, don't you worry about the money, that's what were 'ere for, to help people in trouble…'

*

I ask the taxi to drop me at the bottom of Horsehold, I need to walk that last quarter mile. I have rallied. It is late afternoon on the fourth day, and I am walking up Horsehold.

'I am walking up Horsehold,' I say aloud, involuntarily.

It is a miracle.

So much has changed in the town, traffic lights, new houses, shops, a café, so many cars, girls in bright colours, boys with long hair, and yet, it seems the same. Here it *is* the same. It is September. I breathe in the air, already a promise of winter in it. It has been raining and the earth smells of late fruit and rotting leaves. Also, weirdly—Jake—a warm leathery smell, so much so, I stop, look up, as though half expecting to see him. A blackbird wheels into the air and flies off.

The road feels steep. I had forgotten hills; my breathing is heavy, laboured. I stop, putting off the moment of turning the bend. I need to savour this last minute of aloneness, prepare myself for what I may find. As I pause, I spy on the ground in front of me, a small curled white feather. Not wet or bedraggled, perfect. Just one. I stoop, pick it up, hold it up to the light. I feel myself smiling. I put the feather in my pocket, hold it lightly between my fingers.

I look around me. A weak sun is low in the sky, my hair frizzes with the dampness, I feel a heat burn inside me, my forehead moisten. The moors are olive in the frail light and a ground mist is already swelling, curling against the stone walls. There are blackberries in the hedgerow, worms in the puddles. Stoodley Pike suddenly emerges faint and high in the distance from behind a drift of low cloud.

I continue walking and see the house, so small, and I am reminded of my picture of it on the yellow nursery wall that Carl painted over, sometime after my miscarriage. I notice each bulging stone of black millstone grit, a chimney with smoke curling, sinking onto the roof. I am lost in a dream. I don't quite know if I am sane. I gaze, while a sense of profound contentment settles on me like a warming sun. For a moment, I cannot go forward, but there is no going back. Ever.

Then I see her, an outline in the window looking out. There is something familiar, but the reflection of the light on the glass makes it difficult. The figure then sees me, moves closer to the glass with an air of someone wary of callers, then withdraws when she sees me staring back.

I go to the door, the smell and look of fresh paint, and knock. I remember the door of the Amish house I knocked on all those years ago and am filled suddenly with foreboding. A bustling elderly woman comes to the door as though slightly irritated by a caller at this time and my apprehension dissipates into the air.

'Yes, can I help you?' She looks over my shoulder to check whether I am alone.

'Mam?' My voice is barely audible.

'Beg your pardon?' She looks at me, unsure.

I clear my throat. 'Mam…it's me…Alice.'

Chapter Thirty-Three

Hebden

October 1963

It is Sunday. *Sing something simple*...plays softly on Mam's radiogram. There is a smell of roast beef in the oven, the clanging of cutlery from the kitchen. Outside, rooks caw and wheel in the grey air, their nests high and dark in ancient oaks. I am in a time-warp.

Ned's voice is raspy, as he ponders aloud the passage of time, filling in the gaps. His head tilts to one side as though the patch over his eye weighs him down, while 'little' Alice, his lovely daughter, who at thirteen is going to be the tallest female in the family; her long legs amply displayed in Capri pants, sings Gerry and The Pacemakers: *I like it, I like it, I like the way you run your fingers through my hair*...while brushing mine.

She sees me as a project. *Loves my accent*. The conversation circles on itself as though we can think of little else than my *absence* to speak of; and yet we can't speak of it. Each time I pick up the photo of Dad on the mantlepiece, which draws me like a fire, everyone goes quiet, exchange glances. One day, Mam speaks.

'He didn't mention your name for six months, Ali, not once he didn't. Walked out of the room, his eyes brimming, whenever you were mentioned. Years later, we couldn't shut him up. He talked of you constantly. He never admitted he'd been wrong—'

'He wasn't wrong.'

'...he never admitted he was wrong...' she speaks over me, tilting my chin with her hand so that she can look me in the eye, 'but we all knew he felt it. I don't know whether Ned told you love...but two weeks after he... you know... passed on...' she hesitates, as though speaking about it makes it more real, 'he was due to be sailing out to try to find you. Had a ticket and everything. You know, we never had much money to speak of...but he cashed in his Post Office savings for the ticket. This was well before we got your telegram. But his death…well, and after that, Vincent was going to come.

'Dad tried before, of course. He got as far as Southampton back in '55 but suffered his first mild heart attack whilst there and after treatment, they told him to come home. He waited, Ali, always. Always believed that one day you would knock on the door. Said all those years without contact was…well, he wanted to see you before he… He'd begun to be afraid.'

'Mam, don't.' Vincent puts his arm around her. A fleeting look at me speaks of the need for caution. 'She's back now, Mam. Dad knows, wherever the old sod is—he knows.'

'Sorry love.' Mam turns her back, sweeping away tears. 'He was afraid, you see… had a bad feeling… he loved you, Ali, more than anyone…'

'I know, Mam, I know… it's okay.'

For some reason, my father's death seems to affect me less than perhaps it should, as though I can only cope with things one at a time. They have all been dead to me for so long, it is their *aliveness* that seems more difficult, as though I must stem my resentment of their carrying on as normal for so long. And we are all different people; I have been alive almost as long without them as I have with them.

'Have you seen Walter yet, Ali?' Vincent asks directly. 'You two were pretty sweet, I seem to remember.' I can tell the subject has been discussed.

'No… I haven't. I thought… well, I don't know what I thought really. He's nothing to do with me now… that was all a lifetime ago… I suppose I don't want him to see me looking like I'm ninety.' Everyone laughs nervously.

'I should think she's had enough of men.' There is a gritty edginess in Mam's voice. Vincent winces. 'Anyhow, it's amazing what that haircut and a good rest has done. Alice, leave our Ali's hair alone, you're spoiling it.'

'Can I do your make-up, Auntie Alice?'

'Yes love, see what you can do with me.'

I haven't told Mam half of what happened at Home Farm; shall never tell anyone the worst of it, can't even record it here. Back in this sane world, my experiences seem so extreme. Talking about it to her, with her Catholic view of things, would not only make me feel in some way culpable. Also, I squirm when any mention of sex is made in front of her; there have been no intervening years where we have communicated as adults. I think Ned is the only one who guesses exactly what my life has been.

At that moment he puts his hand over mine, I almost flinch, he smiles, picks it up and kisses it.

'How is he? Walter, I mean,' I ask almost perfunctorily.

'You know he married?' Vincent says.

'No, I didn't.' Even after all the years, I feel a pang, then am angry with myself for learning nothing.

Mam says he wrote to you about it, I'm sure…'

'I didn't get…' It must have been in one of the letters still in the box in the attic at Home Farm. A strange thought that. Part of my life and that of my family is still trapped up there, the swing of sunlight moving over the treasure chest every day from the round window.

'Oh…' Mam's hand clasps melodramatically over her mouth. 'Sorry love I forgot…your old Mam is a bit forgetful now.'

'It's okay.'

'He married Shirley Grey, from over Rawtenstall way,' Margaret, Vincent's wife, says casually, unaware of the shifted dynamics introduced between us at the mention of his name. 'Nice, we thought…They had no children; I think that's what broke up the marriage. She didn't want any apparently. Then she went off with another bloke and was pregnant within six months.'

'Fancy any woman not wanting bairns…it's not natural,' Mam adds, then darts a nervous glance at me. I hate feeling that I am being watched for any adverse reaction to what is said. The doctor has told Mam that trauma can alter someone psychologically, which of course, being Mam, she told me. Now everyone is looking for it.

'I think he was a bit weak about the whole affair, if I'm honest,' Vincent says, as though it is important, tugging at the grey hair of his temples. 'I mean I'm not sure he really cared that much.' He crosses his legs, folds his arms. He has become a little smug. Cocksure.

Over the month since I have been home, I have come to realise that Vincent disapproves of Walter's wartime 'desertion'; never loses an opportunity to criticise him.

'We're all weak, Vincent, one way or another,' I say. 'I can tell you all about weak.' Suddenly self-conscious, I get up from the settee and gaze out over the moor.

'Anyhow, they split up a long time since. She remarried, moved back to Rawtenstall and he bought a flat in Manchester where he works for the newspapers, though he still keeps his mother's old house here. Sold the shop, of course. You know she died?' Ned says.

So many deaths, so much bad news.

'No,' I say quietly.

'Always liked Walter, Dad and I did,' Mam says wistfully. 'Always thought you and he would…well, you know…all water under the bridge now.'

'Look…we've all got to stop being awkward with each other.' I turn from the window.

'We're not, love…are we, boys? Not awkward.' Mam stands leaning forward, wanting it to be right. I smile weakly, turn back, talk to the window, suddenly have a memory of my face squashed against it.

'What happened, happened. So, I've thrown my life away, I know it. But I'm back now. New slate, you know? It's going to take a long time…' I feel my voice falter, I bite my lip, blink my eyes.

Ned pulls himself up out of his chair with the help of his sticks, then very deliberately puts them down, turns me around and pulls me to him. His wife Helen, as I am beginning to realise is her way: saying little, seeing all, watches her husband. He holds me very tight, pushing the breath out of me, causing me to whimper.

I don't know whether it is the conversation, his gesture, the smell of his skin, his kindness, but I cry on his shoulder in front of everyone, sobs heaving from my belly until I am close on distraught. I see that Helen's cheeks are wet. It is the first time I have cried to someone in over seventeen years, and I cannot stop. Mam comes over and puts her arms around the pair of us and bawls too.

'Gee, why is everyone around here scrikin'? Didn't you want tea?' David, Ned's son says, returning from the kitchen, mimicking my accent, bizarre mixture of northern vernacular and American, a tray of crumpets and pot of tea for us all in his hands. Everyone laughs, including me through my tears.

'How about a ramble up over't moors tomorrow, Ali, to Stoodley, remind yourself what the wind can do up on the tops?' Vincent says suddenly.

And that's how it is. Everyone pussyfooting around me, whilst I try to be the girl I used to be, before I realise, she is never coming back. It must be difficult for them all; whatever they say is wrong, and my responses are snappy, defensive. Lingering at the back of everything is the resentment, theirs and mine, that I chose Carl above all of them. I want to say to them—I was just a girl, a silly headstrong girl, but I say nothing.

Jake told me once that all experience, even bad experience makes us grow: *what doesn't kill you feeds the soul*. Well perhaps I have grown, and I have to get used to it, and so does everyone else. Though, all things considered, it is the cocoon of my family that is helping me make the transition. I avoid contact with anyone outside because I imagine my return as something shameful, a failure, something to hide and I don't want to keep dredging up all the evasions for coming back alone. And because I simply can't bear to see what time has done to folk, with the implication that I have missed out on all the years between.

The visit to old Father Martin has promised to be difficult.

'You've got to see him, Ali,' Mam said at least once a day for the first couple of weeks at home. The conversations always go the same way.

'I'm not the same, Mam.'

'Once a Catholic, my girl—'

'No Mam, I'm not anything, not anymore.'

'I don't understand…'

'I know only that I don't want to get back into that particular cage.'

'Cage!'

'All my life I've been wearing a hair shirt, apologising for living. Oozing guilt. The church gave me that; men in black cassocks and rosary beads that had no idea what they were doing.'

'Oh Ali, you exaggerate…'

'Mam, you have no idea…Your life just happened to fall in with the Catholic ideal. Try to imagine what it's like going through life as a failure, a *sinner*. But I know now, I'm not a sinner. I'm flawed like everyone else, that's all.'

In the event, my meeting with him is productive and in a funny sort of way, cathartic—helps me make peace with my demons. Coming home is proving to be neither an end nor a beginning; I've been here before. I've had two lives; just have to ensure that the weight of one doesn't crush the life out of the other.

Chapter Thirty-Four

When the letter comes, it is a shock. I had expected to deal with things through Mr Slattery. When we were going over everything and he asked me whether I had adequate grounds for divorce, I laughed. Where did I start? Adultery, mental and physical cruelty, unreasonable behaviour… He stopped me. I needed only one. Which, he asked, would be the most likely that Carl would accept? *Accept?* Surely the truth is the truth, I said. It was his turn to laugh. As it turned out, it really made no difference; the law is the law. No matter what our personal sense of grievance, threat, need, the sense of rightness of it all—we are all the same when it comes to divorce, bound by the same rules.

It was pouring with rain when I arrived at his office in Manchester, flat with wet clothes and chilled by a wind that had suddenly come up, and at what I had to face behind his closed door. For some reason, I felt like some plaintive confessor as I pressed the bell, as though the muck of marriage I would have to excavate would somehow implicate me, and that I would reveal myself to be, after all, the culpable one. Less afraid, I think, that he would objectively judge me to be that, than that I myself, on hearing out loud for the first time how it was, might judge myself to be. I realised in that moment that the black crow had not gone from my shoulder; it was merely dormant.

However, I told myself, I had to take a business-like approach to this, put in the relevant investment to get the return that I wanted. Guilt and blame were irrelevant; I just wanted an end to it.

His receptionist smiled broadly in *a poor you* sort of way when I came in and dripped all over the floor. She rushed into the back room only to rush out again with a tired looking towel for me to wrap about myself. Almost immediately a smiling Mr Slattery, Ned's solicitor and friend, opened the door to his office, looking very dapper in a dark pinstripe suit and crisp white shirt. It was a smartness I hadn't encountered in years and made me glad to see it for some reason. He greeted me warmly, placating my anxiety, and bade me sit, leaning back to the receptionist through the door asking for a pot of tea for two and to hold all calls.

I sipped my tea, as he took notes of all our finances and assets, perversely enjoying the ritual and the drama of the occasion after all, perhaps it was the cosy indulgence of being benignly listened to, I don't know. *I don't want any money,* I said. *Just to be free of him.*

'It depends,' he said. 'Is he, notwithstanding what you have told me, in any sense a reasonable man?' I didn't reply, just gave him a look. 'Besides, you simply can't walk away from this marriage empty-handed after seventeen years, you're entitled to reasonable financial provision, including maintenance.'

'Everything he has is worth nothing to me,' I replied. 'Half of nothing is still nothing. Do what you have to.'

'Well, to be honest, it probably won't be up to you—you can't really dictate to the courts what you do or do not want, they will decide.'

He remained silent for a few moments mulling over all I had said, his closed fountain pen poised between two index fingers, his wedding ring yellow against his white skin. I knew from Ned that he was a good and decent man with two grown children. I had liked him instantly. While he pondered what I told him, taking his time—this was a man that wouldn't be hurried—I looked out of the rain-smeared window, out over the roofs of the law courts.

A pigeon sheltered on the windowsill, turning and cooing and pattering its feet. Below, a world turned. Buses and cars revved and hooted, and people, oblivious to my personal hiatus, moved along the pavements, carrying shopping, babies, pushing, pulling, living, laughing, hoping, dreaming. All I wanted now was to be one of them without always looking over my shoulder. I told him again, I wanted nothing of Home Farm, nothing of Carl. I'm not sure he was entirely convinced; thought it was grief or anger talking. Or both. But it wasn't, it was indifference.

'Of course, Mrs McCullough, the *problem* of maintenance aside, there is the question of whether the English legal system would have jurisdiction in this case. You can only bring divorce proceedings in England if you are domiciled or permanently resident here. If you have returned to England and were domiciled in America, you can only start proceedings here after 3 years of residence.

'Otherwise, I am afraid, you will have to bring proceedings in America, specifically Montana. Then you would be bound by the decisions of the US court and if that be the case, you, as the petitioner, would have to appear in court in America for the hearing at least once, possibly twice.'

If it meant going back to the States, I would have to remain married, I told him. Nothing would induce me to return. It just wasn't physically possible for me. I pictured the scenario—standing in a courtroom with Carl, knowing what I know about the attitudes of those in authority towards Overcomers. I thought back to the one time in all those years that I tried to get some justice for Jake at the Sheriff's Office... No, it couldn't go that way.

'Oh...and it's Alice please.'

'Alice.'

'You've known my brother for many years and besides, I no longer consider myself either a Mrs or a McCullough, Mr Slattery.'

'Okay Alice, and it's Mike...'

'Pleased to meet you, Mike,' I smiled and stretched across his desk to shake hands again.'

'Right. Right then...Alice. Well, as you can see, the whole domicile thing is slightly complex in this case, given that you lived until recently in the States. When you married and moved there, did you intend to come back here at some stage in the future?'

'Well, no... I don't know... I suppose not. But things change, don't they? I am resident here now. I shall be always.'

'They could take a different view on that. However, if you really cannot go back to America then you cannot. In which case, we must wait and go for the three-year residency and then divorce should be pretty straightforward given your personal history, or the worst-case scenario, the five-year without consent.'

I felt a sinking sensation. It seemed that Carl was capable of trapping me even from three thousand miles away.

That was over a month ago. And now the letter I hold in my hand, its distinctive child-scrawl enough to make my legs go from under me, is an unexploded bomb, so that as I open it, I am on my knees.

Home Farm
3 December 1963

Hello Alice,
Remember me? So you want a divorce? Well, your just going to have to come here and plead for me to forgive you and then I'll think about it. You deserted

your husband, I think you'll find that's plenty grounds for me to divorce you, Alice, if I were so inclined. All your claims that I treated you bad have no proof. I treated you better than you deserved. You were nothing but trouble, you stole my money, and now you want to twist the knife by accusing me of everything under the sun. Where's your proof, that's what I say. Where's your goddamned proof? You are a bad wife, always were and not worth the effort.

You want something from me? Your going to have to come and get it, then we'll talk about it. Who knows, being back in England may have made you realize what you left behind. Your home is here. I can forgive you if you ask real nice.

Your husband,
Till death parts us,
Carl

PS: I told you once I'd never let you go. Remember?

I can hear his voice as I read it, feel the incipient threat, see the child-bully, also his personal desperation. I imagine Home Farm with its winter white wrapped around it like a forever chrysalis, and him buried deep within it, dying a long slow lonely death. He is going to fight in the only way he knows. I force myself to stand, look around me. I move into the sitting room, look out through the window, over the moors, on all that I love.

I breathe again, smile thankfully that I am here and not there. Carl was right in one thing; being here *has* made me realise what I have left behind. Here he cannot reach me, here he cannot hurt me. Empty threats; I've been living with them for years. There is nothing he can do. It is the death rattle of a dying man. I can deal with this.

When I take the letter to Mike, he tells me that because of the adultery and cruelty within the marriage, I would have sufficient grounds. *Is there anyone there that can vouch for you? Witnesses?* No, I say. Sheila and Jake are dead. Then I wonder about the Amish minister all those years ago. Would he remember what I told him? *The way is hard that leads to life*...No, even if he did, it would go against his principles, far easier, by silence, to condone the actions of a violent dysfunctional man, than to assist a woman in the breaking of a *divine institution*.

Ten days later, while Mam is out at a Christmas 'evergreen' meeting in the town, I am going through a prospectus I picked up whilst in the city: courses at

Manchester University. There are exemptions for mature students, which means that an interview and a two-hour examination on a previously set topic by the university will decide whether one is a suitable applicant. I allow myself a frisson of pleasure at the thought: Ali Conroy, a university student. How could that be possible, after all? Better late than never.

I go to fetch a pen from the hall table to begin filling out the relevant application forms when I catch sight of my reflection in the full-length mirror and the new purple A-Line Mam got me in the sale. What strikes me is the comparative youthfulness of my demeanour; I am only forty after all and I think I look pretty good.

Perhaps it is the mascara and lipstick that I have begun to wear, or the haircut, but I prefer to think that it is the way I move and the expression of calm that has settled onto my features over the last few weeks. It is more than well-being that crosses my physiology, it is the idea of a renaissance. I wander into the kitchen pleased with myself in a way that seems unfamiliar, but reminiscent of how I used to feel most of the time. I think it is optimism.

I look at the clock; Mam will be home soon. I switch on the transistor and listen to The Beatles singing: *With love from me to you...* while I put on the kettle, take pleasure in preparing tea: warming the pot, one spoon of tea-leaves each, one for the pot. *All these friggin' rituals...* I take the milk from the step and pour enough into the tiny jug on the side with its lace cover—wonder when I can persuade Mam to get a refrigerator.

Whilst I perform these mundane tasks, I am conscious of each and every step towards reinventing myself, or perhaps rediscovering what I once was. Small acts such as this are the outward evidence of my new freedom. I cut a slice of cake that Mam has made in her continuing effort to feed me up and sit at the kitchen table for my little snack whilst I wait for her. The radio station is now playing a Christmas carol and I find myself singing softly along while pondering what I shall write in my university application.

I take a sip of tea gazing about me thinking of essays and books that I shall read in preparation, random thoughts interjecting: I must clip back the dormant climbing rose that overhangs the window and taps on the glass every time the wind blows. Then, before my conscious mind can register it, Carl's face is peering in through the glass. And then it isn't. I freeze. I know it can't be, but stand up wide-eyed, my stomach lurching, to look out in any case. No one. Then a knock at the front door. I wilt, feel the familiar sinking sensation that the idea of his presence evokes: the nausea, the chill. Another knock. I walk slowly to the door, tremulous like a leaf fluttering in the cold December wind and open it.

'Sorry love, I forgot my key, I'm getting careless in my old age.'

I can't speak, instead lean out, look around, my hands white-fingered gripping onto the door architrave. Nothing. I smile, remember the man at the airport in Calgary.

'Cat got your tongue?'

'Sorry Mam, you're back. That's good. I…I didn't expect…I…so it was you at the window?'

'What? Just take this shopping, will you, love. Are you all right, you look like you've seen a ghost?'

'Not a ghost no, but…oh it's, you know, my mind playing tricks. Look, I've made us some tea. Cake?'

Two days later, I leave the house and walk into Hebden to post my application to the university. I stop and have a cup of tea in one of the cafés that have appeared since I left, enjoying that feeling of being around people—in the centre of something as opposed to the periphery of nothing. I like to *potter*, as Mam puts it, remembering afresh all that I have never forgotten and discover all that I have never known. The place still has my imprint on it; my childhood is here.

The Monkey Puzzle tree that I sat drawing patiently for hours for my primary school nature project, the mill chimneys that stand high over the town, about which, in school essays, I weaved fantasies of ghostly residents, being, as they were, at the margin of my known world and towering over it. The ducks on the canal, which as I cross, I think of a lovely summer's morning before the war… The old red brick pub that sits, out of context, in the middle of the main street, which my mother bade me avoid for the *riff-raff* that, according to her order of things, hung about there of an evening. All still here.

I wonder to myself whether Walter will be at his Mam's house over Christmas. I'm not ready to see him yet; want to be the some-one that I remember first, but I wonder, nonetheless. I put him out of my mind like a parcel one can't open yet.

I want to buy some baubles for the Christmas tree that Mam has ordered from the local farmer. I have no money for presents—the family don't expect it, but shopping money that Mam gives me from time to time will be enough.

As I walk back up Horsehold, feeling the steep in my knees, I think about the family coming up on the twenty-fourth and realise it will be my first Christmas at home since the war. We shall have turkey cooked just right with crispy bacon. No goose and no fat. I shall be with my family. I smile, can't stop smiling.

But in the night, I dream. Know things. Things I don't want to know. There is always the sense of a ticking clock in my dreams as though I am waiting but I don't know for what. Last night I dreamt I was still at Home Farm. I was cooking pieces of chicken that sizzled and spat sharp, coating me in a fine spray of heat and fat until I was drenched with it, until it splattered greasy around my feet where there were chicken feathers and bits of straw, and my red dress was there and a pair of worn-out red shoes with a broken heel.

Then I saw Jake at my side, his brown skin and hazel eyes, could smell his warm skin and I was filled with a nostalgia that I didn't understand. He was asking me a question, but I couldn't hear what he was saying for the sizzling from the range. Then the dream shifted, I was in his home, I didn't sit down, instead wrapped my coat around me trying to shut out what I didn't want to see. The bare light bulb was swinging in the December cold, and I could see a hoarfrost, crystallised over snow, covering a body, his body, and I was alone witness to this. Blood had seeped and dried brown into the icy blanket and I could see that he had been dead for a long time.

I woke crying out, soaking wet, when Mam's voice from next door shouted, gentle, asking if I was all right.

'Yes...yes. Just a dream, Mam. I'm fine.'

'Try and sleep, love. Night, night, God bless.'

But as I lay there waiting for sleep, I remembered what happened to Jake and began to unearth the whole thing again in my mind. How did he die? I felt uneasy, stopped feeling safe. Then I reasoned with myself, Carl was bad, he was an abuser, but he wasn't born that way. He wasn't a murderer, just a man that spent his life trying to take the control he'd never had. He didn't kill Jake, couldn't have done. He wouldn't hurt me. Not like that. Couldn't hurt me; I was here, and he was there.

Then as the dawn quietly stole into my room and took back the dark, I pulled back the curtain and stared out over a fresh blue snowfall where, in the garden, past the apple tree and out through the gap in the dry-stone wall, a solitary fox; silent visitor in the night, had left footprints. I relaxed, wandered downstairs to find Mam in the kitchen filling the kettle.

'Couldn't sleep, love, not after you woke me. Tea?'

'Thanks Mam, lovely.'

And now, as the purple grey light pinks on the freshly painted earth, Mam and I talk about things I never thought we could. I tell her what Carl has done to me; what his father had done to him, to Sheila and doubtless what had been done to his father in his turn. She speaks of Dad, his yearning for me and her grief, freshened by my reappearance and the knowledge that if he had lived just a little longer…

There is something cosseting about the winter morning, as though what we talk of, in soft reverent voices, can only be done in the hush of the surrounding insulating whiteness, before the world wakes up and is witness to it. I feel safe. See that I *can* be open with her; that she understands more than I suspected, that she has gleaned something of my life by my reticence to discuss it. She is wise and generous. We cry good tears, hold each other. I realise with some regret how much I had shut her out in my childhood, how much I have missed her since.

Chapter Thirty-Five

'Alice, put the crackers on the table love, would you? No…little Alice, I mean.'

'Nana, I'm taller than Auntie Ali, you can't keep calling me little Alice!' She takes the crackers and puts one by each place setting.

'The 'little' has nothing to do with height, my dear girl. You'll always be little Alice to me.' Mam laughs, easy in the knowledge that she has her clutch about her and that her daughter has finally come home, in the real sense. It would be the best Christmas ever.

Ned's son David fiddles with the parcels under the tree, feeling their shapes that feed his imagination and his hopes, desperate to open those he can see clearly have his name scrawled on them, but Mam has a rule: no presents before church. *White Christmas* plays softly in the background.

'All right. Everything's in the oven, table's set, are we ready to go? Alice, switch off the radiogram.'

Little Alice begs her mother to be able to stay behind and not go to church, reasoning that as she doesn't go normally, it would be hypocritical to go on Christmas morning. To no avail.

'It's not for you, or even for God,' Ned whispers covertly, 'but for Nana. Okay?'

We slither, a motley, muffled group in Christmas colours, down Horsehold towards St Thomas,' Ned insisting on walking with us, clinging onto Vincent and David for support, whilst I carry his sticks. The church is full and there is some sort of arrangement of *Adeste fideles* being played that makes Alice and David giggle, as the organist habitually hits a wrong note or doesn't pump enough air into the pipes to ensure clarity.

The resulting din is like a welcome old friend. The neighbours greet each other with wry smiles and compliments of the season, before sitting down to the opening address of an elderly Father Martin on this 'special Christmas morning', as he casts a surreptitious and colluding eye in my direction.

I realise that this is the first time I have entered a church since my marriage. Somehow it feels like the beginning of the undoing of it. There is a benign, suppressed joy in me that makes my stomach flutter with expectation that I cannot identify. The smell of old incense and flowers, the Christmas hats and lace mantillas, the children squirming—repressing Christmas excitement for a little while, the safety of neighbours, people with Christmas faces on, all feel like a renunciation of my solitariness—an extension of family. Mam, as though reading my thoughts, whispers smugly: *once a Catholic*...I nudge her in the ribs and she laughs.

As we walk back up the hill slowly, Ned holding on, picking his footsteps carefully on still firm snow, we talk about the service: Mrs Owen's ridiculous hat that no one could see beyond. Josie Watson's shrill soprano that could crack the stained glass if unfettered, and little Johnny Riley's loud swear word in the quiet of the gospel while his mother wrestled with him to sit still. We admire the loveliness of the moors in the now lilac-white light that moves in and around the heaped dry-stone walls as snow clouds move heavily across an opaque sky, causing a shy muted sun to peep in and out.

'Who is that by the house, Nana?' Little Alice asks casually.

Waiting by the front door with its wreath of holly and red apples, is a very tall man holding a pile of parcels in his arms, a nervous smile stuck to his face like a cardboard cut-out.

I stop. Ned looks up at the figure and back at me, beckons Vincent and his son David to move in front of me, as he takes my arm, in an effort, presumably, to prevent me from freezing in my tracks, and to reassure me that this time I am not alone.

'Merry Christmas, Alice, Mrs Conroy, Vincent, Ned and er...everyone.'

No one speaks.

Mam opens the front door and beckons little Alice into the house, casting a look like a frightened fawn over at the group that stands about me like tall sentries guarding their property.

'I thought we could talk, like sort things out if I came over. I flew. In an airplane. All this way just to see you, Alice...my wife...I brought some gifts for you and your family. I been staying in the hotel in the town a few days...I saw you...shopping and stuff...'

I remain stone-silent, unblinking, unbelieving, as though he couldn't really be here, as though he might suddenly disappear if I stare long and hard enough.

My body loses its energy, I feel weary in a familiar way that prevents any kind of forward motion.

Eventually, Vincent speaks: 'You must know you are not welcome here. We know all about you. Please take your gifts and leave us to celebrate our family Christmas.'

'I'm not looking for trouble—I come in a spirit of…you know…peace. And I'm family too, you know, whether Alice wants to acknowledge that or not. Legally—'

'Legally, this could be seen as harassment, Mr McCullough,' Ned says, stressing Carl's full title, unable to call him by his first name. 'Alice does not wish to see you, nor have anything more to do with you. I'm sorry if you have had a wasted journey, but as you can see, Alice is not alone now. All is in the hands of the solicitor, as I'm sure you know. There'll be no intimidation here.'

'Intimidation…?' Carl looks genuinely aggrieved, a look that could quickly turn to anger, I know, but he looks at the three men as though searching for some parity, expecting male support and seeming genuinely surprised not to get it.

'…and if you don't leave immediately, we shall call the police.'

'You can't just walk away from a life, Alice—it doesn't work like that. I think you'll find that the law will support me.'

Carl says this while putting down the gifts in the snow, then pushing his hands into jacket pockets, sinking his jaw into the upturned collar of his coat and staring at me, not untenderly, as though expecting me to soften or capitulate. I look at this caricature of a husband, this boy-man in his green trousers and hostile vulnerability. Somewhere, a blackbird flutes a lonely note and there is a skittering in the hedge. He is out of place in this landscape, like a bull in a field of sheep.

'And the law will do what?' Vincent asks, his voice rising. 'Force your *wife* to put up with being beaten senseless every time she has the temerity to disagree with you? You really believe that? Then you are a seriously deluded man.' Vincent sweeps a hand through his hair, his lips squeezed together like a boxer squaring for a fight, a gesture I recognise from childhood, just before a scrap.

Carl takes a step forward, whereupon my brothers close in front of me, Vincent folding his arms and tilting his head in a *what are you going to do about it?* demeanour; Ned squarely, unsteadily, in front of him and standing tall. Carl looks at the scene and begins to laugh.

'You can't be serious? You're not 'tail-end Charlie' now, you know, Vincent. And a one-eyed cripple…and a boy?'

'Get in the house, Alice,' Vincent says.

'No Vincent.' I push past my brothers until I am almost touching Carl, who towers over me. 'This has always been my battle. It still is.'

Ned rests his hand on my shoulder. I breathe in, think of Jake. I am no longer the bird with a broken wing walking in circles.

'Don't speak to my brothers and my nephew like that. Each is more of a man than you could ever be.' I can't, it seems, be strong for me, but for Ned… 'My brothers are right and there is nothing you can do to alter that. It would be in your interest however, as you are here, if you want to keep the farm, to sign some papers.'

Suddenly, I become business-like and feel instinctively that if I show no weakness, he cannot hurt me. 'I have it on good advice that I am entitled to half of everything you own and maintenance for the future, and though I have no real say in the matter, I shall make it clear to the courts that I wish to claim only enough to pay my keep here and virtually none of that to which I am entitled. On that, you have my word.'

Carl takes a backward step, his eyes moving rapidly from side to side as though absorbing for the first time what this could all mean to him personally.

'I'm sure you'll agree, Carl, that if left to the courts alone to decide—for me, that amounts to a lot of money—for you, ruin. I'm sorry that our life together has brought no happiness to either of us but know this: if you do not contest the divorce, which as you may know by now must wait three years, I shall do my best to influence the courts.

'If you fight what can only be a losing battle, I shall still get my divorce eventually, but you will lose a lot more than your wife. Now, if you'll excuse me, I intend to spend the first Christmas in too many years with the family that you kept from me for so long. My solicitor will be in touch with you at the hotel in two or three days' time. If you are not there, if it is in my power, I shall press for the maximum. You shall not win this battle, Carl; your size and your strength cannot help you now. Do not, in any event, attempt to see me or my family again; we are finished and no good can possibly come of it.'

As David chatters incessantly in the kitchen, washing pans, and little Alice dries, the rest of us sit with our coffee around the fireside. We are talked out. The flickering flames bathe our faces, with their family likenesses, revealing the depths of our thoughts, all of us now silent, the day clearly present before us, each in our own interpretation of it, in the red coals of the fire. Around us, imperceptible for a long while, the dark creeps in from outside like a heavy blanket around our backs.

'Put on the lamps, would you, Vincent,' Mam asks absently.

The meal, though a little delayed, revealed that Mam has not lost her touch in the kitchen, and now, her cerise-painted nails on long slender fingers rest in her lap as she stares with a faraway gaze, aware perhaps of the one person that should have been here. It seems she has exchanged her husband for her daughter.

Despite efforts to the contrary, all afternoon the subject of Carl had bubbled up to the surface of conversation, each of us reacting characteristically: Vincent spoiling for a fight, Ned the peace-maker and Mam going back repeatedly to the past: what she could have done differently...aware, like a black crow on *her* shoulder, of the wasted years when we could have been together.

Strangely though, I am the only one that is not anxious. Seeing Carl again on home ground has somehow removed the sense of threat. He seemed to be so much less than I thought, almost a caricature. He *will* stay at the hotel, he *will* sign the documents, he *will* agree to all the conditions. I could see it in his eyes; the same look Sheila described to me in detail on her deathbed, the look he had after his father beat him: resignation.

Besides, there was one thing more important to Carl than me: money.

Chapter Thirty-Six

June 1967

The invigilator moves slowly, desk to desk, putting the exam papers face down, exuding an air of self-importance mingled with a kind of ho-hum anticipated boredom at the prospect of invigilating on such a lovely day as this. She casts suspicious looks panoramically; we are all potential cheats.

'You have three hours. When I give the instruction to turn over your paper and begin, be sure to write your name and examination number clearly. Good luck everyone. Begin.'

I turn over the last examination paper in the final year of my English degree. My hands shake as I cast a look at the clock.

I was not surprised, when I ran into the hall, to see that a brilliant June morning had succeeded to the tempest of the night...Nature must be gladsome when I was so happy. (*Jane Eyre*, page 286)

"Consider Charlotte Bronte's use of Nature in the novel *Jane Eyre*."

I write steadily, thankful that I have prepared adequately, and find myself with time to spare. I read and reread my answers and after a couple of minor alterations know that I am unable to do better. All around me, students, mostly 21-year-olds, but one or two mature students like me, are either writing furiously or casting anxious eyes at the clock, clicking their ballpoint pens whilst searching out appropriate conclusions.

As I gaze, I wonder that I am here instead of three thousand miles away on a continent the other side of the Atlantic Ocean. I smile, *gladsome* in the knowledge that I am not. I feel as though I have at last grown up. I jump, still, when I hear a door slam, freeze when male voices are raised and have an instinctive distrust of my own judgment, which has been more irritating for those around me than it has for me. But here I am, I smile to myself, a divorced woman, living in a small house in Didsbury. I have a garden with two apple trees and a greenhouse for my plants.

Ten minutes left.

I try not to inhale too loudly, impatient, as I am, to be out in the sunshine. I stare from the window at the cherry tree in the courtyard, the last remnants of blossom tumbling like snowflakes in the warm breeze. I think I shall go home this weekend and see the family. Hebden. I sink into old thoughts, ignore the impatient shuffle of others around me, remember, amongst other things, *that* meeting…How could I forget it? Three years ago, on the hill just below Stoodley.

Vincent and his family had long returned to Hampshire and Ned's visits had grown more casual. How long had I been home? Five, six months? Just Mam and I with our new understanding of each other: no longer that of parent and child, but two women sharing a household. It seems our essential femininity had finally crossed all barriers and love of family negated all transgressions as we each recognised our mortality and the necessity to concentrate on what was important. Still, there was one thing we could not discuss.

I had decided, almost without premeditation, to use the new telephone to call Walter in Manchester. Mam was busy in the kitchen listening to *Women's Hour*. It seemed a good moment. It was a shame, after all Walter and I had been to each other, not to at least let him know I was home. At least I think that was my motive. A woman with a Salford accent answered the phone and I almost replaced the receiver. Instead, after a pause, I asked to speak to him. She told me he was over at Hebden, and could she take a message. I said no and hung up.

'Just seen him, funnily enough, walking up yonder, towards the Pike.' Mam had crept out of the kitchen, having heard the tinkle as I picked up the receiver. 'He always walks up that way when he's home. Had his Mam's dog with him, he's got it now you know, bonny little Jack Russell. You could catch him up if you're quick.'

'Why didn't you tell me?'

'You said you weren't ready for people.'

'Walter's not *people*…'

I pulled my coat about me as I walked, a breezy day as I recall, sunny but cold. I wrapped my scarf around my head and kept up a steady pace, keeping Walter and the dog at a consistent distance in front of me. I wanted to be well out of Mam's sight when I met with him. I pushed my hands into deep pockets to still their shaking, felt my chin tremble. All the years were suddenly a patch of green between us. I looked around at the moors I had loved so much from a distance, thought how mangy the grasses looked with their reedy winter coat, knew that within a week or two, yellow celandine would be pushing through, and a pale green coat would transform them.

I lost sight of the pair as they rounded Stoodley and thought perhaps they had cut down to the town the other way. I felt breathless, panicked, didn't want to miss this opportunity, so I put on a spurt, only to almost bump into him as he descended the collar of the hill, returning the way he had come. As he came adjacent to me, I stopped, looked at him and saw a man that, at first, I barely recognised. He was taller than I remembered, wiry, his hair was grey-flecked; salt and pepper, flopped over his eyes, but I saw that his face, though lined, was unchanged; *David*, his green eyes…he had aged well. He nodded as he passed.

'How do.'

I did not speak, could not go after him; he did not know me. Then I heard the brush of grass as he slowly retraced his steps behind me. The terrier ran back, sniffed at my feet. I did not turn around but bent down to pat the dog.

'Ali is it you…?' the faint voice said.

I stood up and turned.

'Yes Walter, it's me.'

We stared, taking in each other's faces. He lifted a hand and moved a curl from my forehead.

'You still swimming?' I asked smiling.

'Oh well…treading water, you know…'

'Yep. I know what you mean.'

'Ali…Ali…I know what happened to you.'

He moved towards me and put his arms around my shoulders, I slid mine around his waist. He felt so slim; my *Angular Saxon*. I felt him inhale. Neither of us spoke, we just stood there, the cold wind snapping at my scarf, the dog barking.

During those moments on that hill, holding each other, I thought of the weeks and months after his 'death' when I prayed to see him; a phantom, just one more time, to say the things I never said. I thought of all the years in between. And now I could say nothing. Needed to say nothing. I just held onto him, felt his ribs through his clothes, his breathing, smelt his skin, air-washed, wind-scented, salty, his warmth sinking into me, his aliveness, the brush of stubble in my hair.

It is the single moment of my life in which I have felt most alive; the miracle of an impossible yet realised dream: a life given back.

'You have five minutes remaining. Five minutes.' The invigilator's heels click as she paces the aisles, leaning over desks, her chin jutting forward, arms folded across a hefty bosom giving her the look of a figurehead over a ship's cutwater. Outside, a teenager in a miniskirt looking like Twiggy wanders past the window, a transistor radio tucked under her arm. *Whiter Shade of Pale* is blaring; the sound of the organ filling the silent examination room. Everybody looks over, smiling. The invigilator scowls, but the skinny girl drifts past, oblivious.

I look again at my paper; check I have filled in all the details, left nothing undone. I chew on the end of my pen, look again at the title of my first essay: *...a brilliant June morning had succeeded to the tempest of the night...* Smile.

What is life but a lived narrative? They must stop somewhere. Perhaps it is time to cease keeping a journal—I have reached where I want to be—want to *live* life now, not write about it. Perhaps, when I can, I shall reread the story of my life, shape it. Then, finished, I can put it on the bookshelf beside Walter's journal. Two lives together, side by side. Testimony.

*

Walter and I are close; he is the lover I knew he would be. I wonder whether he is free this weekend.

He would like me to move in with him, but I smile my silence. He knows I would never marry. I tell him, when I close my door, no one can tell me what to do, no one can hurt me. I like it that way. Sometimes when we loll on the sofa enjoying the feel of each other, an old tune comes to my lips...*I don't want to play in your yard*...and makes us laugh.

But when he stays over, like last night, and we wake in the morning, I watch him move around my bedroom readying himself for work, and I wonder...

I like to watch him. He knows I am doing it and he nods, smiling to himself, knowing I am hunting, following his movements like a cormorant eyeing its prey. Then I smile back, in a way he understands, a secret smile that tells of all things, past and present, before he blows me a kiss and goes, leaving the bedroom door open, like a wide-open gate, on his way out.

To the soft shuffle of the clock: sl-ip, sl-op, as though time is sliding, infinitely patient, delaying itself, I awaken to a new day, stretch out wide and fill the bed in luxurious comfort. I sink into the smell of the sheets, lavender and something male and musky, sea-like. I stroke the silky label of an old red dress pushed under my pillow and remember all the things I want never to forget.

And then I slip out of bed and stretch again in front of the mirror, where a small, beaded thing, with a feather attached, hangs and reminds me where I have been, whom I have loved. I see myself anew. I am not what I was, before the knowledge, nor am I that I had become. Now I am just me, with my crow's feet and scatter of grey hairs, and that's enough for now.

'Pens down. Stop writing.

*